CW00521495

DON'T FO
THAT TEXT!

'Amit Schandillia's book has come at a time when the distinction between fact and fiction is almost entirely blurred. Misinformed history has been in circulation for long, but it has set new standards today. Nowadays, history is perceived by many as a means to fulfil one's present political and social needs by treating the past as "pliable". When facts are created through viral message sharing, followed by history based on these expediently used "facts", Amit's book will be of immense help to sift actual fact from fiction.'

—s. irfan habib, historian, author of *Jihad or Ijtihad* and *To Make the Deaf Hear*

'His tweets are legen ... *finishes reading the thread* ... dary! Amit translates that same style into this thoroughly engaging read where historical misinformation is debunked using deep research and data—but conveyed with the ease of a social media post. In this age of post-truth madness, one can read this book for some much-needed sanity and clarity.'

—Akash Banerjee, satirist and political commentator

DON'T FORWARD THAT TEXT!

SEPARATING MYTHS FROM HISTORY ON SOCIAL MEDIA

AMIT SCHANDILLIA

WITH A FOREWORD BY
DEVDUTT PATTANAIK

HarperCollins *Publishers* India

First published in India by HarperCollins *Publishers* 2022
4th Floor, Tower A, Building No 10, DLF Cyber City,
DLF Phase II, Gurugram, Haryana – 122002
www.harpercollins.co.in

2 4 6 8 10 9 7 5 3 1

P-ISBN: 978-93-5629-080-8
E-ISBN: 978-93-5629-095-2

Typeset in 11.5/14 Garamond Premier Pro at
Manipal Technologies Limited, Manipal

Printed and bound at
Thomson Press (India) Ltd

MIX
Paper
FSC FSC® C010615

This book is produced from independently certified FSC® paper to ensure responsible forest management.

To you, dad!

'The quickest, most direct way to ruin a democracy is to poison the information.'

—Scott Pelley, 21 November 2016

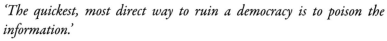

Contents

Foreword

POLITICIANS PREFER BARDS OVER HISTORIANS. A BARD does not always bother with facts. A historian necessarily does. A bard makes people feel proud about their past. A historian carries no such burden. Pride can be transformed into votes, not facts.

British politicians are well aware that most white parents do not want their children to learn how their ancestors colonized and plundered the world. American politicians know that a majority of white parents will not allow their children to learn how their ancestors stole Native American lands and enslaved African Americans. White parents invariably seem to prefer a history that shows Europeans as people who gave the world Science and Enlightenment. And we know that is, at best, only partially true.

Indian parents also want their children to feel proud of India. However, as per many politicians, historians have been privileged over bards in India since Independence. Some well-known historians present Hindus as casteist, Buddhists as pacifists, Mughals as monument builders and the British as social reformers. As a result, they have been accused of being not only Left-leaning, but also overcritical of all things Hindu.

Everyone now accepts that historians do bring prejudices into their work, and often sacrifice their academic credentials on the altar of activism. There is a Left-wing view of history constantly pointing only to the injustices of the past. In India, it currently overshadows the Right-wing view of history that seeks only to glorify the past. Yet, irrespective of the type, historians have to contend with bards—both Left- and Right-wing ones. This makes the past really confusing.

Which is why the writings of Amit Schandillia are so joyful.

I encountered him on Twitter accidentally. His lengthy Twitter threads were fascinating; he drew you into a world of facts and showed how they can be interpreted and misinterpreted. It made history interesting and was done with a sense of humour, often pointing to the pomposity of academicians and the maliciousness of politicians. His writing shows a love for India, without being needy or desperate. It is the kind of scholarship I enjoy.

We bonded on the observation that while Right-wing bards are easy to discredit, Left-wing historians are often too slippery to pin. While the former ignore facts altogether, the latter twist facts subtly to suit their agenda. We also bonded over foul-mouthed trolls, who we realized were merely desperate, unemployed youth of India clinging to that easily available opium—pride. Amit chuckled when I referred to the trolls as creatures who lack the ability of the mythical swan, to separate milk from a mixture with water. That is to say, they cannot separate fact from fiction, historians from bards, and those who can give them jobs from those who only want their votes.

Today, bards are favoured on social media, especially Right-wing ones, and Left-wing historians are feeling an acute push-back, although both argue that the truth is in peril. This is how narratives of the past emerge, with emotions and agendas often at odds with facts. Through the haze of opinions, we have to work with facts, gathering them meticulously, and studying them comprehensively.

That is what Amit does brilliantly. His research is deep but, more importantly, accessible. He makes us aware of how difficult it is to know the past, with a few pieces of precious data tossed into a political ecosystem yearning for pride and revolution.

We need to throw light on India's real and imagined past. We have to listen to bards, to understand the insecurities of people. We also ought to lend an ear to historians, to separate fact from fiction, data from opinion. We need to start appreciating the process by which history can be constructed, deconstructed and reconstructed. We must become aware of the fragility of our self-esteem, which often prevents us from confronting the truth of our past. And every bit of information should be bite-sized, as that's what works better than vast tomes for the current generations. We get all this and more in Amit's tweets, which are now part of this wonderful book.

Devdutt Pattanaik
Ashtami, 2022

Preface

MISINFORMATION HAS BECOME AN INALIENABLE part of our lives, and the trend seems to only get grimmer by the year. What would be a laughable conspiracy theory and fodder for wholesome amusement back in the day, is now threatening to become mainstream scholarship.

Our society isn't exactly a stranger to misinformed history. Partially or entirely incorrect narratives have cascaded as historical gospels since forever. Some are so deeply embedded by now that it's almost blasphemous to even question them. A case in point is hotly disputed topics such as the Aryans; the others are less contested, but still surprisingly erroneous, like the history of zero.

This work is an attempt to examine some of these myths and much of the rhetoric in the interest of erudition. My research is ideology-agnostic, indifferent to religious and political sentiments. My only affiliation is to the spirit of inquiry; so I have relied only on evidence that comes from either primary sources or those that are close enough. I have, to the best of my ability, stayed away from personal blogs and unpublished research. I have also drawn heavily on works that, although now out of print given their vintage, are the timeless products of eminent minds. At times, newspaper articles have been used for reference, but those instances are minimal and only from recognized publications with a reputation for quality journalism and significant circulation.

That said, everything I have put out is a result of research and is limited by the resources available as of now. Naturally, such a work cannot be stagnant and must be revisited as we make new discoveries and findings. So, readers must keep that in mind. As and when new facts emerge, one hopes to incorporate them into future editions.

In short, this is my attempt to lay bare everything either supportive or dismissive of the narrative in this book with minimal value judgement or an ideological slant.

I hope it's consumed in the same spirit.

Introduction

ONE SUMMER DAY IN THE YEAR 2005, AN EMAIL LANDED in my work inbox. Not spam, nor from an unknown source. It was a piece of enlightenment from an acquaintance, blindly forwarded to dozens.

As co-workers gathered around my desk, the collective response was that of ridicule and derision rather than shock.

What a lunatic!

What's he even smoking?

We had a hearty laugh and, within hours, forgot the whole episode. I don't remember who the sender was any more, but I do remember the email quite well. It was about a certain 'discovery': that the Taj Mahal was, in truth, a Hindu temple usurped and converted into a mausoleum by the Mughals.

Casual googling later revealed that the idea wasn't really a novelty. A gentleman named P.N. Oak had already filed a serious court petition years earlier to have the alleged temple 'restored'. Of course, the court had refused to entertain him. *Preposterous* and *pedestrian scholarship* were some of the expressions used in the press.

That was 2005. There was no social media and no instant messaging. Sure there were Orkut and Yahoo Messenger, but they weren't as pervasive as today's Facebook and WhatsApp, even at their respective peaks. Even the Internet was largely off-limits to vast swathes of the subcontinent, for cell phones those days were neither smart nor ubiquitous. So 'enlightenment' had only one medium—email forwards.

Fast forward to 2014. News started travelling at speeds unimaginable five years ago. There was a phone in every hand and the Internet on every phone. Misinformation could now be seeded in a Facebook post or a WhatsApp text and relayed to millions of gullible takers in a blink. This put immense power in every hand, quite literally.

My first interface with this power came about when I received a very long-winded text forward that spoke of how the Jama Masjid in Delhi was actually the ancient temple of some Hindu goddess Jamuneshwari Devi, before the Mughals turned it into a mosque. Only a few days down the line, another forwarded text dropped in to educate me on how Nehru sold Coco Islands to Burma and betrayed India.

Neither of the two claims made any sense because a) there is no Jamuneshwari Devi in all of the Hindu pantheon, and b) Coco Islands already belonged to Burma long before India's Independence.

Back in the day, everybody had laughed off Oak's claims as a joke. Not this time. Both Jamuneshwari Devi and Coco Islands started showing up in various Facebook posts, at times even posts shared by those that we'd call learned in the conventional sense—doctors, professors, bureaucrats, scientists, you name it. It was like a pandemic of misinformation.

History was being edited in the most absurd ways imaginable, right before our eyes. And we could do little more than watch crestfallen. Many had hoped that the twenty-first century would be the pinnacle of human enterprise and scientific rigour, predicated on the democratization of humanity's collective knowledge, enabled by the myriad technological breakthroughs.

Two decades into the fabled century, we ought to take stock of where we are. Are we there yet? Sure, we've become technologically unrecognizable to our ancestors from just years ago. The sheer information output of our generation has far exceeded the sum of all our predecessors' put together. But how much of it is factual?

The answer lies in the way history has been treated these last few years. After decades of collective unrelenting pursuit of knowledge, we now seem desperate to blur the line between history and myth. Old superstitions are making a comeback, and new ones are being manufactured on an industrial scale.

In our own country, an entire buffet of historical misinformation has been rehabilitated, and not only by mere conspiracy theorists and shady godmen. Men and women in extremely responsible positions have become earnest proponents. From imaginary ancient sciences to misinterpreted scriptures, unfounded claims are being put out with carefree abandon. And this isn't even confined to a particular ideology. More battles are being fought *over* history than have been fought *in* history.

This is a dangerous rabbit hole, one that ought to be plugged while there's still time. One step towards that is awareness, which is where this book comes in.

The idea is to pick some of the commonest, most dearly held popular narratives and test them for veracity against the litmus of available scholarship. I endeavour to do this in the most nonpartisan way because truth demands a dispassionate engagement with reason and research.

This work comprises thirty chapters, each dealing with one piece of misinformation. The language is consciously simple, with as little technical jargon as possible, to keep it universally accessible.

What I cover are topics that are extremely loaded with misinformation and are hard to ascertain as such, even by inquiring minds. Some of these are things that have long been held as historical truisms, while they actually aren't. I have chosen them to inform and disabuse readers but, above all, to shake up the narrative. The chapters, for the most part, have been kept short so as not to intimidate or stultify. The only emotions I endeavour to inspire are those of intrigue and inquiry.

Is Damascus Steel Really from India?

Damascus steel is unarguably the most storied piece of metalwork to have ever left the forge. A star attraction during the Crusades, swords made out of it were fabled to be able to slash feathers mid-air. But where did it come from? The name says it's Syria, but India says it's Indian. Seems plausible given the general antiquity of India's relationship with iron. Then why Damascus? Let's settle the debate scientifically.

On 1 November 1856, Britain declared war on Persia. Spearheaded by a coalition of the Emirate of Afghanistan and the East India Company, the campaign was to rid Herat of a recent Persian occupation and curtail its influence in the region. The campaign was part of a much larger international confrontation called The Great Game.

Those leading the British side of operations consisted, among other soldiers, of about 3,500 Indian sepoys of the Bombay Sappers and Miners. The valiance and grit of these sepoys became the subject of lore and helped Britain prevail when the war finally ended the following spring.

At the time, the Persian army came clad in armour; all that the Indian sepoys had were swords. When a colonel got killed on the battlefield, the sepoys, filled afresh with rage, were determined to avenge his death. And within a few quick days, a large part of the armoured Persian infantry had been liquidated by Indian swords.

Having taken their revenge, the sepoys announced that they had 'given their *jawab*'.[1]

For a long time, *jawab-i-Hind*, Persian for 'Indian answer', had been used as a martial expression in Persia. While it's easy to see *jawab* (Hindi for reply) as a metaphor for revenge, the terminology goes deeper. More than revenge, the idiom refers to a cut made by a sword. And not just any sword, but a very special kind, highly prized for its durability and sharpness—one made of *faulad-i-Hind*, or Indian steel. In short, anyone receiving the Indian answer was doomed to die; there was just no coming back from it.

The Anglo-Persian War happened in 1856, but the legend of Indian steel goes back at least 2,300 years, if not more. That's when Persia had switched to non-Persian rule, after spending over two centuries under the Achaemenids. The non-Persian ruler was Alexander from Macedonia. In his quest to expand eastward, he is said to have reached Hydaspes or Jhelum around 326 BCE, where he was confronted by a local ruler named Porus. This is recorded in history as the Battle of the Hydaspes.

Alexander emerged victorious and appointed Porus his local satrap, or governor. In return, Porus gifted the Macedon with thirty pounds of a very special kind of steel made in and known nowhere else but India. It was the same steel that Persians would later hold in much awe and esteem as faulad-i-Hind.[2]

The story of steel is the story of iron, one that began long before even the Iron Ages. While the first culture to inaugurate an official Iron Age did it as early as 1200 BCE, the oldest iron artefact to have ever been discovered in recorded history goes back to 3200 BCE. This was in Egypt.

But this and other artefacts from the period were made of iron retrieved from meteorites, the only source of useable iron at the time. This was more a matter of chance than science, as there was no technology yet to extract iron from ores. That's why the period doesn't qualify as Iron Age. The jump from iron to steel wouldn't come for another 1,000-odd years.

Iron that's freshly extracted from the ore is of terrible quality. The reason is, among other things, carbon. The more the proportion of carbon, the greater the brittleness of the iron. Harder, but more brittle. The iron that comes fresh out of a blast furnace has as much as 4.5 per cent carbon, which makes it pretty much useless for toolmaking. This is called pig iron.

So, since carbon is the problem, taking every last bit of it out should yield the best iron, right? Not really, because carbon also offers an advantage—toughness. Iron without carbon would lack the hardness needed for toolmaking or weaponry. The lowest we can go seems to be around 0.1 per cent, and that would give us wrought iron, which is pretty much useless for making tools. But this kind of iron finds application in areas that warrant flexibility.

As we can see, crafting the perfect iron weapon is a matter of balance—the metal used being a trade-off between hardness and flexibility. That balance comes with steel, in which, to put it most simply, the carbon content is higher than in wrought iron but much less than in pig or cast iron. Of course, there's also other metals involved here, but we won't get into those.

Steel emerged around 1800 BCE in Anatolia.[3] And once it did, it revolutionized warfare. Swords and knives could now be made to withstand far more than any iron weaponry until that point ever could. But this was just the beginning, for even steel could be and was, in fact, further improved with new techniques.

To a bladesmith, the ideal steel is flexible enough to be beaten into the sharpest possible edge, while still retaining its hardness. The sweet spot for this purpose is 0.7 per cent carbon. That's the starting point. Then comes the long and painstaking process of repeated heating and cooling. If the cooling is rapid, the process is called quenching. Otherwise, it's annealing. The two processes are performed alternately to imbue the blade with the desired mix of flexibility and toughness.[4]

Fine-tuning carbon content to a desired level isn't exactly an easy task. One way to accomplish it is by heating pieces of wrought iron with fluxes such as limestone or some organic matter. This process allows finer control over the amount and kind of impurity that is introduced to the resulting steel. What comes out of this process is expectedly known as crucible steel. This is one of the most primitive ways of doing the job.

The earliest textual record of crucible steel comes from the writings of the celebrated eleventh-century polymath and Indologist Al-Biruni. He elaborated on three different methods of producing crucible steel, depending on the kind of iron used.

The first method involves the addition of carbon to low-carbon wrought iron, by heating it with charcoal.

The second method starts with high-carbon cast iron; carbon is removed from it by heating it.

The third uses a mix of both in varying ratios to achieve the desired carburization level.

It's the first method that we'll confine this discussion to, for it's the one that gave us our steel in the beginning. But who came up with the technique in the first place? Available clues take us a long way back in time, as far as the first millennium BCE. Some of the earliest Greek trading accounts mention a highly prized form of steel being imported from the East into Abyssinian harbours. They call it *sideros indikos* (lit. 'Indian iron'). Later, Latin writers such as Pliny reinforce this with their mentions of *ferrum indicum* and *ferrum sericum*!

This takes us to India. Some historians further narrow it down to the Golconda region. The process began with magnetite—a most abundant, naturally occurring source of iron. A measure of this ore was moistened and packed in a sealed clay crucible along with pieces of wood and covered with leaves. This crucible was then heated for about three hours to achieve an egg-shaped piece of wrought iron.

This piece of low-carbon iron was then heated on a charcoal fire, to just below melting point, for a desired level of carburization.[5] It was then quenched and annealed repeatedly over several days for further fortification. The result was a fine variety of crucible steel about half a foot in diameter and a couple of pounds in weight—enough for two good swords. The locals called it *ukku*. Ukku hit the envious sweet spot of about 1.5 per cent carbon, which gave it the best balance between hardness and malleability. This is the steel Indian traders brought to the ports of Abyssinia along with spices and other exotic Indian items.

Over time, this alloy came to be known by different names in different cultures. While the Greeks noted it as *sideros indikos*, the Romans called it *ferrum indicum*, also meaning 'Indian iron'. Some Romans also called it *ferrum sericum*, and the credit for that goes to the Arabs.

Much of the south Indian west coast was once under the rule of the Chera Dynasty. When the ukku steel began its journey, this is the dynasty that ruled the region. Arab merchants of the time mispronounced the dynasty's name as *sera* and the wonder alloy became popular among them as Seres steel or, 'Chera steel'. Later Romans translated it to *ferrum sericum.*[6] The English, who seem to have come last, just stuck with the original ukku, but mispronounced it as 'wootz'.

Do note that the Cheras didn't really export finished products, but raw steel. The importing nations then used this steel to forge a wide range of items to fulfil their needs, both industrial and military.

At some point, wootz steel made its way into the bustling Levantine metropolis of Damascus. By then, several other centres producing the alloy had emerged around India—most notably Sri Lanka.

Once in Damascus, the steel found a whole other application, one that would propel it into renewed stardom. Wootz steel had been used to forge swords for centuries, but the forging method that emerged in Damascus produced a very distinct kind of sword that was said to be the sharpest ever produced by mankind. Legends claimed it could slice through a handkerchief mid-air!

These swords became an instant hit with the Europeans during the crusades. Much of this had to do with the fact that for centuries, they could not be reproduced in Europe despite several untiring attempts. We'll come to the swords a little later, but first, a bit about the exotic steel itself.

By the Middle Ages, the wootz process had reached many parts of the world, including China and the Middle East. This knowledge meant that this type of steel could now be produced on site instead of having to be imported from India. The imports continued, just in reduced volumes. A whole new steel industry came up in the Levant, and Damascus became its epicentre.

When carbon meets iron during the forging process, some of it goes through a chemical reaction to form iron carbide. This compound is hard and brittle, and is commonly known as cementite. When steel containing a certain amount of cementite is polished, the 'impurities' are revealed as silvery, wavy patterns against a black matrix. Some Arabs referred to these patterns as the 'Ladder of the Prophet', among other things.[7]

These cementite patterns are the single most defining feature of wootz steel. But that's just visually speaking. The alloy was treasured for far more than just its beauty. The optimized carbon content meant the blades could be beaten to incredible sharpness without falling apart. It also meant the sharpness thus achieved could be retained much longer than regular, non-wootz steels would allow.

The wootz produced in Damascus came to be known as Damascus steel. Several theories exist around this nomenclature, the most common one being that it was named after the city. One theory also pegs it to *damas*, Arabic for 'watered', alluding to the water-like cementite patterns on Damascene swords. On the other hand, Al-Biruni attributes it to a Syrian bladesmith named Damasqui.

Whatever the motivation behind the name, Damascus steel is how it came to be known in the Western world from this point on.

Wootz ingots continued to be imported from southern India, albeit in diminishing volumes, until as late as the seventeenth century. Much of wootz' popularity goes back to the thriving war business in the Middle East at the time, which kept demand high for centuries.

Now here's a little surprise: the blacksmiths of Damascus weren't just reproducing wootz steel, they were also improvising.

Wootz steel is crucible steel and is perhaps the most primitive kind of steel on record. But a new kind emerged around the second century CE—pattern-welded steel. This is where multiple different kinds of steel are forged and welded together to create a new patterned alloy with its own distinct characteristics, both visual and physical.

The blacksmiths of Damascus employed this process to create their own kind of alloy not found anywhere else. They used thin strips of steel and those made of soft iron in alternating layers to create a kind of steel sandwich. This sandwich was then welded together and the resulting block wrought into swords. This is also what came to be known as Damascus steel.

So now we have two different kinds of steels being forged in the Middle East of the Middle Ages. One, wootz imported from India, later also made locally; the other, an indigenous pattern-welded innovation that has nothing to do with India. For the sake of easy reference, experts have given each of the two forms a name. Oriental Damascus is the crucible version or wootz, and welded Damascus is, as the name suggests, the pattern-welded version.[8]

This diversity in the steel forged in the Levant is key to establishing the alloy's genealogy. So, if the question is, why did steel from India get named after Damascus, the answer is this: it wasn't entirely. Wootz became popular as Damascus because the city was at the heart of the crusading world during the Middle Ages. For many European knights, this was their first acquaintance with exotic oriental steel, and it was just natural for them to name it after the city.

But we cannot afford to ignore the other kind of Damascus steel, the one that was produced using an entirely local technique not known to India. This non-crucible steel had every reason to be named after Damascus because it truly was theirs.

In fact, some experts posit that the primary form of Damascus steel was not even oriental. Their claim is that the rapid quenching involved in wootz production would produce a different pattern than the one produced by forge welding. And since the dominant pattern found in damascene swords resembles the latter, it's incorrect to call it a form of wootz. If that were to be believed, Damascus steel has nothing whatsoever to do with India.[9] Fun fact: claims are also made that there is no archaeological evidence of Damascus steel being actually forged in Damascus.

So where do we stand? Whether or not Damascus steel was a rebranding on steel from India, two things remain largely uncontested—that India is the birthplace of steel, and that for the longest time, India's steel was the only kind prized for its properties. Wootz steel emerged over half a millennium before the common era and remained an exotic eastern marvel nobody could reproduce until the Middle Ages. Nothing can take that away from it.

China Gave Us Silk, but Who Gave Them Cotton?

No single commodity has impacted world history the way cotton has. It once enriched India enough to make it the world's largest economy. But who was the first to grow it? Egypt? China? Or India? Every civilization has laid claim to the marvel, but only one can claim to have been the first. Which one is it?

THE ANSWER COULD START WITH A FABLE. A HUGE crowd has gathered on either side of the road. Men and women of all ages are pushing and jostling for a better view. That's when it happens. Followed by a grand train of attendants, walking proudly under a beautiful canopy, the emperor makes his appearance.

The crowd, at first unsure how to react, soon begins to cheer him for his incredible new dress. And just as the strange procession reaches halfway through, a loud voice brings an abrupt pause to the revelry. It is a child.

"Look, he's naked!"

A child couldn't be wrong, everyone thinks, wondering if the emperor really is in the nude after all. The mood changes from confused awe and admiration to confident mockery and ridicule.

That's the legend of the emperor's new clothes. Anyone who couldn't see the non-existent clothes was considered stupid. Of course, it's just a story, and invisible fabric can't possibly exist for real.

But what if it did? What if there really were a fabric so flimsy, it almost disappeared? That's an interesting question, and we'll revisit it a little later.

Today, we wear all kinds of fabrics, but only three remain in use as far as those derived from natural sources go—cotton, silk, and linen. Of these—surprising as it might be given its ubiquity—cotton is the most recent! Both silk and linen came before and remained the mainstay for centuries, until cotton's emergence.

Textile itself has a relatively short history that only goes as far back as 10,000 years. That doesn't mean people walked naked until that point. It's just that they did not make fabric. Instead, animal skins were just sewn together for use as a cover against the elements.

Both linen and silk showed up around 4000 BCE, albeit in completely different parts of the world, each created with no awareness of the other. Silk, as is easy to guess, first emerged in China. At least that's what archaeological findings thus far seem to indicate. The earliest real piece of fabric we've found so far has been dated to the latter half of the fourth century BCE. It was found in Henan province in central China, and was likely used for a child's wrap.. The region back then was home to the Yangshao culture, a Neolithic settlement that is recognized for housing the world's earliest known dragon depictions.

An even older possibility comes from the Zhejiang province, where fragments of looms were unearthed at various archaeological digs. These fragments have been found to be from around 4000 BCE and are believed to have been used in the production of silk fabrics, although that proposal remains open to debate.[1] The hut settlement that inhabited the region back then belonged to the Hemudu culture and was likely contemporaneous with the better-known Majiabang culture.

After remaining confined to China for over 2,000 years, silk finally spread to other cultures just before the beginning of the common era. By the time of the Achaemenids, the textile reached as far as Persia and Korea. In order to facilitate the trade, later Han rulers even built a whole network of caravan roads called the Silk Road.

Meanwhile, at least one civilization had learnt to produce silk long before the Achaemenids and the rest. This civilization was around the Indus Valley. In 2000, archaeologists digging at Harappa found samples of silk dating to around 2400 BCE.[2] This makes India the oldest producer and consumer of silk outside of China. That said, it's not unlikely for the idea to have been a Chinese import, given the good 1,200-year gap between the samples found in each territory.

China still remains, by all estimates, the world's silk pioneer. Either the silk in Harappa came from China, or it was indigenous. In both scenarios, it came more than a thousand years after China first produced it. But what about the other two—linen and cotton?

Linen is instantly associated with people who made mummies, and for good reason. Ancient Egypt had an abundance of flax, the plant linen comes from. They not only lived in but also died in it. The bandage-like wrappings that covered their dead were all linen. But Ancient Egypt was not the first to do this. That credit goes to a lesser-known Neolithic settlement in Anatolia called Çatalhöyük. These people were burying their dead wrapped in linen as early as 6500 BCE![3] That makes linen the oldest fabric woven by humanity to continue to be in use. The Mesopotamians wore linen too, and some of the earliest flaxseed findings in Europe have been dated almost to the time of the Neanderthals![4]

India was never big on linen because flax isn't native to the region. But India has plenty of hemp, which was a source of textile for a long time before other finer fabrics took over.

And finally, we come to cotton. No other item of textile has impacted human history as dramatically as this one. From the Atlantic slave trade, to the American Civil War, to the rise of Bombay as a commercial powerhouse, to the British Industrial Revolution—cotton has touched every major historical milestone. Let's chart this revolutionary textile's very eventful origin story.

Europe has been wearing cotton for well over a thousand years, but the landscape only took its now-familiar form as recently as 200 years ago, when an American named Eli Whitney invented a new mechanism to speed up the process of cotton ginning.

Cotton, when harvested, comes in pods called bolls; the fibre in the bolls sits tightly studded with seeds. Needless to say, the seeds ought to go. So, for the longest time, workers would manually pick them out, one at a time. The leftover fibre would then be spun into threads which would, in turn, be woven together to make the fabric. Now, picking seeds by hand is as painstaking and slow as it sounds, which is why cotton remained an expensive piece of textile for a very long time. Until someone invented a machine to speed up the process. A *ginning* machine.

Whitney's machine was a cotton gin, short for 'cotton engine'. Not the first, but certainly the most efficient of its time.

Before Whitney, the work was handled by a different kind of contraption that involved two cylinders rolled by a hand crank. The gap between the two is where raw cotton went for *de-seeding*. These dual-roller cotton gins had been the standard all over Europe for at least two centuries until Whitney's machine took over. And those came from India. Indians had used the device since at least the thirteenth century if not earlier still.

But cotton gin is only one part of the story, the other part being cotton itself. While we know that the double-roller gin originated in India, can the same be concluded about cotton itself?

Remember how Columbus set out to 'discover' India and wound up in a whole new place instead? Well, the man never really got to realize his mistake. In fact, when he reached what's today Bahamas, he saw something that only further reinforced his conviction that he'd reached India. He saw native men and women clad in garments made of cotton. Those days, cotton was still an expensive novelty in Europe.

But the fact that Columbus associated cotton with India does imply two things—that cotton was already believed to be far more commonplace in India than elsewhere, and that the Europeans were well aware of that belief even though their interaction with India was far from close.

This is not to say that there was no cotton in Europe. It was just not abundant enough, as it had to be imported. Ports such as Venice and Antwerp became some of the biggest cotton hubs on the continent.

So far, we've seen cotton and cotton gin. But that only gets us to the pristine, seed-free lint. This fluffy product still needs work. First, the unwieldy cloud of lint has to be spun into yarn. Only then can it be woven into fabric on looms. The spinning was also done by handheld contraptions back in the day. But in the mid-fourteenth century, a new kind of mechanical device emerged that made the task much easier—the spinning wheel. Back home in India, they called it the *charkha*.

While some historians trace the device to India, many others attribute it to the Islamic world. Either way, Europe only got those in the fourteenth century. So it was only by then that they had the gin, the spinning wheel, and also cotton, even if not in abundance. But the question remains, when did all this even start?

The first time most Europeans got acquainted with cotton as a textile was when the Normans took Sicily sometime in the eleventh century. Until that point, the island had been under Muslim rule and officially known as ʾImārat Ṣiqilliya, or the Emirate of Sicily.

Cotton was pretty much the mainstay on the warm Mediterranean island when the Normans arrived. Taking an instant liking for this exotic fabric, the Normans not only adopted it but also helped spread it to the rest of Europe.

Now the question is, who brought cotton to Sicily? The Arabs? Turns out, yes. In the year 718, the entire Iberian peninsula was brought under Umayyad rule and was reorganized as the province of al-Andalus. This Muslim rule lasted well over half a millennium, with the reins changing several hands during the period. It is widely accepted that these Muslim invaders, also known as the Moors, introduced cotton to the region.

It's now getting increasingly tempting to credit the whole thing to the Arabs. What further bolsters this notion is the fact that Egypt had already domesticated cotton and started cultivating it by the middle of the first millennium. When the Moors arrived in Iberia, the Egyptians were not only producing textile out of cotton but also wearing and exporting some of it to the rest of the Arab world. Before then, the only thing they knew was linen. So, it seems, Egypt is where the world found its cotton and learnt to wear it for the first time.

But then, there's one small hitch—cotton gin. The dual-roller gin, as we just learnt, came from India between the twelfth and the thirteenth centuries, almost six centuries after the Egyptians learned to use cotton. But so did the older, single-roller edition. This was just a handheld contraption and took a lot of effort, but had been in use in India since at least the sixth century. That certainly predates both al-Andalus and Islam, and it rivals, if not beats, Egyptian cotton in vintage. But the story goes even further.

Arrian of Nicomedia was a unique person who lived in Ancient Greece in the second century CE. Unique because he was a philosopher and a military commander—not a terribly common combination even for his time. Around 150 CE, he completed *Indiki*, a brief historical account of Alexander's military exploits in the Indian subcontinent. The man himself never travelled to India, though.

Of our interest in this work is chapter 16, where Arrian describes Indian fashion and clothing. In it, he speaks of ivory earrings, colourful beards, white slippers, and a characteristic white tunic worn around the calf and thrown over the shoulders. This tunic has been identified as being made of cotton, although he erroneously called it linen.[5] The Indian cotton claim now almost breaches the common era, but we're still not done.

A few decades before Arrian lived yet another Greek historian and philosopher. His name was Strábōn, better recognized as Strabo. This man is best known today for his encyclopaedic compendium of seventeen volumes, titled *Geōgraphiká*. Most theorists place the work in the earliest years of the common era.

The first chapter in the fifteenth volume of this work describes a plant that gives 'wool blossoms', which the locals draw into fine threads.[6] Furthermore, he claims that the Macedonians who came with Alexander used these blossoms as pillow stuffing. The only Indian plant that fits this description and use case is cotton.

Both Strabo and Arrian speak of India in the context of Alexander's invasion—an event that took place more than 250 years before their time. So while we can surely consider their accounts, something more contemporary would serve better.

And that brings us to Hēródotos.

Although not really a contemporary, Hēródotos is better for our purpose, as he died nearly seventy years before Alexander was born. In 425 BCE, the year of his death, this man published his magnum opus, a nine-volume work on world history, unassumingly named *Histories*. This was the first written work of its kind, which is why Hēródotos, despite being notorious for his literary licence, is unanimously called the 'father of history'.

In book VII of this collection, titled *Polymnia*, we find references to Xerxes' army of 1.7 million—a highly exaggerated number for sure—consisting of men from various nations. Among these, Hēródotos says, was a contingent of Indians who were 'dressed in cotton and shot iron-tipped cane arrows'.[7] Interestingly, Hēródotos referred to the Indian cotton plant as 'wool-bearing trees'. That's because the only textile the Europeans knew at the time was wool. In fact, when Alexander invaded India a hundred years later, his men were elated to find cotton, a fabric that offered the softness of wool but the lightness of silk.

Can we now conclude that India pioneered cotton? It would seem so. Especially since the association between India and cotton is evidenced by no less than the Indus Valley Civilization itself! Traces of cotton found at both Mohenjo-daro and Harappa suggest that its vintage could be pushed to at least 3000 BCE. And if that weren't enough, there are references to cotton from Meluhha in Mesopotamian tablets as well.[8] So yes, India does seem to have been among the first in the world to use cotton.

Why among? Because the top spot, in fact, seems to go to a very unlikely contender, the New World! Excavations at pre-Inca sites in Peru and Mexico have thrown up cotton plants and specimen that go back more than 5,000 years, clearly predating the oldest dated samples from Harappa.[9] Remember the cotton garments Columbus saw in the Bahamas?

Even if the New World got around to using cotton before the rest of the world, it's India that gave the world its cotton. The pre-Inca fabric remained confined to that part of the world. A few records indicate there was some native acquaintance with the fibre in China concurrently with the Indus civilization, but it was India that took to exporting the fabric to Europe, China and the Arab world—becoming one of its oldest exporters.

The most definitive support for this argument comes from an ancient Greek text titled *Períplous tis Erythrás Thalássis* (lit. 'Periplus of the Erythraean Sea'). Although its authorship is yet to be established, we know it was composed during the earliest decades of the common era. This book carries a description of life in the ancient city of Ariaca, not far from today's Mumbai. Here, merchants from Egypt are said to have traded in, among other things, Indian cotton.[10]

On the eastern front, India is said to have exported cotton to China until fairly recently. The famous Chinese pilgrim Faxian reported finding Indian cotton during his Indian sojourn in the fourth century. Even as late as the sixth century, Gupta kings were routinely sending cotton to China.[11] So, yes, it's indeed safe to assume that cotton is India's gift to the world.

Coming back to the emperor's new clothes before we conclude, here's an interesting theory. Sure, the story is entirely fiction, but a fabric, made using cotton, and so fine, it's almost transparent does exist, even if the original and most fine art of weaving it seems lost to time. The Romans wore it and so did the Medieval royalty that followed. Apparently, the whole length of this legendary fabric could be contained in a matchbox, and it once made Dacca, its birthplace, one of the most prosperous metropolises in the world. You guessed it right. It's muslin!

Is India Truly the Birthplace of Toilets?

The India of today is the butt of toilet jokes in a way no other country on Earth is. This has led to the notion that while the world has continued to step up its hygiene game, we as a nation have remained largely unfamiliar with sanitation. Was there ever a time when Bharat was actually *swachh* when the world wasn't?

IN 1596, A MAN NAMED JOHN HARRINGTON PUBLISHED A book titled *A New Discourse of a Stale Subject, called the Metamorphosis of Ajax*. In it, he elaborated upon and advertised a new invention of his own. It was a flush-toilet, the earliest in recorded history. Before putting out the book, Harrington had already installed the apparatus at his home in Somerset and intended to make a living out of it.[1] He called it a 'water closet'. The book was meant to be, besides a veiled attack on the British monarchy, an advertisement for his invention. Queen Elizabeth I, the reigning monarch at the time and Harrington's godmother, banished him from her court for his insinuations.

Interestingly, an innovation that ought to have been an instant hit and a lifelong cash cow for its maker, failed spectacularly. Besides the one at Harrington's residence, the only other place where it got installed was at Richmond Palace—one of the myriad residences of the British monarch.[2] But why? The answer was two words—running water.

It's not that Harrington's idea wasn't welcome or revolutionary. In a world of stinky chamber pots, where excreta stayed within the room until a servant emptied it into a cesspit that may or may not have already filled to the brim, the idea of a contraption where excrement could just be flushed away with the turn of a lever would have surely been more than a relief. But a water closet, by definition, needs water. And plenty of it. Without a consistent supply thereof, the whole contraption is rendered useless. This is where Harrington flunked.

He just assumed running water would be taken care of beforehand by anyone considering installing his system. But in seventeenth-century England, running water was practically non-existent. That's one of the reasons the royal family had so many palaces. They constantly moved from one to another so the servants could clean the place once it got too smelly!

As we just established, no decent waste disposal system can be imagined without provisions for a robust water supply. In short, the history of sanitation is the history of plumbing. The second part of the equation is sewerage. Until fairly recently, much of Europe was just evacuating in pans, which were then emptied either in an open drain just outside the house or, if wealthy, in a cesspit on the estate. Neither solution was optimal for public health and led to multiple typhoid and cholera outbreaks until as recently as the mid-nineteenth century.

But Europe wasn't always this filthy. In fact, the Romans had a relatively 'advanced' water delivery and sewerage system for their time. They built enormous aqueducts to bring water from remote reservoirs into city dwellings. So that took care of the water problem. But disposal was still less than optimal, at least by modern standards.

While poorer Romans did the same thing the Englishmen would centuries later, i.e., evacuate in a pan and empty in a sewer, many chose to go out. Every Roman city had at least one building that served as a public toilet.

The building consisted of a single row of stone or wooden benches running along the walls. These benches had suitably spaced holes on which the user could sit and defecate. This arrangement offered zero privacy as there was no partition between adjacent seats. Under the bench ran a stream of water connected to an aqueduct that served as the source. This way, the waste did not have to be carried as the running water did the job. Once they were done, people would use a long wooden stick with a loofah on one end to clean themselves up. There was also a large tub of water in the centre to rinse the waste off the stick. Typically, they all shared the same stick. It must be noted here that some scholars reject the idea that these 'sponge-sticks' were a part of Roman life.[3]

While all this sounds gross, the system was a pretty radical one for its time. We're talking the BCE era here. These toilets doubled as places to socialize and unwind after a hard day's work. The Romans called them *lātrīnum*, the word later British borrowed to create the English latrine.

This system remained in place for centuries, until Rome's fall led to their disuse in Western Europe.

But the Romans weren't exactly the pioneers. They got the technology from the people who inhabited Rome before them—the Etruscans. Sometime around the middle of the first millennium BCE, these people built Rome's first sewage system.[4] But this was less for waste disposal and more for drainage. Their sewers helped drain water out of low-lying parts of the city after heavy rains or flooding.

Even the Romans took time to turn this into a waste disposal system. Initially, they continued to evacuate and dispose in the streets. Some disposed of their waste in the drains outside their homes that emptied into a large city-wide channel called Cloāca Maxima (lit. 'the greatest sewer'), which in turn emptied into the Tiber River.[5] Others just tossed it out into the street.

Naturally, this created problems. Not only due to the stench but also because of the injury to unfortunate passers-by. To that end, the practice of reckless street disposal was outlawed once sewage lines started being connected to individual households. By 100 CE, many wealthy homes had their own private latrines.

So the British learnt from the Romans and the Romans from the Etruscans, even if the transfer of technology wasn't always seamless and lossless. But who did it before the Etruscans? Were they the first to have sanitation in any form?

Before we explore earlier times, it's important to note that public toilets equipped with some kind of automatic waste disposal, say, running water, were not exclusive to the Romans. While they picked sewerage from the Etruscans, they picked the latrine itself from yet another culture that thrived for centuries before them.

The Greeks.

For a long time, it had been held that the Romans brought the latrine culture to the East after their conquest of the Mediterranean. Today, that theory has been discarded and the reverse seems to be the case. And the evidence comes from, among other sites, the island of Santorini.

Back in the day, this was home to the ancient Greek city of Thera. Excavations on this island have revealed that the people living here were already enjoying the luxury of private toilets with running water as early as the sixth century BCE. Of course, communal toilets existed as well.[6]

But washing up was a rather unpleasant process even here. Of course, there was no toilet paper. Instead, the defecators of Ancient Greece used the same stick-with-a-sponge that we saw the Romans use. It's actually the Greeks that gave the Romans this idea. But before the stick, the job fell on discarded shards of pottery called óstrakon.

Often, disgruntled individuals would write their enemy's name on the óstrakon just before using it. This is how we got the word 'ostracize'.[7]

So now we know that flush toilets were not a Roman innovation but a borrowing from the Greeks. So was it a Greek innovation? Or did they, too, get it from someone who came before?

Long before the Greeks or the Romans, came the Minoans. This was a Neolithic culture that inhabited a city-state called Knōsós, or Knossos, on the Greek island of Crete. After having lived and prospered for almost 6,000 years, the settlement seems to have suddenly ceased to exist sometime in the second millennium BCE.

Nobody knows why.

Archaeological works on the island have revealed several palaces and mansions from the Minoan period, some dating all the way back to the third millennium BCE. One such palace is said to have belonged to the legendary king Minos. This palace, it seems, had not only running water but also rainwater harvesting, covered sewerage, manholes, airshafts, and fully-functional private toilets![8]

Now that really pushes the envelope. But what about before them? What did humans do before the second millennium BCE? Had any other culture beaten the Minoans to it? Let's see if the answer can be found by turning east, the part of the world most conversations around hygiene seem to unfairly ignore.

During the eighth century CE, from the deserts of Arabia, emerged a whole new system of faith that endeavoured to bring together the myriad disparate tribes and their traditions under one theology. This was Islam. Being as prescriptive as it was, the religion dictated practically every aspect of its adherents' daily life in its quest for perfection.

Among such prescriptions were a few that pertained to hygiene and sanitation.[9] The rules were strict and room for deviation practically non-existent. Individuals were required to bathe regularly; they were also to wash up before each of the five daily prayers. To add to this, there were also mandates on how to pass urine and defecate; thoroughly washing up after each was a ritualistic compulsion. And it was forbidden to stand while passing urine, lest a single drop splatters on the feet!

This motivated a whole new level of sanitary innovation unheard of in many parts of the Medieval world. Elaborate sanitation systems involving cesspits, sewerage, airshafts, and even flush toilets emerged and became mainstream all over the Arab world. Since Islamic rules strictly mandate washing up with water, the Arabs dispensed with things like the leaves, paper and sponge used elsewhere. Evidence of this was unearthed in Egypt when archaeologists exploring the medieval city of Fustat found the remains of what they called 'toilet flasks'.[10]

A tenth-century Persian mathematician by the name al-Karajī offers a most detailed and insightful account of what sanitation must have been like in the region during his time. Towards the later years of his life, the man published a book titled *Inbat al-miyah al-khafiya* (lit. 'Extraction of Hidden Waters'). As the name suggests, it's a remarkably elaborate treatise on hydrology and sanitation under the Abbasid rule. The book covers everything from groundwater extraction to wastewater disposal and even touches upon various processes of water purification.[11] This, at a time when the rest of the world was not even familiar with the concept of waterborne diseases, was nothing short of ground-breaking.

These elevated hygiene practices were among the highlights of the Golden Age of Islam. That said, the toilet was certainly not their brainchild as we have seen, at least for now, the story dates to the Minoans.

Coming back to Europe, there does exist another culture that developed its own sanitation system, either before the Minoans or at least concurrently with them. A nineteenth-century winter storm ripped through Mainland, an island in Orkney, Scotland, and killed 200 inhabitants. Tragedy aside, the storm also unearthed a settlement that had remained buried there, undisturbed and unexplored, for centuries.

By the 1930s, the whole settlement had been recovered. It was a Neolithic settlement named Skara Brae, and its story went back more than 5,000 years. By 2500 BCE, the settlement had already been abandoned. What makes this dig important is the discovery of some of the oldest signs of a well-developed sanitation system.

The dwellings discovered here are generally small, about half of a typical British apartment today, and were made of stones. The walls had recesses and alcoves of varying sizes, likely for storage. Archaeologists call them *cells*. Many homes had a cell that didn't store anything. Instead, they had drains running underneath the floor. Experts read those as a smoking-gun for some of the earliest and most sophisticated indoor toilets in all of Europe,[12] going back to nearly 3000 BCE.

Do we then hand it to the British on vintage, if not sustained sophistication? We could, but another culture seems to have done it even earlier. Again, this time, it's to the east—Ancient Mesopotamia.

By the Euphrates, in modern-day Syria, once sat an early Mesopotamian settlement named Habuba Kabira. Today, it lies submerged under Lake Assad, an artificial reservoir created by the al-Thawra Dam. Prone to flooding, the settlement was built on elevated land surrounded by walls for protection from invasion. Archaeologists working the site have discovered pipes made of baked clay, a sign of some kind of primordial sewerage system. Wastewater was carried through these pipes and dumped straight into the Euphrates. All other cities in the vicinity, such as Ugarit and Eshnunna, have been found to follow the same practice.

The Mesopotamian region was initially just a collection of city-states with varying degrees of autonomy. Broadly speaking, two different cultures existed in the region, the Sumerians and the Akkadians. Both spoke different tongues. Towards the latter half of the third millennium, a man from Akkad named Sargon rose to become a king and then proceeded to conquer Sumer. This conquest brought the two disjointed polities together under what became the first empire in recorded history. The Akkadians introduced many landmark innovations in both sanitation and construction.

One such innovation from the time was a highly sophisticated water management system. At the Akkadian palace in Eshnunna, there were toilets along the exterior of the building with pipes carrying the waste directly into an underground sewer made of baked bricks and lined with bitumen.[13] This sewer ran along the length of the street, collecting waste from as many homes as possible, finally emptying into the Euphrates. Things only got better when the Babylonians took over later. They replaced bitumen with asphalt and invented knee and T-joints for more sophisticated waste routing. And all of this happened more than a thousand years before the Romans and the Greeks, whose system not only came later but was also demonstrably inferior.

But before we hand it to the Mesopotamians, let's see if we have forgotten anything. Looks like we have.

There is one civilization that had its own highly evolved system of water management thousands of years ago.

This was the Indus Valley Civilization.

Although no Harappan artefact pertaining to sanitation has so far been found to date earlier than those found in Mesopotamia, there are indirect clues that indicate otherwise.

For starters, Ancient Mesopotamians—Sumerians, in particular—are known to have routinely conducted business with the Indus Valley people, Meluhha being the port of call on the Indian side. Consequently, it's quite plausible that many Indus merchants may have made permanent homes in Mesopotamia. Much material evidence, in fact, exists to establish the presence of Meluhhans in Sumer.

Secondly, remember the amazingly sophisticated sanitation found in the Akkadian capital city of Eshnunna? Well, a large number of seals and toilets here have been found to bear motifs of animals that aren't native to Mesopotamia, such as elephants and Indian gavial.[14] Experts have sometimes studied these artefacts to conclude that the technology was a Harappan import rather than indigenously Mesopotamian.

This, of course, is little more than educated speculation, and the house remains divided on the final verdict. While the seals and their depictions sure indicate a Harappan connect, they fail to conclusively establish a Harappan precedence over Mesopotamia on the subject of sanitation and toilets. It might as well have been an influence in the opposite direction. Then again comes the Great Bath of Mohenjo-daro, an artificial open tank of water meant for public use that goes back to nearly 3000 BCE! No similar structure has ever been found in Ancient Mesopotamia. One may read that as an argument in support of the Indus Valley Civilization's primacy or await further archaeological reinforcement.

Either way, one conclusion remains unchallenged—that Eastern nations had a remarkable headstart on public and personal hygiene, as compared to their Western counterparts.

Even though the balance seems to have flipped in modern times.

Was the World's First University Indian?

Many claim it was the one at Bologna, others credit the academy started by Plato. And then there's India, which calls it all a lie and prefers Nalanda and Taxila. So who's right anyway? Which culture had the world's first university? Is the Indian claim just unsubstantiated nationalism, or does it actually have merit?

DORABJEE NAOROJI MITHAIWALA WAS AN AMBITIOUS Parsi entrepreneur from early nineteenth-century India. He is best known for migrating to Hong Kong as a stowaway and setting up a successful shipping business that still exists as Star Ferry. In 1843, his son Dhunjeebhoy Nowrojee, a fresh convert to Christianity, arrived in Edinburgh to join the Free College Church as a student of Christianity. He'd finally graduate three years down the line, get ordained as a preacher and return to India to evangelize.

Dhunjeebhoy was not the first Indian to visit Britain, but he was the first to do so for educational purposes. The trail having been blazed, many others followed. By the end of the century, there were no fewer than 1,700 Indian students in Europe, over 200 of those in Oxford and Cambridge alone.[1] This was about twenty years before India's formal introduction to the English education system.

In fact, Dhunjeebhoy might as well be the first Indian student anywhere in the West, not just in Britain. For the first student in America would not travel there until the beginning of the twentieth century. That was a young Calcutta University graduate named Girindra Mukerji who went to Oregon to study agriculture.

But the history of education is far older than the West, as is the history of Indian's contacts with distant lands. Take, for instance, Iran's Farhangestân-e Gondišâpur, better known as the Academy of Gondishapur. Its history goes back to a time when Persia was under Zoroastrian Sassanian rule, and Islam was not even born. Under Khosrau I, a great patron of the arts, philosophy and sciences, many Greek and Syriac academicians fleeing religious persecution in the Byzantine empire found refuge and work in Iran.[2] With them came Greek knowledge and wisdom, as they translated a large number of Greek works into the local language, giving a fresh boost to Sassanian education. As many as three hubs of academic activities came up under this regime, and Gondishapur was one of them.

In his quest to make Gondishapur an international centre of learning, Khosrau I also sent one of his physicians named Borzuye to India. The mission involved bringing home all the texts on Hindu medicine he could get his hands on. Borzuye went a step further and returned with not only texts but also a team of Indian experts to help understand them.[3] This is also when the Indian game of chess entered Persia.

From that point on, the Academy of Gondishapur grew into a university of international renown, where the best of all cultures could be learnt and explored. Since Indians had already travelled there as experts in the beginning, it's quite likely at least a few more would have followed over the ensuing centuries as students. This takes us to the sixth century CE, more than a good thousand years before Dhunjeebhoy's Oxford stint. But can we go even further behind? That depends on how we define education.

Formal education at universities in the modern sense of the term is a fairly recent phenomenon, and most experts attribute their emergence to the universities in places like Bologna, Oxford and Cambridge. Informal learning, however, is a different matter altogether. The idea of curious students congregating at a place in order to acquire unstructured knowledge and exchange ideas is at least 2,000 years old and is generally attributed to Ancient Greeks. Two great examples are the institutions floated by Plato and later, Aristotle.[4] In fact, the word 'academy' traces its origin in the estate of Attica's Hekademos, on whose property Plato ran his school.

Now, the Greeks and the Indians have been in contact since as early as the fifth century BCE, quite likely even earlier.

We know this because when the Achaemenid king Xerxes the Great invaded Greece around 480 BCE, Herodotus notes in *The Histories* 7.65.1[5] that he had many Indians in his army. Although Herodotus is known for his liberties with facts, his description of Indians wearing cotton clothes and shooting arrows shows he was, at least, aware of India and Indian ways to a degree. The level of awareness he displays could only stem from some kind of pre-existing Indo-Greek contact. Does this establish academic links as well? Not necessarily. But, again, it isn't entirely implausible for at least a handful of early Indian immigrants to have joined one of the Greek academies of higher learning.

For contacts of a more academic nature, we need to move forward by about half a century, to the time of Alexander the Great.

Plutarch was a Platonist philosopher and a priest at the Temple of Apollo in Delphi. He is best known for his seminal work titled *Parallel Lives*. It's a collection of biographies of Greek and Roman men of repute, forty-eight in total. One of the men profiled therein is Alexander. Here, Plutarch offers an account of Alexander capturing ten Indian ascetics to test their wisdom.[6] Plutarch, and later Greeks, called these ascetics gymnosophists due to their extreme austerity.

They shunned all worldly necessities, most notably clothes, in their quest for enlightenment, a practice seen as extreme and exotic by the incoming Greeks. *Gumnós* is Greek for naked.

When Alexander heard of this practice, his curiosity naturally aroused, he arranged for ten of those ascetics to be brought to him. They had to answer a series of questions; the caveat was that while correct answers would attract handsome rewards, incorrect answers would get them killed. All were subsequently released after having correctly answered all questions.

The account further states that Alexander then sent for another Indian ascetic, one of a much higher repute, named Dandamis. At least that's the name he's known by to the Greeks. Alexander told him that he first heard of him from a man named Sphínēs.

Sphínēs was an Indian ascetic, a gymnosophist, who had travelled to Greece with Alexander on one of his earlier campaigns. Plutarch recorded his name as Sphínēs but he later became popular as Kalanos, proposed by some as a Greek corruption of his original name Kalyāṇa.

Kalanos is said to have later killed himself by jumping into a burning pyre while in the Ancient Greek city of Susa, now in Iran, leaving Alexander and his army looking on helplessly. This episode was later also corroborated by other historians such as Megasthenes and is today part of the Alexandrian lore. This is the first extant record of an Indian presence in Ancient Greece.[7]

Before dying, Kalanos had issued a curse against Alexander—that he'd meet his end in Babylon. The curse turned out to be a prophecy that came true. It's through this man that Alexander first learnt of Dandamis.

While this was definitely an academic exchange (unless the whole story is mere legend) it does not establish the fact that Indian students visited Ancient Greece for higher learning. On the other hand, Kalanos is recorded to have offered his services as a teacher during his Greek sojourn. His pyre was built specifically by Ptolemy on his instructions, which further corroborates his position as a senior educator. Before dying, accounts posit, he wore nothing but a garland of flowers and chanted Vedic hymns.[8] Could this mean he also taught Vedic philosophies to local Athenians? Not improbable.

Kalanos' feat was later matched by another Indian—this time in Athens. Known to the Greeks as Zarmanochegas, he was most likely a Buddhist monk who lived and taught in Athens before his death. They even built him a tomb just outside Athens, as recorded by Plutarch in his works.

Do note that in those days, there was not much separating science from philosophy, and philosophy from religion. As a result, there was not much separating education from proselytization either. Or, for that matter, a monastery from a university. So, a preacher was a teacher and so was an ascetic or a monk. Acknowledging this ambiguity is key to understanding the state of learning in antiquity.

The contact between Indian and foreign cultures for academic purposes doesn't stop here, though. We can go further back, and by centuries. But in a different direction.

Now that we know monasteries often doubled up as schools back in the day, a whole new system of learning emerges from Ancient India. As the Aryans graduated to a more sedentary lifestyle in north-western India, they absorbed and internalized a number of indigenous religious practices. One such practice involved sacred groves outside native villages used for occasional religious rituals. These came to be known as *chaityas*. Aryan ascetics started using them as sanctuaries where they could go to pray and meditate.

Chaityas also became a big part of many other non-Vedic creeds that emerged around the fifth century BCE. Some started being built atop reliquaries containing remains of a dead Buddha, a practice added by the emergent Buddhist creed.[9] With time, some chaityas were extended with living quarters for monks who wished to live there permanently. These 'proto-monasteries' were called *vihāra*s. The word is older than the dwelling, though, and initially referred to inns for weary travellers. It's only with Aśoka's decision to repurpose them as monasteries that they acquired religious significance.[10]

One such vihāra is said to have come up at a sleepy little village about fifty miles from Patliputra (today's Patna) when Aśoka extended a pre-existing chaitya after his conversion to Buddhism. The name of this place is Nalanda. Although this information comes from scriptural sources, it still awaits archaeological corroboration. If true, however, the vihāra at Nalanda should be among the earliest ever, going back more than 2,200 years.

But why are we even discussing vihāras in a conversation about universities? Because the one at Nalanda eventually grew into a full-blown centre of Buddhist and Brahminical learning, with students from as far as China and Tibet on its rolls. This didn't happen overnight though. The process was gradual and spanned centuries.

In fact, the first record of an academic activity in Nalanda only comes from a fourth-century Buddhist account of three resident students—two Buddhists named Nagarjuna and Arya Deva, and a Brahmin named Sudurjaya. What this means is that Nalanda must have already been established as a widely acclaimed centre of learning by that time, with expansive courses being offered in at least Buddhist if not Vedic theology.[11]

Interestingly, Nalanda bore a striking resemblance to modern universities in character and operation. For starters, there were 'entrance tests'. The only way an aspiring monk could get in was by correctly answering the gatekeeper's questions!

Later Chinese accounts describe the place as a bustling settlement of nearly 10,000 students and 3,000 teachers living on campus for a period spanning years. Classes were held on 100 lecterns, and teachers were assigned courses based on their mastery.[12] It was a remarkably structured system and continued in operation for centuries, before finally being destroyed by invading Khilji armies in the thirteenth century.

If evidence of academic activities at Nalanda could be traced to the vihāra itself, the institution would be among the oldest on the subcontinent. Unfortunately, until concrete archaeological remains of the original structures emerge and all scriptural inconsistencies are resolved, a case for the university's pre-common-era vintage is hard to make. Having said that, it sure was an impressively sophisticated centre of learning, with few parallels anywhere else in the pre-medieval world.

Let's now go further back in time and see if anything predates Nalanda as an educational institution. Sure, Plato's Akademia was already up and running when Aśoka built Nalanda's first vihāra, with a headstart of over a century. But what about other civilizations? Do we have anything like a university that predates the Greeks?

Turns out we do.

Deep in the Punjab province of today's Pakistan lies an archaeological site where remains of an ancient site have been excavated over the last several decades. The earliest any structure from this site has been dated to is 518 BCE,[13] placing it firmly within the pre-Hellenistic Achaemenid period. Since 1980, this site is called Bhir Mound on the UNESCO World Heritage List. It is part of the much larger, ancient city of Takṣaśilā. The city still exists, some twenty miles from Rawalpindi, but as Taxila.

For whatever it's worth, though, 518 BCE has recently found challengers who propose a much older dating. They use the features found on excavated pottery as evidence to suggest it is more likely to belong to the period between 800 and 525 BCE.[14]

Be that as it may, the region went under foreign occupation for the first time in the sixth century BCE when it came under the Achaemenids. From that point on, it switched between the Greeks (Indo-Bactrians), the Scythians, the Kuṣāṇas, and the Hunas, before finally returning to native rule after more than half a millennium.

Throughout its existence, Takṣaśilā managed to retain its prominence regardless of who occupied it. Every occupant kept its regional capital or satrapy here. With this prominence came attention. People from far-off places came here for a better life and learning opportunities.

Although no archaeological evidence exists to corroborate this, the Jātakas, a Buddhist body of work, speak of Takṣaśilā as a major centre of Buddhist studies as early as the seventh century BCE. If true, this makes Takṣaśilā the oldest such centre in human history. One must note that the Jātakas themselves came only around the fourth century CE though.

But a university did exist here, even if it came much later than the Jātaka claim. The heavy Greek influence in the region puts Takṣaśilā in a unique position. Along with Indian languages such as Sanskrit and Pali, and philosophies arising from this part of the world, like Vedic philosophy and Buddhism, students could also learn Greek at this university. In fact, Greek was a popular subject here, given its prospects in the Indo-Greek Bactrian rule.

Unlike modern counterparts, the university at Takṣaśilā had no affiliated colleges or schools. Each teacher was an institution unto himself and was free to recruit other teachers to assist him. Students joined individual teachers for the chosen course and not the university. Takṣaśilā was not meant for kids. Only those who had completed elementary-level education went there for further 'specialization' under a teacher of choice, typically at the age of sixteen.[15]

All students lived with their respective teachers on campus. While those from wealthy backgrounds paid for boarding and other living expenses, others made up with manual labour. Tuition is said to have been free of cost, though. There was education for all. Thanks to its proximity and protracted exposure to foreign cultures, Takṣaśila hosted a thriving community of international scholars and students from places such as Persia and China, not unlikely even Greece. This community was believed to consist of as many as 10,000 students by some estimates.[16]

So, is it possible to think of a university older than Takṣaśilā? As per the body of evidence at our disposal right now, not really. This really seems to be where the journey ends. One still can't conclude for sure that there was no education before Takṣaśilā; it's just that this seems to be the oldest example of an organized institution of learning with a comprehensive curriculum and a truly cosmopolitan attendance. Takṣaśilā was, for all intents and purposes, the ancient world's Harvard. Except, it did not have much of an admission barrier.

Who Truly Owns Biryani?

Biryani has now become the single most communally polarizing dish in this country. For the longest time, the dish has enjoyed unquestioned association with Muslims. But a new thought has started gaining currency in recent times: the recipe had existed in India since long before Islam. Is it true? Let's examine all available evidence for either claim and try to settle the debate.

INDIANS HAVE MIXED MEAT WITH RICE SINCE AS LONG AS they have cultivated rice. Although it's hard to see why other rice-eating civilizations wouldn't have done the same, given the ubiquity of meat and the straightforwardness of the idea. But merely mixing rice with meat doesn't a biryani make. It takes a series of very deliberate manoeuvres, improvised and fine-tuned over centuries. Long before biryani, came its humbler ancestor, pilaf. So that's where the story has to begin.

Etymologically, pilaf is a later development. The word's lineage goes all the way back to *puṛukkal* or *puzhungal*, Tamil for 'cooked rice'.

This could have initially just referred to boiled rice, not necessarily with meat, as the name itself derives from *puṛukku*, which means to 'boil paddy before husking'.[1] Later, the Aryans borrowed it into Sanskrit as *pulāka*. Now things start sounding familiar. From Sanskrit pulāka to Persian *pelâv* to Turkish *pilāf* and Hindi *pulāv* was a pretty straightforward journey. Somewhere along the way, meat hopped on to the bandwagon, if not already part of the puṛukkal, and pulao assumed its current form.

Some authors have claimed a reference to the dish in the fifth century Yājñavalkya Smṛti. Others take it further back to the first millennium BCE with references to preparations resembling pulao in the Mahābhārata. Be that as it may, one can safely accept the Indian origins of pulao in its most primitive form.

Interestingly, the dish did not remain confined to India for very long. Nearly a thousand years before the Yājñavalkya Smṛti, came Alexander the Great. The map those days looked very different from today. What's now Uzbekistan, Tajikistan, Kyrgyzstan and Kazakhstan, was then Sogdiana. Together with Bactria, its better-recognized southern neighbour, Sogdiana made up the eastern fringes of the Achaemenid Empire. The two provinces were the wealthiest of all, and the reason was a bustling trade route that cut right through them. Historians call it the Silk Road. In fact, three of its biggest cities—Bukhara, Samarkand, and Khujand—sat right on this route and hosted enormous markets where merchants from lands as far as China, Venice, and India came together to exchange spices, horses, tea, and stories. This sustained interaction also helped introduce travellers from distant lands to each other's cuisines.

The early decades of the fourth century BCE saw the emergence of an ambitious Macedonian who dreamed of conquering not just the Achaemenid country but also whatever lay further east. And he even succeeded to a remarkable extent. By 329 BCE, Alexander's army was in Sogdiana. When the Macedonian entered the capital Samarkand, then named Marakanda, he discovered many culinary novelties, among them a luxurious dish of rice and meat locally known as pilāf.[2]

It's likely the dish was a Sogdian variant of the pulāv brought to the bazaars by merchants and traders from India.

Alexander must have thoroughly enjoyed the dish, for when he returned to Macedonia, he brought the recipe with him. That, one could say, was Europe's first interface with pilāf. So thus far, we have a rice-and-meat dish that emerged in some prehistoric Dravidian culture and then spread to the rest of the subcontinent with the Aryans, to Central Asia with Indian traders, and to Europe with Alexander the Great.

Unfortunately, the exact recipe Alexander carried home is lost to time. It sure was written down but is still awaiting discovery. The earliest written recipe wouldn't come for at least another 1,300 years.

Abu Ali Sīnā or Ibn Sīnā, better known today as Avicenna thanks to European merchants who couldn't pronounce his name correctly, was a Muslim polymath who lived and worked in Sogdiana towards the turn of the tenth century CE. Although this prolific writer authored more than 400 books on subjects ranging from medicine to astronomy and from poetry to geology, he's arguably best known for putting to paper the first ever extant pilāf recipe. For this, he's still celebrated in Uzbekistan and Tajikistan as the 'father of modern pilāf preparation'.[3] But make no mistake, the dish itself is far, far older than this 'father'.

Either with Ibn Sīnā or before him, but certainly long after Alexander, the preparation reached Persia. The region was under the Abbasid Caliphate at the time. And the Abbasids were voracious eaters. Abū Jaʿfar al-Manṣūr, the second caliph in the line-up, had made himself a new capital city and named it Baghdad. This was a time of great affluence, especially for the seat of the biggest Muslim government of its time. Thanks to this affluence, the city became a fertile ground for some of the best gourmet cuisines from around the world. Naturally, the residents indulged generously. And so did the rulers. In fact, al-Manṣūr himself is said to have died from overeating![4]

The fifth caliph, Hārūn Ar-Rašīd, was so worried by this trend that he even hired a personal dietician to approve his menu. But the practice died with him, and the Abbasids returned to their gluttonous ways. His grandson, al-Wāthiq bi'llāh, who took the throne as the ninth caliph, was commonly referred to by a very unflattering nickname, al-Akūl (lit. 'the glutton').[5]

Such was the gastronomical ambience when the star of the Sogdian kitchen made its way into Baghdad. The Abbasid kitchen being the melting pot of world cuisine, pilāf felt right at home, right off the bat, and quickly became a delectable royal fare. The journey doesn't end here, though. Earlier, the Umayyad Caliphate had already taken it to Western Europe as the Andalusian paella. Later, centuries of culinary evolution down the line, the dish would return home to India as pulão.

In the first half of the sixteenth century, less than a decade after the fall of the Abbasids, emerged a new empire-builder from the heart of what once used to be Sogdiana. It was a semi-Mongol warlord with a titanic ambition of building a transcontinental empire. His name was Zahīr ud-Dīn Muhammad, better known as Bābur. With some minor initial hiccups, he eventually succeeded in seeding an empire of his own on the Indian subcontinent, thus establishing the Mughal dynasty. The name, of course, wasn't his idea. It was an appellation that came with the Persians as a corruption of Mongol.[6] Instead, early Mughals used the term Gurkani, a reference to his great-great-great grandfather Timūr Gurkānī or Tamerlane.[7]

Bābur, although from less than opulent origins, was a lover of good food and good poetry—both of which would become the hallmark of Mughal life despite the extreme austerity adopted by some of his descendants.

But the man could never develop a palate for India or its food. In fact, he didn't even intend to build an empire in India. His original mission was just to conquer as much of the subcontinent as possible, rake in all the gold he'd heard about in legends, and then retire to Samarkand.[8] For better or for worse, that never happened.

Among the things he missed the most, besides fruits like melons and grapes, was good meat. Meat was, and continues to be, a staple from where he came. But India was predominantly vegetarian. It hadn't always been the case though. Early Aryans were not all that averse to meat, and there are references to meat as food in both Vedas[9] and the epics.[10] Caraka-Saṃhitā, one of the best-known authorities on Ayurveda, even prescribed things such as sparrow semen, crocodile eggs and buffalo beef as aphrodisiacs.[11]

But things had changed by Bābur's time, and meat had mostly vanished from the mainstream Indian gastronomy. Killing animals for food had come to be seen by most Hindus, and Brahmins in particular, as a barbaric practice. This was in sharp contrast with the pastoral, meat-centric diet Bābur and his men were accustomed to. Bridging this gap wasn't exactly easy.

Little is known for sure about his son's culinary preferences, but we do know that he spent a good decade and a half in Safavid Persia, the land where pelâv was perfected as a royal fare half a millennium ago. Thus, it should be safe to assume he had enjoyed enough of this dish and likely brought it back to India in its flavourful Persian avatar. Humāyūn's reign also witnessed heightened Indo-Persian contact and much cultural and culinary exchange. Many Persian cooks, artists, and bureaucrats migrated to work in the Mughal court during his time. The prevailing anti-Sunni sentiment in the Safavid country had a major role to play in this exodus. Iran's loss became India's gain.

Humāyūn's son and the third of his dynasty, Akbar, was the first truly Indian Mughal. Unlike his predecessors, he was actually born and raised in India and felt a natural connect with the land. His reign saw a period of relative prosperity and a great deal artistic, philosophical, theological and culinary innovation. Akbar believed that cultural synthesis was the key to empire-building and pulled out all the stops to make this the leitmotif of his rule. Perhaps the most well-known manifestation of this endeavour is Tawḥīd-i-Ilāhī, a new syncretic system of faith he invented by bringing together best practices from Hinduism and Islam. Later historians called it Dīn-i-Ilāhī. His kitchen became a bustling laboratory of Indian, Persian and Uzbek chefs exchanging ideas and creating new delicacies in the process, under the watchful eyes of a Mīr Bakāwal or Master of the Kitchen.[12] A whole new kind of food began to take form—the Mughal cuisine. Ironically, Akbar was one of the most frugal eaters in his dynasty. The emperor spent much of his adulthood as an active vegetarian. He even observed fasts on certain days of the week in compliance with Hindu traditions.

Among the many syntheses Akbar's kitchen produced was one that introduced India's spicy richness to Persia's aromatic pelâv, by now fully 're-Indianized' as pulāo. This is also when some cooks added a new elaboration to its preparation: they started cooking rice and meat separately.

This called for skill, as both rice and meat were to be cooked only partially, then the two were layered one above the other multiple times while being infused with aromatic essences such as saffron, rose, or screw pine (kewra). Finally, the mix was sealed off and cooked on low heat until done. The process was extremely sophisticated, and the result tasted luxurious. Although the experiment was based on pilāf, what came out of it tasted very different. It needed a different name.

The dish was predominantly rice and, thanks to the spices involved, looked yellow. These are the traits the new name had to express. After much deliberation, the kitchen finally settled on a name that addressed both—*zard birinj*. A brief list of ingredients for the dish, along with many others popular at the time, first appeared in *Ain-i-Akbari*, an exhaustive three-volume part of a much larger treatise on Akbar's life and administration titled *Akbarnāmā*.[13]

Zard is Persian for yellow or pale. That's the colour part. Now comes rice. Birinj has a long etymological story that goes all the way back to where pilāf first caught international attention—Sogdiana. Birinj is Persian for rice, but descends from Sogdian βrinč. In fact, the recipe section of *Ain-i-Akbari* contains at least two rice preparations with birinj in their name. One, of course, is zard birinj, which is made with meat. The other is *shīrbirinj*, which is made with milk and isn't very different from kheer today. Kheer itself is a corruption of *shīr,* which comes from the Sanskrit word for milk.

Although a consensus is yet to be established, some linguists further extrapolate the Sogdian word to Sanskrit *vrīhí,*[14] which itself could have Dravidian or some other non-Aryan, Austroasiatic origins.

But zard birinj being a mouthful, the name was slowly abbreviated to just birinj. Although the word meant just rice, everyone understood what it referred to, at least in the Mughal court, where the dish quickly became the mainstream rice preparation. Further down the line, birinj itself corrupted to its now-familiar morphology, biryani.

Interestingly, while the evolution from pulāo to biryani was nearly seamless, both were essentially meat-based dishes, contrary to one of the popular modern notions of pulāo being vegetarian and biryani non-vegetarian. The only major distinction one could make between the two is the layering, which is exclusive to biryani. But even that line starts to get blurry when one takes into account the concept of kutcha biryani, where both meat and rice are cooked together and layering is eschewed in the interest of simplicity. Some purists refuse to even consider them biryani, but there's a whole repertoire of variants that are made that way and are mighty mainstream in their respective capacities. Case in point, Bombay biryani.

So, again, who truly owns biryani? The south Indians who invented puṛukkal? The later Aryans who adopted it as pulāka? The Uzbeks who introduced it to the world as pilāf? The Iranians who perfected it to pelâv? Or the Mughals who turned it into what we know as biryani with the invention of its most characteristic trait—layering? Do also note that coastal south India's contacts with the Arab world predate the Mughals by centuries, if not millennia. So, it's not unlikely that their variants developed under Arab and Persian influences independently of the north, even if with a different name than biryani.

Truth is, the preparation is too ubiquitous, has too many contributions, and exists in too many forms to be conveniently assigned a definitive ethnic claim. That said, one can safely place its origins in India, developed under Muslim influence from many distant lands.

Aryans: How Indian or Foreign Are They Anyway?

The notion that Aryans originated in the Indian subcontinent and spread out to the rest of Asia and Europe has gained unusual momentum of late. But does it hold water? Let's do a holistic deep-dive into archaeological, linguistic, scriptural, and anthropological proofs to get to the bottom of the dispute.

WHEN ABRAHAM HYACINTHE ANQUETIL-DUPERRON first landed in Pondicherry in the fall of 1755, the prevailing notion was that all Asian theologies derived from the Vedas, and all languages, at least the ones in currency in India at the time, from Sanskrit. Besides European imperialists such as Britain and France, much of India was under the Mughals at the time. And the lingua franca of this empire was Persian, which was also assumed to be a Sanskrit derivative then. Keen to learn all there is about the Indian way of life, Anquetil-Duperron spent several subsequent years mastering the three languages he thought crucial to his endeavour—Sanskrit, Persian and Avestan.

In 1771, the French orientalist published his first work, a three-part compendium that included a translation of Zend Avesta and a few ancillary works. While working on this project, Anquetil-Duperron noted some curious etymology behind the name Iran.

Among Ahura Mazda's 'sixteen perfect lands', he observed, was one named *Airyanəm Vaējah*. Although the actual location of this perfect realm remains uncertain, it's widely assumed to be Iran. Anquetil-Duperron was the first to draw the etymological parallel between Airyanəm and Iran. But more interestingly, he also saw a parallel between this Zoroastrian realm and Areoi, the name Herodotus gave to the Medes, an ancient Iranian people. Having drawn these parallels, he introduced a new ethnonym to mainstream European scholarship—Aryan.[1] The name caught on, and by the end of the century, it had already entered the English lexicon. By now, most mainstream scholarship was unanimous on there being a common anthropological thread linking Europe with South Asia and on the Aryans being that thread. What still remained to be resolved was where this race originated and how it came to populate the two continents.

The following hundred years witnessed a frenzy of scholarly interest in India's past. The subcontinent had thoroughly captured Europe's imagination as not just some exotic land of sorcerers and jewels but a possible cradle of human civilization. In India, this interest was pioneered by an East India Company judge William Jones, who meticulously researched Sanskrit and other languages as a side project. Until that point, the opinion was split on whether all languages came from Sanskrit. Jones changed that by proposing a third alternative in 1784—an extinct 'Indo-European' tongue ancestral to both Sanskrit as well as Ancient Greek and other languages spoken on the two continents.

A common tongue naturally implies a common people. Now the question was, where was it spoken?

The next big leap in this research came around the middle of the nineteenth century when a German philologist postulated Central Asia as this primordial Aryan homeland. His name was Max Müller. He suggested that the original speakers of the ancestral Indo-European tongue split several thousand years ago and migrated along two divergent routes—one group went west and settled in Europe, and the other went south to settle in Iran and India.[2] This was the birth of the controversial Aryan Migration Theory.

Müller's ideas didn't start off as controversial. If anything, they received massive acceptance right off the bat, both in India and in Europe. Among the names they resonated with instantly was the Hindu nationalist Bal Gangadhar Tilak, who placed the original Aryan homeland in the icy Arctic in his quest to bring Müller's Nordic Aryans closer together with the Vedas' Hindu Aryans. He even wrote a whole book elaborating on this notion in 1903.[3] The only major departure from Müller's suggestion was on the date of the Rigveda. While Müller had suggested 1500 BCE, Tilak pushed it further back to 4500 BCE.

Just as Müller pondered over an Aryan homeland, another gentleman named James Lewis got busy throwing the spotlight on a whole other civilization lost to time in the Ravi basin. By 1842, he published his findings in a book and inadvertently introduced the world to Harappa.[4]

Over the following half century, Indian and British archaeologists working further along the river managed to unearth another prehistoric metropolis in Mohenjo-daro. It was quickly understood that all these sites belonged to a single civilizational continuum that thrived long before Müller's Aryans showed up in the region. They named it the Indus Valley Civilization.

This changed things. Only a hostile takeover could explain a band of pastoralists taking over a settlement as urbane and advanced as the Harappans. Migration was now invasion, and it elegantly explained everything from race relations to the caste system. India came to be seen as home to an indigenous dark-skinned race that once populated the Indus valley, and a foreign light-skinned race that drove them out of the north. The Aryan question seemed finally settled.

But things, as it'd soon become clear, were far from settled. As the nineteenth century progressed and further studies concluded, the Aryan Invasion Theory threw up its first deficiencies. Despite decades of meticulous digging, archaeologists failed to get their hands on any material evidence of this invasion—no weapons, no injured warriors, no warhorses. Violence is a prerequisite for an invasion, and in the absence of any archaeological corroboration thereof, the theory quickly reverted to migration.[5]

By the latter half of the twentieth century, voices rejecting any kind of foreign origin had started acquiring prominence in certain circles. Three theories now competed for acceptance—invasion, migration and out-of-India. Of these, the theory involving invasion grew weaker by the day and is now almost completely rejected in favour of a nonviolent migration.

Before we proceed to examine the controversy, it's important to understand its reason—foreign origin is seen as an academic justification for the British rule over India. Colonizing India wasn't such an evil move because India is a nation of colonizers anyway. That's the notion this theory empowered. On the other hand, an indigenous origin lends Indian nationalists a measure of ethno-cultural superiority by making India a veritable *cradle of civilization*. It empowers nativist sentiments.

But truth warrants a more dispassionate investigation, one that follows evidence and reason rather than politics and sentiments. And those, it seems, favour a foreign origin more than indigenous. Let us see how, but first a brief on what the theory entails.

The north Indian story began with the Indus Valley Civilization some 5,000 years ago. We say north Indian and not Indian, because the latter includes a much older (but still not indigenous, as often claimed) Dravidian reality outside the scope of this conversation. Having enjoyed a good 1,400-year run, this culture entered a phase of steady decline around 1900 BCE and eventually ceased to exist about half a millennium later. Contrary to some beliefs, this was not triggered by foreign invasions or territorial hostilities but by more organic factors, most likely climate.[6]

Concurrent with the later years of the Indus Civilization, two settlements that emerged in the steppes of Eurasia—the Sintashta culture and the Andronovo culture—are crucial to our discussion. So let's focus on them by rewinding a little more—to about 3000 BCE when, one could say, not without a hint of exaggeration, language was born.

The Yamnaya culture, also known as the Ochre Grave or Pit Grave culture, was an early civilization that thrived on the transition from the Copper Age to Bronze Age in the cold stretch between the Black Sea and the Caspian, the Western or Pontic–Caspian steppe. We don't know what they spoke, but whatever they did, experts now believe, was ancestral to most tongues spoken in India and Europe today, including Greek, Latin, Persian and Sanskrit. Hence, they call it Proto-Indo-European (PIE).[7] The Yamnaya people buried their dead in pit mounds, much like their contemporaries, around the Indus.

In the second half of the third millennium BCE, these cattle-herding people started migrating eastward in search of greener pastures and resettled in the Ural–Tobol steppe as the Poltavka culture. But only a few generations down the line, the Poltavka people too came in contact with various Corded Ware settlements nearby and evolved into the Sintashta culture. It's during this phase that a dialectical offshoot of Proto-Indo-European (PIE) is believed to have evolved into the Proto-Indo-Iranian tongue.[8] By the end of 2000 BCE, the Sintashta people further expanded and evolved into what we now call the Andronovo culture in the region along the Ural River.

The Andronovo people are today accepted as the progenitors of the later Indo-Aryan tribes.[9] Driven by ecological and geographical contingencies, they had moved into Anatolia and northern parts of South Asia by 1600 BCE. As of now, this is the mainstream narrative. Evidence supporting it can be assorted into four groups—linguistic, archaeological, genetic/anthropological and cultural/scriptural.

Of these, the linguistic evidence continues to be the oldest and strongest. Several studies have established a seamless family tree of languages that connect Greek, Persian, Sanskrit and Latin to each other with roots in a common PIE spoken by the Yamnaya people more than 5,000 years ago. The language has even been successfully reconstructed by eminent linguists after decades of comparative studies; reconstructed because, of course, its speakers didn't leave written records of what they spoke and how.

But why exactly is successfully charting this tongue so crucial to our discussion anyway? Well, because whoever spoke PIE also spawned Sanskrit, i.e., the origin point of this extinct tongue is also the original homeland of the Aryans.

The existence of PIE can mean one of two things with respect to India: either it migrated *from* India and evolved into other tongues, or it migrated *into* India and the migrating branch was corrupted into Sanskrit along the way. So which one of the two is it? There's only one way to settle this—the Linguistic Centre of Gravity principle (LCG).

Pioneered by American linguist Edward Sapir and popularized by Joseph Greenberg in the 1960s, the principle posits that the most likely birthplace of a language family is the one with the most linguistic diversity within the family.[10] In other words, areas where the family has lived the longest ought to have accorded it the maximum opportunity to diversify into sub-families or dialects. This rules out India right off the bat, as it's home to only one branch, the Indo-Aryan. On the other hand, the areas around the Ural mountains offer the maximum density of Indo-European families, coinciding with the idea of a Western steppe Aryan homeland.[11]

While the argument seems compelling, it's not without its fair share of problems. One glaring issue is the non-contemporaneous status of the language families being compared. Also, depending on the languages we consider, the PIE nucleus moves wildly from the Balkans to even Italy,[12] rendering it highly unreliable as the only indicator of Aryan migration.

This brings us to another set of evidence buried in the various Indo-Iranian scriptures, notably the Vedas and the Avesta.

Vedic Sanskrit, the language of the Rigveda, has been established to have shared origins with Persian, Greek, and Latin, whereas the language of the Indus Valley remains largely undeciphered till date.

Vedic Sanskrit goes back to a few centuries before 1500 BCE, which makes it almost 2,000 years younger than whatever it is the Indus people spoke.[13] But some of the earliest references to Vedic deities come not from India but from Asia Minor.

It's called the Boğazkale Inscription, after the village it was found in. Digging the site in 1906, German archaeologist Hugo Winckler found a clay tablet with cuneiform inscriptions that were subsequently interpreted as an agreement between a Mitanni king and his Hittite neighbour. Winckler dated it to c. 1380 BCE. The three most conspicuous names invoked in this inscription are Arunashshil (cognates with Varuṇa), Mitrashshil (cognates with Mitra), and Indara (cognates with Indra).[14] The presence of these undoubtedly Vedic names in a polity so far away from India has been seen as evidence enough to establish an Aryan presence there more than 3,000 years ago.

Further bolstering the argument is the fact that the Zoroastrian Avesta and the Hindu Rigveda share not only a common vintage but plenty of overlaps in naming too. For example, the deity Mitra is common to both. Other Avesta–Rigveda overlaps include *zaotar*/*hotṛ* (priest), *haoma*/*soma* (ritualistic drink), *daēva* (demon)/*deva* (god), and *ahura* (god)/*asura* (demon).[15] The name Iran itself comes from Avestan *Airyan* via Middle Persian ērān. These similarities are only possible if the authors of both texts had access to a common origin story or at least some linguistic and cultural exchange. Either of these possibilities widens the Aryan-homeland sphere.

All of this, however, may or may not establish a concrete path of migration beyond doubt, as one could just as easily read it all in favour of Aryans originating in India and later migrating westward. Therefore, we need something more unassailable—genetics.

Every living thing is defined in character, nature, and appearance by its DNA—the most basic building block of which is a nucleotide. Each individual is unique because the way their nucleotides are arranged is unique. The most common variation in this arrangement is called a Single Nucleotide Polymorphism or SNP (pronounced 'snip').[16]

In 2010, Scientists at the Harvard Medical School and the Centre for Cellular and Molecular Biology studied more than half a million such SNPs across fifteen Indian states and six language families including two from the Andamans. This study found the majority of Indian populations split between two broad genetic groups—Ancestral North Indians (ANI) and Ancestral South Indians (ASI).[17]

While the ANI pool showed greater affinity to the Middle Easterners, Central Asians and Europeans, the ASI pool resembled none from outside the subcontinent. The conclusion was clear—the Aryans, represented by the ANI genetics, are closer to the people from Central Asia than they are to those from southern India. This establishes the most scientific ground thus far, for the idea that the Aryan gene isn't native to India. Ergo, the Aryans migrated *into* India and not *from* India.

So it's settled, right? That the Aryans aren't indigenous? Well, almost; only one problem—Sinauli.

In 2005, archaeologists digging at a prehistoric site in western UP's Sinauli found a Late Harappan culture they subsequently dated to around 2000 BCE. While interesting, this find was barely remarkable in the context of this discussion. Then in 2018, a second round of excavations revealed more. The dating that was done this time around places it right in the middle of the Harappan-to-Aryan transition. Among its finds was identified a large cache of funerary artefacts, including wooden coffins and chariots.[18] Wooden coffins have earlier been found in Indus Valley sites like Harappa and Dholavira, whereas chariots are an established Aryan mainstay. This makes Sinauli the perfect missing link in the Harappan-Aryan continuum, and Aryans a mere eastward extension of the indigenous Indus Valley peoples.

But the whole thing hinges on a couple of assumptions—one of them being that the Vedic people buried their dead, which they mostly did not. The notion of the indigenous Aryan is further complicated by the presence or absence, in Sinauli, of chariots.

Why chariots? Because where there are chariots, there are horses; and where there are horses, there are Aryans. From Daśaratha's *aśvamedhá* ceremony to Abhimanyu's broken chariot, the two epics are packed with equine themes of all kinds. Horses also feature heavily in the Rigveda as draught animals and, in at least one post-Vedic text as Hayagrīva, an avatar of Viṣṅu.

Horses are traditionally wild beasts and, for the longest time, roamed the vast Pontic expanse freely, with zero human interference. Then one day, man learnt to tame the animal and put it to use for a wide range of domestic applications, including nutrition. These were the Yamnaya people, the first to domesticate an otherwise extremely unwieldy beast.[19] The Sintashta people further extended their utility with the invention of chariots around the turn of the second millennium BCE.[20] Now, entire settlements could traverse vast distances with relative ease, which explains the sudden explosion in the area of influence when the Andronovo culture came about.

So, once again, horses and chariots are an absolute prerequisite for any archaeological finding to be called Aryan. And that's where Sinauli falters.

What they found in Sinauli were wooden carts, not chariots. What's the difference, you ask? Spokes. Carts have solid wheels; chariots have spoked wheels. Sure, impressions of some triangular copper embellishments have been identified on Sinauli wheels, but the wheels themselves remain solid. Those copper pieces are not spokes—not by any stretch of the imagination.[21]

Vedic carriages are chariots and not carts; there's little ambiguity on that bit. Carts drawn by bulls are no stranger to Harappan digs, spoked chariots drawn by horses are. Just as they are alien to the landscape of Sinauli.

Another nail in the Sinauli coffin comes from the complete absence of horse fossils in any of its digs. Not in Sinauli, not in Harappa, not in Dholavira, and not in Rakhigarhi—no horse remains have ever been dug out of any site contemporaneous with the Indus Civilization.[22]

Does that mean Aryans came from abroad? In light of all the evidence, both archaeological and genetic, available to us right now, most likely. Interestingly, so did the folks at Sinauli, it seems. The Copper Hoard culture that peopled the settlements at Sinauli and Daimabad has been now understood to be part of a 'first wave' of pre-Sintashta immigrants, most likely from the Bactria–Margiana Archaeological Complex or BMAC, commonly referred to as the Oxus civilization. It's in a 'second wave' that the chariot-riding Indo-Aryans familiar to us as the warrior-class Vedic people finally showed up.[23] Thus, once again, it's perfectly safe to conclude that the Indo-Aryan peoples weren't indigenous to the Indian subcontinent.

But that's not to say that the situation can never change. New findings can always flip the whole story in ways we can't predict. Who knows, we might just dig up spoked wheels or even horse fossils at one of those sites tomorrow? But until such a time, all evidence of Aryan origins—horse, chariot, spoke, genetics, language — points to the grassy plains dominated by the majestic Urals.

Is the Swastika Exclusively Hindu?

It's hard to imagine the Swastika and Hinduism as distinct thanks to an association that goes back millennia. But many Europeans have now started claiming the symbol as theirs. Whose claim does archaeology support? It's certainly not the Nazis as, if anything, they were the last to the party. But did anyone use or even know it before it entered Vedic iconography?

IN 1920, THE NAZI PARTY ADOPTED AS ITS SYMBOL A symmetrical black cross tilted at 45° with arms bent 90°. By 1933, it was on the national flag. They called it Hakenkreuz, the crooked cross; Swastika to the rest of the world. What we think of as a Hindu symbol now stood besmirched for the rest of its time due to this association.

But Germany's troubled relationship with the Swastika is far older than Hitler or his outfit. Völkische Bewegung, a lesser-known precursor of Nazism, had used the Swastika as the symbol of Aryan supremacy since at least 1907. Of course, even this isn't where the Swastika story begins. Going further back, we come to 1870.

Enter Heinrich Schliemann, a German businessman, archaeologist, and above all, the man who brought Swastika to Germany.

Schliemann dug up a private property on the fringes of Çanakkale, Turkey, because someone told him it was the site of Helen's Troy. Here once stood the ancient city of Hissarlik. Although he didn't find Troy, Schliemann did stumble upon nine buried cities and what he called 'Priam's Treasure', a cache of gold and jewels dating back centuries, maybe millennia. And a vase with a familiar symbol painted on its side—a symmetrical cross with arms bent at 90 degrees.

A Swastika.[1]

Ensuing digs yielded another 1,800 of those. Schliemann rushed to discuss this with a friend and fellow German who shared his passion in history and archaeology, but for India instead of Greece. His name was Max Müller.

Müller was convinced the symbol came to Ancient Greece from India via the Silk Road. The Greeks, you see, are themselves no strangers to crosses. In fact, one where both arms are of the same length is called a Greek Cross.[2] The symbol predates Christianity.

One of the letters in the Greek alphabet is gamma, the uppercase of which (Γ) if rotated 90° thrice around its base, gives what looks like the Swastika. The Greeks called it *tetragammadion* (lit. 'four capital gammas').[3] This was, thanks to the general esteem commanded by Greek scholarship across Europe, the most common name for the symbol until the turn of the nineteenth century.

Then came a new crop of Indologists and Orientalists like Müller, who replaced Ancient Greece with India as the centrepiece of European scholarship. The symbol that so far had enjoyed a Pelasgic origin, now became Indian. Tetragammadion was now Swastika.

But before we debate whether the symbol is Greek or Indian, let me introduce a third contender—a piece of silk that was dug out of sites in El Etmannyieh near Egypt's Coptic hub of Asyut and now sits in London's Victoria and Albert Museum. Known by its accession number, T.231-1923, the artefact has been dated to around 300 CE.[4]

That's when El Etmannyieh was Qau-el-Kabir. The off-white piece of textile carries painted motifs that include pink pyramids, green squares, and green...

Swastikas.

Four around each square.

So the options for the origin of the Swastika now become Greece, India and Egypt. But which of them, if any, owns the symbol? Well, for now, the answer seems to favour India. That's because the Indian story goes way back from here, right into antiquity.

The world's first grammar was written for the Sanskrit language by a man named Pāṇini. The book is called *Aṣṭādhyāyī* (lit. 'eight chapters'). Pāṇini is said to have lived anywhere between 600 BCE and 300 BCE. It's in this work (*adhyāya* 6, *pāda* 3, *sūtra* 115) that Swastika makes its debut as a written word.[5] Here, it features in a compound form, *Swastika-karṇa* (lit. 'Swastika ear').

Cattle branding was a common practice in Pāṇini's days. Much like today, this was for easier identification. Different owners used different branding signs, and the Swastika was one of them. The term Swastika-karṇa referred to an ear (karṇa is Sanskrit for ear) branded with the Swastika. This makes the symbol at least 2,300 years old. But we're not done yet.

Cattle branding as a practice predates Pāṇini by centuries and finds reference even in the Vedas. The name Swastika itself is a compound of *su* meaning 'good', and *asti* meaning 'to be'. Sure, the word Swastika itself doesn't appear in the Vedas but its two linguistic components do. With that information, it's safe to assume that early Aryans were well aware of the symbol, at least in some primitive form. This pushes the Swastika further back to at least 1200 BCE and makes it firmly Indian. And not just Indian, but Hindu.

There's a small issue with that last bit, though.

Some 250 miles north of Khartoum, Sudan, by the Nile, is a place called Gebel Barkal. Named after a solitary hill standing roughly

320 feet above the Nubian desert, Gebel Barkal was once part of an autonomous Kingdom of Kush. Although vassal to the Pharaohs in Egypt, Kush managed to retain its cultural autonomy for the most part.

Just like their Egyptian neighbours, Kushites were prolific temple builders. Gebel Barkal alone has over a dozen temples dedicated to deities such as Mut, Amun, and even members of the royal family as was common in all of Nubia in those days.

But it wasn't until the nineteenth century that the world even learnt of its existence. By the end of the century, a decent amount of Kush had been pulled out of the ground. This snapshot of sandy prehistory has thus far yielded many artefacts that tell us how ahead of its time this culture was. Among these artefacts are shards of ancient pottery. And spindles. Today, one such spindle whorl sits in the Sudan National Museum referenced as SNM 9935. The whorl comes stamped with what looks like a Swastika.[6]

Although the Kushites were contemporary to the Vedas, no evidence of Indo-Kushite contact exists as of today. So now it's between the Egypt–Sudan region and India. But even that isn't the only contender for India.

Koban is a village in North Ossetia-Alania, a semi-autonomous republic in the Russian part of the Caucasus. This village, like villages in general, had lived in blissful obscurity since forever. But that changed when a bunch of archaeologists showed up and started digging in 1869. What emerged soon was a whole Bronze Age civilization never heard of before. Among the finds was a piece of what they presumed to be a girdle. A sash, if you will. Meticulously etched with Swastikas.[7]

This changes things. At 3,200 years, the Koban culture is far older than Pāṇini and far too unrelated to both Ancient Greeks and the Kushites.

Is there anyone else who can claim to own the Swastika now, if not Indians, Greeks, or Egyptians?

Let's see, we'll now make one last trip to India before exploring more candidates. There was another culture in this part of the world that thrived and vanished even before the Aryans showed up.

Most experts place the Indus Valley Civilization between 3000 and 1200 BCE, making it significantly ancient.[8] Archaeologists began digging here in 1921 and have built an enormous inventory of artefacts since. Part of one of these artefacts is a Swastika-bearing clay seal dated to c. 2000 BCE. It comes from 'room 202, trench 43' of Harappa and is referenced as H99-3814.[9] Being older than Kushite spindles, this seal brings the Swastika comfortably back to the subcontinent. And it's not the only one.

The Indus Valley Swastikas are the oldest ever discovered on the Indian subcontinent. But since the Harappans left before the Aryans showed up, are these Swastikas older than Hinduism itself?

Almost a thousand years before the Indus Valley Civilization was the Samarra culture of Mesopotamia, roughly today's Iraq. These were a socially complex people that thrived off the Tigris not far from the modern city of Samarra. From here comes the famous Samarra bowl. They've dated it to 4000 BCE, which makes it older than Harappan seals and Kushite spindles. There's a Swastika painted on the bowl.

The first Hindu wouldn't appear for another 2,000 years at the very least.

Of course, even this isn't final.

Not far from today's Shanghai, some 7,000 years ago, there flourished a lesser-known Stone Age civilization fed by the Yangtze—the Majiabang culture. Among the wares unearthed at this Neolithic site is a remarkably intact jar adorned in rich patterns that are interspersed with a very familiar symbol. Any guesses which one?

The Majiabang Swastika predates its Indus Valley counterpart by centuries, if not millennia. But don't hand it to the Chinese just yet.

So far, we have Egypt, Sudan, Iraq, Russia, and China. And, of course, India. Complicating the matter further is a piece of evidence from 6000 BCE Bulgaria.

Now we're solidly beyond the realm of history. The right word here would be 'prehistory'. About a three-hour drive from the capital of present-day Bulgaria is an enormous limestone cave with many prehistoric artefacts and many more bats. It's called the Devetashka

Cave. This cave is a cornucopia of Palaeolithic wares going as far back as 9,000 years, maybe even longer.

A piece of painted ceramic ware found here was dated to 6000 BCE. Painted with, among other things, Swastikas. It's exactly the kind of Swastika you see today, except in the opposite direction. Sanskrit calls such Swastikas, Sauwastika.

But the Balkans' relationship with the omnipresent symbol doesn't end here. The Swastika has been found all over the place, mostly in Bulgaria but also in Romania as well as the rest of the Slavic world, most of them prehistoric. One such artefact was a Swastika-like nephrite amulet that showed up during an excavation near Slatina in Romania. Nephrite, one of the two forms of jade, was extensively used by the Paleoliths of the region as jewellery and probably also talismans.

Another similar find came from Kardžali, a Bulgarian municipality some 300 miles to the south. Both artefacts bear a remarkable similarity to the Swastika, albeit they also look like frogs. That's why they're called 'frog Swastikas'. Both go back at least 8,000 years.

Also from Romania come three mysterious finds collectively called the Tărtăria tablets. Named after the Neolithic site they were dug out of, these have inscriptions that remain undeciphered to date. Most experts place them around 5500 BCE.

What makes these tablets special is the script of the engraving. Known as the Vinča symbols, this script is far less known than its Sumerian counterparts and, consequently, far less studied. Since most tablets bearing this script have been found in the Danube region, it's also sometimes called the Danube script. Many studies suggest that this is the world's first writing system, predating even the Mesopotamian cuneiform. The reason we're discussing this script is, of course, the Swastika.

The symbol features in the Vinča glyph-set, not once but twice—once clockwise, once counterclockwise. That makes the Vinča Swastika nearly as old as the frog Swastikas of Kardžali. Be that as it may, the Swastikas of the Balkans surely beat the Chinese by two millennia and the Harappans by at least four.

Similarly dated Swastikas have also been found as rock carvings in Italy's Camonica Valley, Lombardy's Camunian Rose being one of them.

Circling back to Europe, where we started this journey, let's head to Ukraine. Somewhere in Kyiv's National Museum of the History of Ukraine sits a figure carved out of a mammoth tusk. It was retrieved from a Palaeolithic site near Mezine. Whether the figure in 1908 is that of a woman or a bird is still the subject of debate. But the mammoths mostly went extinct over 10,000 years ago, so that's how old the item must be, at the very least.

Closer inspection of the figure reveals etchings of concentric straight lines. Think spiral but with straight lines, instead of rings. The etchings are similar to a well-known symbol with similarly squarish 'rings', although with far fewer lines. It is concentric lines, spreading out around a central axis, bent around each other repeatedly at right angles. Think Swastika with extra-long arms!

The same pattern also shows up on other mammoth artefacts from this site, such as the famous Mezine bracelet. Just like the mysterious bird figure, this bracelet has been variously dated to between 12,000 and 15,000 years ago. For perspective, the Vedas were composed around 3,500 years ago.

This right here is the Mezine Swastika of Ukraine, the oldest mankind has discovered so far.

Between Mezine's bracelet and Hitler's Hakenkreuz, is a whole mélange of crooked crosses that have shown up in places completely unrelated to each other. There are Minoan amphoras with painted Swastikas, Roman tiles with recurring Swastika patterns, and Polish Orthodox vestibules embroidered with Swastika leitmotifs. There are Native American peoples that still use the symbol as a good luck charm (e.g., the Navajo tsil no'oli').

The symbol also gets an astronomical interpretation in some cultures such as Nordic, Ashanti, and the Minoan. Two interpretations exist in this class. In one, it represents the Sun; in the other, the pole star with the big dipper constellation around it (four positions in four seasons).

The oldest one from Mezine—not the bracelet—seems to be a representation of either a female form (some kind of a fertility cult) or a stork in flight. This also seems to be the case with the Samarra specimen.

All interpretations point to nature worship. Hinduism, being inherently a nature-worshipping system, can then easily stake its claim on the pagan symbol. That means the Swastika might have originated on the Indian subcontinent and later spread to other parts of the world; but if that were the case, the Carpathians wouldn't be a bigger source of prehistoric Swastika than the Himalayas.

So who invented the symbol that's called, among other things, Swastika?

Short answer, everybody.

How Integral Are Temples to Hinduism?

Just like the Swastika, it's impossible to imagine Hinduism without its mandirs. And Hindus claim they've been building temples since forever. But what does forever mean in a historical context? Was there a point in time we can go back to when the first Hindu temple would have been built? And most importantly, did anyone build temples before that time?

TUCKED AWAY IN THE DUNES OF UPPER EGYPT IS THE nearly 4,000-year-old mortuary temple of Mentuhotep II,[1] some of the oldest extant temples in the region. Far older are the limestone megaliths of Ħaġar Qim and Mnajdra in Malta,[2] both said to have once hosted ritualistic sacrifices as part of a fertility cult.

These are some remarkably ancient complexes we're talking about. And yet, their vintage pales in comparison to what's by far the world's oldest temple. It's a mind-numbing 11,000 years old and predates tools, agriculture, even the wheel.

Three hours from Gaziantep in south-eastern Turkey, close to its Syrian border, is recorded history's oldest megalith and a marvel of human enterprise.

Göbekli Tepe.[3]

Built by a highly ritualistic 'skull cult', the structure was built by literal cavemen!

By 800 BCE, the Greeks had started building their own temples, complete with the colonnade that came to lend them their iconic peripteral appearance.[4] Between 500 and 200 BCE, the region saw a building fad that gave us many structures still standing today.

As we've seen, temple complexes have a rich and long history—one that's much longer than we tend to appreciate. But what about those in our part of the world? Some sources name the Mundeshwari Temple of Bihar as one of the oldest.[5] This building beats even the ones at Elephanta by more than a century. Of nearly the same vintage is the Balaji Temple of Tirupati, but even that doesn't go beyond 300 CE.[6] No older structure has so far been unearthed that could be considered a temple complex with reasonable certainty.

Why did we start so late?

This question calls for a dispassionate appreciation of how Indian traditions have evolved and the various influences that shaped them. For the purposes of this discussion, we'll start with the Indus Valley Civilization. One problem with the study of this culture is that their script remains undeciphered to this day—a fact that makes everything opaque. That said, outside of a few sundry seals that *may* be thought of as religious, no definitive religious artefact has yet been found. The cities of the Indus Civilization exhibit a remarkable degree of urban sophistication. They had grid layouts, sewage systems, bazaars, public baths, and even multi-storied housing. But no temple, much less a temple complex.

That doesn't necessarily mean they didn't have the practice of worship. It's likely they were nature worshippers. We still have tribal traditions such as Sarnaism that worship trees and animals.[7] The

Harappans likely did the same. And nature worship seldom warrants elaborate infrastructure.

Even older are some of the oldest 'sacred' rocks in India from Baghor in MP. Experts have dated them to as far as 8000 BCE. These 'pre-Hindus' (as they had little to do with later Vedic cults that assimilated them upon contact) had no need for grand structures.[8]

The Harappans had a good run for almost 2,000 years, and then they vanished.

Next came the Aryans, nomadic pastoralists who had travelled vast distances over generations, most probably unfamiliar with agriculture. Fire played a tremendous role in the Aryans' lives. Being nomadic, they depended on it for not just cooking but also protection from wildlife and the harsh northern chill. Fire was practically life. Naturally, then, it became an object of reverence over time.

Thus began the cult of fire worship—something the Aryans have in common with their Persian brethren, the Zoroastrians. This devotion manifested in a practice that continues to this day—*yajñas*, one of the earliest cornerstones of Aryan theology.[9]

Yajñás involved makeshift rock contraptions for holding a wood fire to which offerings (*hōma*) were made accompanied by religious chants. Once the ritual was over, the setup would be destroyed and the site abandoned as the tribe moved on. The same process would later repeat at a new location.

The Rigveda, which is estimated to have been composed around 1200 BCE, has no reference to permanent places of worship or temple complexes whatsoever, as affirmed by Scottish Sanskrit scholar and indologist Arthur Berriedale Keith.[10]

But that doesn't mean physical deities and places of worship didn't exist on the subcontinent at all. Indigenous tribes have worshipped natural elements, especially trees, for millennia. They've even had permanent shrines since long before the Aryans—the one at Baghor being a case in point.

One key difference between these primordial shrines and mainstream Hindu temples, though, is that the deity doesn't permanently live in these but only visits on occasions. Many such practices were later adopted into the subsequent Hindu tradition.

These shrines were mostly situated in the forest or on river banks, away from human settlement. Yes, these people lived in permanent settlements and engaged in farming. No formal theology existed back then, and they worshipped forest spirits that later Aryans called *yakṣas* (the name was also attributed to the worshippers themselves at times).[11] These were clothed and fed, especially during a natural crisis, such as a famine. Keeping the spirits happy was imperative, because it was believed that only then would they return the favour. These early Indians also painted on cave walls. Rock-cut structures and cave temples were only a later extension of this practice.

To call them even proto-Hindu would be presumptuous.

Initially, the Aryans had no need for permanent structures, given their mobile lifestyle. In fact, when they started building shrines, they were almost always portable and carried around on carts and chariots. This practice would later develop into the *vimāna* (aeroplane) architecture.

Another remnant of this concept can be seen in the *rath yātrās* still taken out in various parts of the country. A result of the unique blend between the farming and the herding community is the practice of festival pandals, which are dismantled and rebuilt every year.

Depicting Vedic deities in human form had an organic start. But the practice gained visible traction after the fifth century BCE with the Ionian Greeks, whose idolatry was already at a highly mature stage by the time. The Aryans called them Yavanas.

These early European conquerors brought with them a vibrant tradition of fine arts and theatre; theatrical curtains are still called *yavanikā* in Sanskrit.[12] They also brought new systems of divine representation. But temple complexes were still a long way away. The last five centuries before the common era were quite eventful. In this window, Buddhism emerged, Jainism went mainstream, and Valmiki wrote the RāmāyanaRāmāyana. The two new cults pioneered something new during this period. By now, the indigenous sacred groves had been internalized by the Aryans as chaityas.

Buddhism is an atheistic system, i.e., it doesn't posit a creator deity. That said, Buddha was already beginning to be accorded a godlike personality cult within his lifetime. After his death, followers preserved his relics in commemorative chaityas. From this point on, chaityas would almost exclusively be associated with Buddhism. Buddhist chaityas aren't exactly temples; they're more like a sacred mausoleum, a permanent heap of rocks placed atop a buried relic. And they are meant more for commemoration than for worship.[13] With time, their sombre ambience made them ideal haunts for monks looking to meditate.

Chaityas also find references in Hindi epics, especially in the Rāmāyana.[14] The transition from chaityas to formal temples as places of ritualized worship was a gradual, organic one. But so far, no formal temple from before the common era has been found in India.

The epics also reference a characteristic Vedic feature called *yūpa*. Yūpas were sacrificial contraptions. Animal sacrifice is a key Vedic ritual. These were mostly tall wooden posts meant to hold the victim in place.[15] Over time, spaces around these yūpas evolved first into mandapas, then into courtyards of much larger temple complexes.

At this point, two terms need to be introduced—*Shudra* and *Mleccha*. These were broadly names the Aryans gave to the indigenous forest people[16] and non-Aryan foreigners,[17] respectively. (The Greeks were also thought of as mlecchas, but they were also more specifically referred to as Yavanas.)

Interestingly, the Hindu temple system evolved as a cultural borrowing from both shudra and mleccha traditions, which is how yajñá evolved into pooja. Scholarship attesting to this comes from no fewer than four seminal sources, including well-known names such as P.T. Srinivasa Iyengar and S. Radhakrishnan. But these are still secondary expositions prone to subjective prejudices, even if eminent. We need more *primary* references.

One such reference comes from one of the most elaborate authorities on Hindu iconography, the three-part *Viṣṅudharmottara Purāṅa*. Of its 570 adhyāyas or chapters, the one that interests us is no. 93. Part of a set that elaborates on Vedic liturgy and musicology, this adhyāya has something very unambiguous to say about temples.

But before we get to the piece, let's understand one key concept—the concept of Hindu timekeeping known as the *yuga*. In short, Hinduism considers time as a cycle or *chakra* of four finite periods in an infinitely repeating loop. These are Satya Yuga (also called Krita Yuga), Treta Yuga, Dvapara Yuga and Kali Yuga. We're currently said to be in the last one, the Kali Yuga. Once this is over, it's back to Satya Yuga, and the cycle will repeat. Rāma is said to be part of the later Treta Yuga and Krishna of Dvapara. With that in mind, let's return to Viṣṅudharmottara, adhyāya 93, verses 1 to 3, where it's asserted that temples and statues were redundant in those two yugas, as gods lived among humans.[18]

Viṣṅudharmottara itself is considered supplemental to *Viṣṅu Purāṇa*, one of the eighteen Mahāpurāṅas. Naturally, the supplement cannot be older than the main text. Therefore, one way to ascertain the age of Viṣṅudharmottara is to date the *Viṣṅu Purāṇa* itself. Depending on whom we ask, that's between 400 CE[19] and 800 CE[20] (although the author is careful to call this date the date of compilation and not composition), with one theory even positing 900 CE.[21] The latter date comes from none other than the eminent Marathi-language litterateur, historian, and a friend and ally of Lokmanya Tilak, Chintaman Vinayak Vaidya.

Another, slightly older, reference to temples as places of worship comes from a text that continues to trigger much high-octane socio-political debate to this day—the Manusmṛiti. But even this work only goes as far back as 200 CE,[22] which is still centuries after the Greeks invaded, ruled and assimilated into the subcontinent.

Basically, Hindu temples or mandirs, are a Purāṇic feature, as is evident from the *Viṣṅu Purāṇa*. And by the time they did show up, in what's called the Purāṇic Age, the *Śramaṇas* and the *Brāhmaṇas* had already completed their separation, something that started much earlier with Aśoka. Śramaṇa included Buddhists and Jains, among other fringe traditions.

While the Brāhmaṇa orthodoxy continued its focus on ritualistic sacrifices and yajñá at yūpas and *yajñáshalas*, respectively, heterodox Śramaṇas were already building elaborate chaityas and vihāras as centres of meditation.

Long story short, temples as permanent divine abodes (unlike ancient indigenous shrines where gods only visited on occasions) didn't start showing up prominently until as late as 200 CE.

And even when they did, they were mostly commemorative and not religious. Besides being places of worship, they were meant to glorify the royalty, somewhat like the mortuary temples of Ancient Nubia. One of the most instantly recognizable exhibits is the temple at Tirupati, which began with a dowager Pallava Queen's land grant.[23] These land grants became increasingly common, towards the latter half of the first millennium, as a monarch's way of securing their subjects' loyalty and obeisance.

A paper published in 2018, titled 'From Megaliths to Temples: Astronomy in the Lithic Record of South India' also attests to the commemorative nature of structures built by the Chalukyas in places like Aihole and Badami, until as recently as 800 CE.[24]

Most structures in this period were either being carved into hills and rocks, or sculpted into caves. Grandeur was naturally the theme as their main objective was to glorify the royalty. The Kailāsa temple at Ellora and those at Mahabalipuram belong to this genre.

All this would change quickly around the tenth century when temples as places of devotion and worship would go wildly mainstream and become the single-most compelling expression of faith. But why?

The answer lies in the cyclical nature of urban development. As expected, urban peaks bring about innovation and rapid structural changes; decays stall them. The first urban decline came after the first few generations of the Guptas. The dynasty had inherited from the Kuṣāṇas, a territory enriched by steady long-distance commerce with the Persians, the Chinese and the Greeks. The Kuṣāṇas were a Chinese tribe with heavy Greek influence. Their ouster by the Guptas triggered a steady decline in urbanization that lasted pretty much the entirety of the Gupta Era.[25]

Things started turning around in the middle of the ninth century, with the opening up of long-distance maritime trade. Magnificent new urban centres came up all over South, Asia. The epicentre of development now shifted to the south, with the emergence of strong Deccan dynasties such as the Chalukyas and Rashtrakutas.

With this new affluence came new ideas, new expressions. While most of it was in the areas of literature and prosody, much also went into a more material form of vanity—temple building. Just like in Ancient Egypt, kingship now started acquiring a semi-divine character.

This was different from the north where kings were mere kings, not gods. In the south, temples became idioms of power. Kings became Viṣṅu incarnates and started adopting names like Sri and Prithvivallabha. This triggered a building frenzy, and enormous temple complexes started sprouting all over the subcontinent and beyond. Very often, these complexes also doubled as royal headquarters, in keeping with the king's divine eminence.

These complexes were generally built in compliance with *Mānasāra*, a derivative seventh-century text on architecture. The authorship of this text remains unknown.[26] The text prescribed separate sections for the king and the gods, called *rājaharmya* and *devaharmya,* respectively. Even within the rājaharmya, the hierarchies of early Hindu feudalism were elaborately preserved.[27]

The king was even accorded rituals that were originally meant for gods! The most pronounced of these was the *nityābhishekam*, or daily anointment.

The later Chola kings were even more energetic in their expression. Most notable of these was Rajendra Chola I, who openly identified as Rajarājeśvaram or Shiva. In some temples, the distinction between king and the divine just didn't exist. The eleventh-century Bṛihádīśvara

Temple of Thanjavur is also called Rajarājeśvaram after the deity it houses. It was built by Rajendra Chola I.

Much of this can be traced back to a single individual keen on adding grandeur to the Hindu expressions, the great Vaishnava reformer and theologian Śrī Rāmānujāchārya. He lived in the eleventh century and was an enormous influence on the Bhakti revival with his *Arcā Vigraha*, which meant divine representation in material form.[28] This was the first major push towards Hindu idolatry and a radical departure from the *nirguṇa* philosophies of Madhvāchārya (Dvaita) and Ādi Shankara (Advaita).

This fresh injection of reforms fuelled a frenzy that swept through the Deccan well into the twelfth century. The Cholas, although initially averse to this new wave, soon hopped on the bandwagon and started building bigger and bigger temples.

It was practically a contest. The bigger the structure, the more invincible the empire. By the fourteenth century, the frenzy assumed new proportions in what's today parts of Karnataka and Andhra Pradesh. There's a reason for that—Islam.

A series of Turkic raids in the thirteenth century threatened the Hindu way of life for the first time ever. While all the earlier invaders had assimilated, these didn't. Within a century, most of the north was under the Delhi Sultanate, having suffered devastating waves of Muslim invasion mostly by Turkic-Afghan hordes.[29] By the fourteenth century, what's today Telangana and Maharashtra had also been Islamized by the likes of Alauddin Khilji and Muhammad bin Tughlaq.

It's against this backdrop that two Yadava brothers established the Vijayanagar Empire.

The threat of Islamic invasion was real and present; temples were being razed indiscriminately. This triggered the Vijayanagar Empire's fanatical temple-building efforts. The idea was to build as many as possible to ensure that some survived.

Within decades, thousands of new temples and temple complexes sprouted all over the kingdom. The empire itself eventually succumbed to the Turuks (the Indian term for Muslims back then) after a 200–year run, but not before having produced some of the most iconic temples in all of the Deccan. The evolution of temples from here on is more or less unceremonious.

That said, it'd be highly reductive to blame the absence of all structures from antiquity on Muslim invaders. It's true they tore down many, but not all. They couldn't.

For example, places such as Sudan, Egypt, Turkey and Mesopotamia were fully Islamized long before India became reasonably familiar with the religion, and far more comprehensively. Yet, those places still have pre-Islamic structures that go back thousands of years.

Therefore, only one thing can explain the absolute lack of temple complexes from before the common era—that they didn't exist.

Āryabhata Gave Us Zero, but Did He Invent It?

We gave the world zero, that's what we've heard countless times all our lives in many a passionate conversation around India. How true is it though? Let's piece together all we have in the way of inscriptions from around the world and India to confirm if Āryabhata was really the first to use the much-discussed numeral in the world. Or in India.

Once upon a time, in the fertile expanse between the Tigris and the Euphrates, in what's today southern Iraq, there lived a people who engaged in commerce, had a system of weights and measures, paid in currency, and most importantly, kept written records of all of this in clay tablets. Part of a larger entity called Mesopotamia, these are said to be some of the first humans to have formed some kind of a civilization. We call them Sumerians. Sumer, their settlement, occupied a major section of southern Mesopotamia.

Writing was a real chore back then. The Sumerians would make tablets out of wet clay and use a hollow reed to etch rough representations of physical elements, such as body parts, trees or astronomical bodies, into it while still wet and soft. We call them pictograms. Once done, the tablet would be baked in a kiln to make the etchings permanent. That's how they wrote. It goes without saying, only the most crucial pieces of information were written and by only a select few. One just couldn't afford to be frivolous with a process this involved and deliberate.

But this was a really long time ago; we're talking 3000 BCE and earlier. Some of the earliest such tablets come from the ancient Sumerian settlement of Uruk, today called al-Warka.[1]

With time, the reed further evolved into a three-sided stylus. Instead of circles and semi-circles, the stylus did lines and wedges, which further simplified and sped up writing. This was cuneiform, a writing system made up of cuneus (Latin for 'wedges'). Unlike us today, the Sumerians counted in 60s (Well, sort of, but we'll get to that later). We call this the sexagesimal system. Ours is in 10s, i.e., decimal system.

Around 2300 BCE emerged the first true empire in recorded history—under Sargon of Akkad. He conquered Sumer and other Mesopotamian territories to build the Akkadian Empire. Here, the Akkadians found not only some of the most fertile lands known to mankind, but also a whole new script along with a counting system. Soon, they were writing in cuneiform Akkadian and counting in sexagesimal. Over the following few centuries, the system was made mainstream all over Mesopotamia and Babylon.

By 2000 BCE, the Akkadian country had expanded to cover all of Mesopotamia. With this, cuneiform came to Babylon. And so did a whole new counting system. Now, it's hard to say with certainty which of the myriad Mesopotamian counting systems made it to this stage, because Mesopotamia had little in the way of standardization. Upper Mesopotamia counted differently from Lower Mesopotamia and Sumer. Even within Sumer, different cities practised different systems.

The two biggest contenders are Sumerian of Kish and Eblaite of Ebla. Both employed the sexagesimal system in some form, and both wrote in cuneiform. So, one of these entered Babylon and, more or less, became standard across the Akkadian country.

Under this system, digits were represented using two cuneiform symbols. One was a straight vertical wedge and looked somewhat like an inverted lowercase 'l'. The other was a 'corner wedge' or 'hook' resembling the modern '<' sign[2].

So, 1 was a single vertical stroke, 2 was two vertical strokes, and so on. From 4 onwards, though, the strokes were also arranged in multiple rows vertically to save space. So, 4 was two vertical strokes above two vertical strokes instead of four vertical strokes in a single file. Finally, 9 was a 3-by-3 matrix of nine vertical strokes. With 10, the monotony broke and instead of ten vertical strokes, a single hook was used.

For 11, it was just a combination of the hook and the vertical stroke, roughly resembling '<l'. Similarly, 53 was written as '<<<<<lll'.

If this sounds like a decimal system, that's because it was. At least partially. Interestingly, the single vertical stroke returned with 60; this means, instead of '<<<<<<', it was just 'l'. Thus, 1 and 60 had the exact same symbol. This could cause a great deal of confusion. But it didn't, and we'll shortly see why. For now, the takeaway is that the Babylonians counted in a mix of 10s and 60s.

Now circling back to the ambiguity between 60 and 1, at first it was handled by making the stroke for 60 a little longer. Do note that most of the time, the context was enough to tell the difference. Of course, the longer stroke would only help when seen relative to another, shorter one, which means a stroke by itself could not be interpreted as 1 or 60 with certainty. So, an easy solution was to never write 60 in isolation, unless the context made it obvious what number was meant.

Since it's a little difficult to represent the longer stroke using English letters, we'll use the uppercase 'L' for 60. So, for our purposes, it's 'l' for 1 and 'L' for 60, while 10 remains '<'. Using this method, we can translate, say, 63, into Babylonian as 60+1+1+1 or 'Llll'. Just to reiterate, the first vertical stroke here would be larger than the remaining three on an actual Babylonian tablet.

Finally, let's try a bigger number before moving on. How about 152? Let's see, we can break it down as 60+60+10+10+10+1+1, which gives us 'LL<<<ll'. On a real tablet, of course, it'd appear as two large vertical strokes followed by three hooks and two regular vertical strokes.

But the similarity between 'L' and 'l' was problematic. Sizes could vary from hand to hand and a 62 (Lll) could very easily be misread, or even mis-etched, as 3 (lll)! To remedy this, someone decided to assign dynamic values to the symbols, i.e., value a digit based on where it sat in the string. Today, we call this the placeholder system. In our placeholder system, each positional shift to the left increases the value of the digit tenfold. We count as ones, tens, hundreds and so on. The Sumerians counted as ones, 60s, 3,600s and so on. Someone decided to make this a written standard.

Now, the size of the wedge didn't matter. What mattered was its position. Thus, 'l' was 1 if in the 1's (first) position, but 60 if in the 60s (second) position, and 3,600 if in the third position. Just keep adding to the power of 60 as you move leftward (just as we do with powers of 10 in the decimal system). The number 152 could now be rendered as 60+60+10+10+10+1+1. That is, 'll<<<ll'. But there's still one problem.

In English, each digit has just one symbol, so it's easy to tell its position in a number. Not so in cuneiform. There's no way to tell the positions apart. Take 'll<<<ll', for instance. Is this two positions (120+32), or seven (60^6+60^5+10+10+10+60+1)? In other words, take the second 'l' from the right; is it one or sixty?

If it's two positions, where do they break? The solution was to group symbols of each position together with spaces between adjacent groups. Thus, 'll<<<ll' became 'll <<<ll' for better clarity (note the space between the first two strokes and the rest of the numerals) when representing 152. This tiny update revolutionized counting. Now, very large numbers could be rendered with both ease and clarity.

Take 1,273, for instance—twenty-one 60s plus 13, i.e., '<<l <lll'. This solved many problems, but not all.

There are things positional counting didn't help with—the ambiguity with standalone strokes, for starters. So, 120 is two strokes ('ll') and 2 is two strokes ('ll'). How does one tell the difference now that all strokes are the same size? One solution is to draw on the context, which is what the Sumerians had done for centuries. So, 'll' is more likely to be 120 than 2 when given as the population of a settlement. But it was only a matter of time that context alone couldn't suffice. The ambiguity had to be killed once and for all.

So the Babylonians, again, came up with an innovation—two slanting strokes that looked roughly like the modern backslash ('\\'). This was a rather late development but definitely before the end of the fourth century BC.[3] So, while the blanks stayed on as placeholder separators, the new symbol '\\' came to explicitly mean 'nothing in this position' Thus, 'l lll' was (1×60) + (3×1) = 63. But 'l\\lll' was (1×3,600) + (0×60) + (3×1) = 3,603. Today, we use a different symbol for the job, we call it zero.

This should've easily resolved the 120-2 dilemma. While earlier both 120 and 2 were rendered as two strokes each, now 2 could be 'll' (two 1s) and 120, 'll\\' (two 60s plus zero 1s).

Could be, but was not.

Because the Babylonians, despite having invented the game-changer of a symbol, never used it at the end of numbers. Why? We don't know. So, 2 was still 'll', as was 120, and the Babylonians still preferred to tell the two apart from context and nothing else. Nevertheless, the slanting strokes to represent 'nothing' was a major leap in the history of counting.

The leap from here to terminal zero would take centuries even though it's impossible to overstate the impact the Babylonian zero-marker, even in its non-terminal usage, had on their commerce in particular and life in general.

One last thing before we leave Babylon—the zero-marker wasn't always '\\'. Different scribes used different 'standards'. Also, the backslash notation was only a later development, and the Babylonians had been writing zero since at least four centuries earlier. Bêl-bân-aplu, a Babylonian scribe, for instance, used three hooks (‘<<<’) for his zero around 700 BCE. Yes, it looks like 30, but that's how he wrote.[4]

So it's clear, the Babylonians were using some kind of a proto-zero, if you will, at least 2,700 years ago if not earlier still. Sure, it needed tonnes of refinement, but a zero it was. So were they the first in the world? Not really.

Turns out, the Egyptians were independently doing their own thing with numbers centuries before the Babylonians, possibly even the Sumerians. Sure, they used hieroglyphs, much of which remains undeciphered to this day, but their number system was surprisingly much closer to what we have today. For one, theirs was a base-10 system, just like ours. (We still use base-60, by the way, in certain niches, such as time.)

We could do a whole chapter on how the Egyptians counted but instead, we'll come straight to the most startling aspect thereof—the Egyptian zero.

It's called *nfr*.

Nfr is ancient Egyptian for good or beautiful and is at the root of Nefertiti, a later queen much known for her beauty. The hieroglyph for nfr looked like an emoji with a cross over its head. Long story short, the Egyptians had a zero at least as early as 1770 BCE.[5]

This makes the Egyptian nfr humanity's first recorded attempt at representing ‘nothing’. However rudimentary, this hieroglyph was a zero-marker.

But the idea of expressing nothingness did not remain alien to other parts of the world for long. By 400 BCE, the Mayans were counting in what's considered the most economical number system ever invented—base-20. Guess what? They had a zero too![6] They initially used pebbles and sticks to express numbers. Pebbles represented 1 and sticks represented 5. After 19, they needed a zero as the units placeholder to write 20. So they brought in a shell. The shell represented ‘nothing’. Later, when they started writing stuff down, pebbles became dots, sticks became bars, and shells became what looked like an eye. This symbol was remarkably similar to how we write zero today.

The Incas of South America, too, had a base-10 system as early as 2000 BCE. But they weren't into writing. Instead, to represent different numerals, they used a system that involved strings with knots called *quipu*. A knotless string represented 'nothing', i.e., zero.

Coming back to the Old World, the first Europeans with some kind of number system were the Greeks. They had a positional lettering system in base-10, sometimes also base-5, which is what the Romans would borrow later. But the Greeks has no zero, at least not until Alexander. They did have trouble counting, and there was too much dependence on context, but they had no idea zero could save the day.

Not until 331 BCE, anyway.

That's when Alexander invaded Babylon and learnt of this wonderful new notation that solved all their problems with just two slanting strokes. Zero now entered Ancient Greece—not as backslashes, but as a circle. There are several theories around how the Babylonian backslashes turned into the Greek circle. The most widely accepted is that the circle is omicron, the first letter of οὐδέν, Greek for nothing.

The first time zero makes an appearance in Asia is, to be generous, at least a hundred years after the Greeks started with the circle notation. In fact, it can all be narrowed down to one individual.

Piṅgala.

One would've, given the popular and mostly uncontested notion, expected the name Āryabhaṭa, but he, in fact, comes much later. Piṅgala is said to have come up with a primitive form of the binary system in his work Chandaḥśāstra. Variously dated to between the second and the third centuries, this work seems to be the first recorded mathematical treatise from the Indian subcontinent. This is where we first meet *śūnya*, a dot that's understood to represent nothingness.

As a notation, this is the first Asian zero. But Piṅgala's zero isn't really the zero we know today. It didn't serve any mathematical function and was just a symbolic representation for nothingness.[7] Even his binary system was not śūnya (0) and *eka* (1), but *laghu* and *guru*. In fact, his counting does not start with zero but with one.

The next big exhibit comes from, by the most liberal of estimates, around 224 CE. It's a Sanskritic text written in the Śāradā script (a third-generation descendant of Brāhmī, itself understood to have some kind of Semitic origin) on a piece of birch bark that was discovered in Bakhshali near Peshawar in 1881.[8]

Āryabhaṭa is erroneously named by most Indian historians as the 'inventor' of zero but the truth is, he doesn't show up until 400 CE, a good 250 years after the Bakhshali manuscript. His system, just like Piṅgala's, does not have a numerical zero.[9] Instead, he used nine vowels to represent nine numerical positions or, as he called them, *kha*. Later, kha narrowed down to zero and became the prevalent Hindu name before śūnya returned to reclaim currency.

Of course, there is also a debate about whether Āryabhaṭa even existed and, if he did, as one individual or many. But that's a debate we won't get into here. Let's just work with the assumption that he existed and as a single individual.

About half a century after Āryabhaṭa came Varāhamihira of Ujjain. He, like his predecessors, did not have zero in any numerical sense but he gave it a new name, *ākāśa*. The word is also Sanskrit for sky. So, now we have śūnya, kha, and ākāśa—all merely notational.

A significant medieval evidence against zero's Indian origins comes from Severus Sebokht, a Syrian scholar and bishop who taught at the Theological School of Nisibis. He was also the first Syrian to mention the Indian number system—as an admirer, no less. He wrote about how the Indians expressed numbers using nine symbols in the year 662.[10]

Nine, not ten.

This is also a practice Indians shared with the Chinese back then. An allusion to nine planets as understood at the time? Possible since most mathematical activities in Asia those days pertained to astronomical calculations.

So who exactly gets to own zero?

The Babylonians who invented the idea of expressing numerically significant nothingness with two slanting wedges about 3,000 years ago?

The Egyptians who repurposed nfr, the hieroglyph for beautiful, to denote nothingness, around 3,700 years ago? The Mayans who first wrote it as an oval?

The Greeks who first wrote it as a circle?

The Indians who first wrote it as a dot but with no numerical significance?

Truth is, it's unfair and immensely reductive to assign something as broad as zero to a single geographical identity. Concepts such as these are civilizational efforts spread over centuries. No one culture owns it all. As for Āryabhaṭa, he wasn't the first to propose a zero, not even in India.

Funnily enough, as if to close the loop, this zero that India inherited from Piṅgala, made its way back into Europe as part of the Hindu-Arabic system in the eleventh century thanks to the Moors of Andalusia, who were voracious translators. The modern name, all said and done, does owe it to India. The Arabs borrowed śūnya as *ṣifr* and then carried it to Europe where an Italian mathematician named Leonardo Fibonacci Latinized it to *zephirum*. Later, as Latin gave way to Italian and other Romance tongues, zephirum contracted to zero. The English word cipher also traces the same etymological lineage. Thanks to this collaboration between Indians and the Arabs, the world still counts in the Hindu-Arabic system.

So that's how zero came to be. Short answer, the world's first zero did not originate in India, and when it did, it wasn't with Āryabhaṭa.

Was Vasco the First European to Reach India by Sea?

The Europeans have known and visited India since long before Vasco da Gama; he was just the first to reach here via the sea, or so they say. But Indians had been venturing out into the ocean since long before him. So how is it that nobody in Europe could find India via sea until so late? Was Vasco really the first to do it? And if so, why? The answer may either reinforce what we've been taught since forever, or upend it completely.

ON THE NIGHT OF 20 MAY 1498, A WEARY SHIP FROM A distant land dropped anchor about five miles off a coastal town on the mouth of Korapuzha in Kerala. The intended destination was Calicut, but a navigational error diverted them to this place instead. Calicut was another two leagues to the south.[1]

The last time this ship had seen land was in Kenya, its last port of call. And that was nearly a month ago.[2]

Shortly upon anchoring, the crew was visited by four boats from the mainland, enquiring about their purpose of arrival and their nationality. The following day, the ship finally arrived in Calicut.

The crew immediately learnt that every legend it had heard of this exotic land and its riches was indeed true. The city was teeming with Christians, spices, gold and gems. Much money was to be made trading with them. But before any of that could materialize, they'd have to secure the royal nod. The king, known officially as *Svami Tiri Tirumulapad*, was at the time not in town. He was fifteen leagues away in what's known today as Koyilandy.

Despite many initial hiccups, thanks to barriers of language and culture, the contingent finally received an invite to meet the king in Calicut, but was instructed to anchor at Koyilandy anyway. The reason offered was better anchorage. Immediately, sails were hoisted for this last leg and one week later, on 27 May, the group was at its final destination. The man helming the expedition then picked thirteen good men, left the rest behind in Koyilandy, and set out for his audience with the king back in Calicut.[3]

That man was Vasco da Gama, and he was here with a letter of introduction from Dom Manuel I, the king of Portugal, himself. Svami Tiri Tirumulapad being a mouthful, the locals abbreviated it to just *sāmūtiri*, which the Portuguese heard as *çamidre*, which itself corrupted to *zamorin* over time.

The audience had its fair share of friction, but da Gama eventually succeeded in securing a deal from the zamorin. This was to make Portugal a very wealthy empire and a pioneer of maritime trade with India.

With the successful conclusion of this expedition, da Gama went down in history as the first European to have reached India by sea. This was nothing short of a milestone, for it gave a new life to Indo-European contacts, consequently changing the course of history not only for Portugal and India but also for the whole world. Indo-European contacts were not a novelty even in da Gama's time. The Silk Road up north had brought Europeans to India for nearly a millennium. But that was overland. The maritime alternative was a Portuguese discovery.

But was it? Let's find out.

Interestingly, inhabitants of the Indian subcontinent have known maritime commerce since early antiquity. Their contacts with the world at large go back to pre-Aryan times, when merchants from Sumer and Babylon made routine voyages to the ancient port of Meluhha. So, Indians were really no strangers to foreign seafaring visitors. And neither were the Europeans.

Sure, Europe did not receive a whole lot of foreigners back in the day, but their merchants did sail to Africa and Arabia for business long before da Gama's expedition. What could possibly have kept the Europeans from venturing further east to India then? The hazards and difficulties of long voyages in uncharted waters could be a reason. Especially in the early Middle Ages, when superstitions and monster lores abounded.

But then, overland routes were no less forbidding either. A typical medieval caravan from Europe to India or China would pass through punishing deserts, desolate rocky stretches and some of the deadliest mountains on Earth—all crawling with murderous hordes, robbers and generally hostile inhabitants. There wasn't enough motivation for them to look for an alternative.

About two years before da Gama's expedition, though, another expedition made it to India and even ventured beyond. This was led by a Genoese merchant and seafarer named Hieronimo di Santo Stefano and his partner Hieronimo Adorno. Unfortunately, not much information remains on them or their work. All we have is a letter Stefano wrote from Tripoli to one Giovan Jacobo Mainer in the fall of 1499.[4]

The letter offers some decent insights into Stefano's voyage to India and beyond, and his experiences along the way. The account is riddled with a generous helping of exaggerations and legends, but much can still be gleaned from a careful reading. Such as the fact that the voyage was a rather tragic one.

So the duo's first stop was Cairo, whence they travelled overland to what's today the port city of el-Qoṣēr. It's here that they embarked on their voyage to India. But they took it easy and made several long layovers. One such layover was in Aden, where they spent four months.

From Aden, the next leg was to India, and the journey was made in a different ship with cotton sails. Another thirty-five days of sailing, and they finally arrived in Calicut.

After spending an unspecified number of days here and making some interesting observations about local customs, such as widespread polyandry and cow-worship, Stefano and his partner left for Ceylon in yet another boat. They even managed to circumnavigate the Indian peninsula to reach Coromandel on the other side! The rest of their trip took them to other uncharted territories such as Burma and Sumatra before turning around and exploring the Maldives and Gujarat on the way back.

Unfortunately, only one Hieronimo made it back home. Adorno fell sick and could not cope with the hardships of the long, punishing voyage. The sickness only grew severe with time and eventually claimed his life towards the end of 1496.

About a hundred miles to the north-west of Moscow is the city of Tver. Here lived, in the fifteenth century, a merchant and explorer named Afanasy Nikitin. This man did not even intend to visit India, much less by sea. He, like nearly every explorer of his time, had grown up reading about India, a distant land of mystique, wealth and exotic animals. But he didn't actually plan on making a trip.

What he did plan, though, was to take a trip to a city called Şirvan (in today's Azerbaijan) in search of financial opportunities. But things did not work out quite as expected, and a series of mishaps only added to his ordeals. Unable to return to Russia, he continued south, where an unfortunate detour landed him in Persia for more than a year. By now, he had probably decided to travel to India. There were several other extended layovers along the way, and he could only get back on track in 1469 when he reached the Kingdom of Hormuz on the Persian Gulf.[5]

From here, it was far easier to just sail down to an Indian port town than continue overland. So he had a ship outfitted for the purpose, and began his voyage. After several pit stops and detours, Nikitin finally arrived at an unspecified port town on the northern end of the Indian west coast. The region was under Muslim rule those days—the Bahmani Sultanate.

This was at least thirty years before both di Santo Stefano and da Gama. Nikitin spent more than two years travelling and observing India before homesickness got to him. He left around 1471. Unfortunately, he never made it home and died near Smolensk.[6]

This firmly places the mantle of the first European to reach India by sea on Afanasy Nikitin's head. But looks like we can go ever further back in time to find another traveller heading to India.

In 1450, an Italian cartographer named Fra Mauro created what went on to become one of the biggest milestones of medieval cartography—a map of the world as known at the time. We call it the Fra Mauro map. This map included, among other things, India. A project this ambitious could not have been a one-man job. Multiple sources contributed their personal experiences to the design, and one of them was a merchant from Venice named Niccolò de' Conti.

Niccolò was young and adventurous, with a keen desire to explore. This quest first took him to Damascus, where he lived long enough to learn Arabic and assimilate, although he remained a devout Catholic.

Then, eager to move east, he left Damascus, crossed the desert with a caravan of 600 other merchants, and reached Baghdad. After a brief sojourn in this grand city, and then in Basra, Niccolò continued until he arrived at Hormuz. There, he teamed up with some Persian traders and together set sail for India. After days of sailing, the team finally arrived in the Gulf of Cambay. A detailed contemporary account of this trip was later published by his friend Poggio Bracciolini. Among other things, the account introduced Europe to the 'bizarre' Indian practice of Sati.[7]

What sets Niccolò apart from other explorers discussed here is that he didn't stay confined to the coast. Once in India, the man travelled all over and even travelled to the mouth of the Ganges, becoming one of the earliest known Europeans to have visited Bengal. Besides India, he also sailed to Taprobana, which scholars identify as either Sumatra or Sri Lanka.

Niccolò de' Conti died in 1469, so his trip to India certainly must predate that, making him the earliest European to have sailed to India so far. But even he was beaten to it—by yet another Venetian!

Mario Sanudo Torsello was an aristocrat, originally from the Greek island of Naxos in the Aegean Sea. His father was a statesman, and so was he. But young Mario was also a Christian fanatic who dreamed of retaking Jerusalem for the Church someday.

In his writings, Mario Sanudo made some detailed references to many distant parts of the world, including India. His claim was that the bulk of his revenues came from the spice trade with India. He even elaborated further that goods from India arrived in Egypt for onward shipment to Venice. From India to Egypt, or Persia, there were two routes, one overland and the other maritime. Sanudo observed that the spices that came overland were of better quality than the ones that came by ship. For the maritime trade, he named two principal ports on the Indian west coast—Malabar and Cambay.[8]

From this, it's not easy to conclude that he personally made a voyage to India, but it sure makes sense that given the prevalence of maritime trade, many Europeans would have. And Sanudo died in 1343, which pushes the date back by at least a century.

The fourteenth century seems to have witnessed a lot of European footfalls on Indian shores, much of it Italian. Interestingly, the purpose of visits during this period was different from commerce. This time, it was mostly evangelical.

The last major name from this period was Sir John Mandeville, an English knight from St. Albans, at least that's what he claimed in his solitary work, titled *The Travels of Sir John Mandeville*.

While much doubt hangs over the veracity of all personal claims in this work, or even the identity of the author, the account itself has been corroborated by multiple sources. Nevertheless, it's these accounts that matter to our discussion more than the identity or the personal exploits of the author. And one of those accounts pertains to India.

In this chapter, Mandeville speaks of 500 islands around India—an obvious exaggeration—some of which are inhabited while others are not. People of India, he continues, do not venture out of their territory and are not into exploration. And then he drops the most important hint of all for our purposes—India's ports. While Indians don't travel much, merchants from Genoa and Venice make routine trips to the ports in India for spices and other merchandise.[9] Whether or not Mandeville was exaggerating, one cannot deny his awareness of oceanic activities.

Among the evangelicals who seemed to have visited the subcontinent during the period was a Franciscan friar named Giovanni de Marignolli. Coming from a long line of nobles established in Florence, Giovanni entered the Ministry at a very young age when he joined the Franciscan Basilica di Santa Croce.

Having spent a major chunk of his life preaching in Mongolia and China, he came to India around 1347. Here, he settled down in the Malabar port city of Quilon and associated himself with the local diocese. About sixteen months later, he would also travel to other parts of the country making a pilgrimage to the shrine of St. Thomas in Madras.[10]

The diocese Giovanni joined was founded by another Franciscan friar, who had arrived in Quilon not too long ago. Born near Toulouse, Jourdain de Séverac is speculated to have made his first voyage to India as early as 1321 when he arrived in Thane. From there, he went on to travel across Bombay and Gujarat before finally turning south and settling down with his mission in Quilon. The diocese he founded here became the first in the entire subcontinent. That was 1328!

Even earlier came the voyage Marco Polo is said to have made to the east coast. Although this explorer is best known for his overland trips, most famously along the Silk Road, he did have a fair share of sea voyages to his credit as well.

In the year 1292, more than two whole centuries before da Gama's anchoring off Calicut, Marco Polo and a crew of about 300 men reached the Coromandel on the way back from Southeast Asia.[11] The port was part of the Pandya territory those days and a whole new experience for Polo. This was the first time he had reached India on a boat, even though he had spent considerable time on the subcontinent before.

We could push the dates even further but let's go all the way to the beginning directly now.

The Romans!

A shipping log published in an ancient Greek dialect, sometime in the earliest decades of the common era, makes an elaborate reference to maritime trades with the Indian subcontinent. It even names ports like Barigaza (Bharuch), Barbaricum (Karachi), Muziris (Kodungallur) and Arikamedu.

This book is titled *Períplous tis Erythrás Thalássis*. In fact, maritime trade with India was already in place for thirty years before the time of Pliny the Elder, who lived in the first century CE.[12] It's hard to say who between the Romans and the Greeks sailed to India first, but either way, the conclusion remains the same, that many Europeans had travelled to India by sea before da Gama did.

Having said that, da Gama does somewhat deserve credit for being the first to chart a direct oceanic line from Europe to India without any land barrier. All his predecessors had made at least part of the trip overland, mostly around Egypt. Vasco was the first to take the long way around Africa. This was a milestone in its own right as it paved the way for Europe to enter trade in the Indian Ocean, without any dependency on the Arabs. And that's what makes him a pioneer.

Was Ujjain the World Capital of Timekeeping?

Ujjain was once a major centre of astronomy in the Indian subcontinent. The city even boasts of a medieval sundial, a wonder in and of itself. Thanks to this fact and a couple of medieval scriptural evidence of Indian timekeeping, Ujjain often gets credited with much significance on this front. Popular notions have even called it the prime meridian of the ancient world. Is this truth or mere revisionism? What if it really pioneered timekeeping for the rest of the world?

TIMEKEEPING IS A 5,500-YEAR-OLD TRADITION THAT goes back to Ancient Egypt and Babylon, where they used giant stone obelisks for the purpose.[1] We call them shadow clocks or sundials. With time, these ideas were adopted and further refined by other civilizations, most notably the Ancient Greeks. Sundials started getting smaller and more accurate after the Greeks introduced trigonometry to the calculations. Here's a quick primer on how the thing works.

The whole idea is that things cast shadows. And depending on the angle of light, the shadow can be longer or shorter. Also, the shadow always points directly away from the light. That's pretty intuitive—nothing complex so far.

A sundial is nothing but a circular plate with a stick at the centre. This stick runs along the plate's axis and is called *gnomon* (lit. 'the one who knows'). The plate itself is the dial. Kept out in the sun, the gnomon would cast a shadow on the dial. The shadow's angle is always aligned with that of the sun, and since the latter moves throughout the day (of course, it's really the Earth that does), so does the shadow. The dial is etched with hour markers at regular intervals, so the shadow falling on them tells the time.[2]

That was a short explanation. Now here's a quick illustration: imagine the Earth as a giant sundial, and its axis as the gnomon. Standing on the North Pole, you can imagine how the gnomon's shadow would move, tracing a circular path with the Earth's rotation. If a circle is taken as 360°, and the day has 24 hours, each hour would correspond to a 15° slice on the Earth dial. Remember, the entire dial is in the light because the Earth's axis isn't exactly perpendicular to its orbital plane: there's a 23° tilt. This hypothetical sundial works because the gnomon is parallel to the Earth's axis, and since the axis is perpendicular to the equator, the dial itself aligns with the latter. That's why a sundial built to this specification is called an equatorial sundial.[3]

The further away you move this sundial from the pole, the more of it falls in the shadow. At the equator, only half of it sees the sun, which means, it's only capable of telling the time over roughly twelve hours instead of twenty-four.

But there's one problem with equatorial sundials. The gnomon must always run parallel to the Earth's axis. At the pole, this is easy, just let the dial sit flat, parallel to the equator. But on other latitudes, it becomes problematic.

At non-polar latitudes, the gnomon can either be parallel to the Earth's axis, or perpendicular to the ground, never both. To keep the gnomon parallel to the Earth's axis, it must be kept at an angle with the ground. At what angle? Brace yourself for some light geometry here. Let's imagine an arbitrary latitude, α° N.

Since a latitude is defined by the angle by which it's separated from the equator, it's always expressed in degrees. Thus, the latitude in our example is separated from the equator by α degrees, and the N implies it's to the north of the equator, and not south. When a straight line or *transversal* cuts through two parallel lines, the angles made at both cuts must be the same or congruent. So says the corresponding angles theorem. Thus, the angle made by a line perpendicular to the surface, with another, parallel to the equator, must be the same as the angle of latitude at the point, i.e. α°.

Now imagine a line tangential to the surface. By definition, this line ought to be at right angles with the perpendicular we just imagined. So if the latter makes an angle α° with the latitudinal plane that makes 90° with the axis, the angle between the latter and the perpendicular must be $(90\text{-}\alpha)^\circ$. But since the perpendicular also makes 90° with the tangent, the angle between the tangent and the axis reduces to $(90\text{-}90\text{-}\alpha)^\circ$ or α°. The tangent is, just to repeat, parallel to the surface of the Earth, which is how the dial would also sit.

In short, an equatorial sundial's gnomon must be at an angle with the tangent, ergo the dial, the value of which is the same as its latitude.[4]

The Greeks had all this figured out, at least by the time of Euclid—i.e., 300 BCE, if not earlier. But they had already borrowed the more primitive obelisk clocks from the Babylonians as early as the sixth century BCE, long before the equatorial or equinoctial sundial.

Do note that a sundial has to be aware of its latitude since that's the value governing the gnomon's orientation. But it doesn't have to know the longitude. This is a very crucial bit that'll come in handy later in the discussion. Now let's take a trip to Afghanistan.

Some 300 miles north of Kabul, where the Kokcha River pours into the Amu Darya and Afghanistan meets Turkmenistan, lies an archaeological dig. Once upon a time, this is where kings would come on hunting expeditions. On one such expedition, Khan Gholam Serwar Nasher stumbled upon an array of artefacts that seemed mighty ancient. Intrigued, he called upon the famous Princeton archaeologist Daniel Schlumberger, Director of La Délégation archéologique française en Afghanistan (French Archeological Delegation in Afghanistan) or DAFA to investigate.[5]

Turns out, this desolate stretch was once a bustling Graeco-Bactrian metropolis named Aï Khanūm (Uzbek for 'Lady Moon'). The Greeks called it Alexandria after the famous Macedonian conqueror. There were many Alexandrias those days, and this one was Alexandria on the Oxus.[6] Oxus because that was the original name of the Amu Darya River back in the day. Aï Khanūm was pretty much the frontier of the Graeco-Bactrian realm, almost bordering the Mauryan Empire of India. To the south, Bactria reached what's today Thatta in Pakistan but was then Patala. Aï Khanūm was completely abandoned by 145–120 BCE.

The city was named Alexandria for a reason. In 329 BCE, Alexander was in the region on an eastward campaign. Aï Khanūm is where he made a pit stop. His men fatigued, his supplies running out, the emperor decided to stay on until ready to fight again.

It's during this period of rest that he founded a city, named it Alexandria on the Oxus, and married a local Bactrian princess called Roxana. This is the magnificent city DAFA had unearthed.

To the East, Bactria bordered the Mauryan Empire, not far from where Aï Khanūm then stood. This empire was divided into four provinces, one of them being *Avantirāṭṭha* or Avanti, the western province.

The capital of Avanti was so grand for its time, it also became the capital of the whole realm—Ujjain.[7]

Ujjain has an interesting location. Horizontally, it sat smack dab in the middle of the Mauryan Empire. Almost vertically so too. Even today, a longitude that runs almost through this city (75° 43' E) is considered the 'unofficial' prime meridian of India.[8]

Of India, not the world.

The longitude is roughly half an hour behind the one that runs through Allahabad, the official prime meridian of India (IST). This astronomical trivia was first recorded in the Sanskrit treatise *Sūrya Siddhānta*. Even today, traditional Hindu horoscopes treat the Ujjain line as its 0°.[9]

The practice of standard time wasn't confined to India though. Throughout antiquity, empires and kingdoms have designated their own 'prime meridians' driven by their own contingencies. There was no universal time coordinate because the need was never felt. While the choice of a nation's standard or prime meridian (a local *0*°, if you will) is constrained by geometry (the closer to the horizontal midpoint, the better), that of the universal prime meridian is rather arbitrary. Any given longitude can play the role.

But ancient Indians weren't the first to have a standard meridian, or even meridians in general. Greek polymath Eratosthenes had propounded longitudes as early as third century BCE.[10] Of course he didn't do it alone and was likely assisted by fellow Alexandrians Timocharis and Aristyllus.[11] That doesn't necessarily mean the Indians learnt it from him. In fact, it's possible that astrologers in Ujjain came up with the concept of longitudes independently, since they didn't measure those in degrees like the Greeks did. The first reference to this in India comes from the aforementioned Sūrya Siddhānta.

Sūrya Siddhānta claims to be from two million years ago, which is obviously scriptural liberty; reality is closer to fifth century CE at best.[12] So that makes Eratosthenes at least 550 years older than this text.

Eratosthenes defined a prime meridian for Alexandria in Egypt. That's because he worked there, as the librarian at the Great Library. After him, other Greek city–states started marking their own prime meridians. This included one at Rhodes.

By 150 CE, Claudius Ptolemy came out with a treatise of his own in Alexandria. It was titled Γεωγραφικὴ Ὑφήγησις (Latinized as *Geographia*). Geographia was an earlier work by Marinus of Tyre rehashed, and it reflects the influence of its contemporary Persian cartographers. With this volume, Ptolemy became the first to propose a universal time coordinate, a single standard prime meridian for the entire known world. This original prime meridian corresponds to the legendary *Fortunate Isles*,[13] which today most likely corresponds to the Azores,[14] way off the line through Greenwich.

Ptolemy's meridian remained the global prime well into the Middle Ages. Two whole centuries after *Geographia*, the line in Ujjain with the Sūrya Siddhānta became prime for territories within the Indian subcontinent. At no point in time was it the universal standard.

So, thus far, here's what we have: Sundials originated in Ancient Egypt and Babylon. The simplest kind is the equinoctial or equatorial sundial. It consists of a dial with hour markings and a gnomon. The gnomon casts a shadow, which tells the time. The angle between the gnomon and the dial must be the same as the latitude at the place of installation. Ergo, the sundial's configuration changes with a change in latitude. No dependency on the longitude whatsoever. This holds true for other kinds of sundials too. That is, two identical sundials on two different longitudes but on the same latitude will function the exact same way, their gnomons at the exact same angle with their dials. They'll give different time readings, but they'll both be equally accurate.

We also learnt that Aï Khanūm was an Uzbek name (meaning *moon lady*) for Alexandria on the Oxus,[15] a military outpost developed into a functional city by Alexander the Great while he was on a campaign trail towards India. The city sat on the eastern fringes of Bactria, not far from the border with the Mauryan Empire of India.

Concurrent to the founding of Alexandria on the Oxus, was the Mauryan annexation of Avanti, an ancient territory corresponding to today's Malwa. Its capital Ujjain was considered the hub of Indian timekeeping because an ancient book on the subject said so. This book was Sūrya Siddhānta and it was the first that introduced India to the idea of longitudes (*deṣantar*) and latitudes (*akṣanṣ*) as timekeeping devices, and named the one through Ujjain, the subcontinent's prime meridian.[16] The idea of longitudes was first conceptualized more than 500 years earlier, by the Greeks. Ptolemy proposed a single universal prime meridian for the whole world in 150 CE. This was a good 200 years before the composition of Sūrya Siddhānta.

With that recap, let's return to Afghanistan, where the idea of Ujjain as the world's timekeeping centre has found its strongest piece of material evidence thus far.

In 1975, the French team digging up Aï Khanūm unearthed a carved slab of limestone with a large cylindrical hole through it. The slab was about eighteen inches high, fourteen inches wide and six inches thick. The hole was about nine inches across.

After much examination, it was concluded that this artefact was an exotic type of sundial—a one-of-its-kind piece—that didn't feature even in Vitruvius' list of thirteen types of sundials from 25 BCE.[17] The inner surface of the cylindrical hole had markings (etched lines). There were two sets of markings, each with thirteen. These lines were arranged in such a way that if the surface were to be unrolled and spread flat, it'd show the two sets running parallel to each other. Each set had a long centre line with six smaller ones on either side.[18]

If the slab were to be laid parallel to the equator and a rod driven through the hole's axis, this could easily become a modified equinoctial sundial. The rod would then be the gnomon. We'll get to the working of this sundial shortly, but first some design details. Unlike a regular equinoctial sundial, this time, the gnomon wouldn't have to tilt. It'd always be perpendicular to the dial, i.e., the slab. Instead, it's the slab itself that'd tilt with respect to the ground in order to remain parallel to the equator.

In order to make the slab tilt, a triangular portion thereof would've needed to be chipped off; and sure enough, the slab was found to have this chipping done. The angle of tilt ought to be the same as the latitude of the slab's installation. Now, if you examine the hour markings closely, you'll find either edge to be divided into twelve sections, six on either side of the long centre line.[19]

These twelve sections corresponded to the twelve temporal hours of the day. The long centre line was the noon marker. This gives us the perfect equinoctial sundial with each hour marker separated from the adjacent ones by 15° (180° ÷ 12 hours). But there's two sets of lines. Why?

Those days, hours weren't uniform. The span between dawn and dusk was divided into twelve hours. Thus, winter hours were shorter than summer hours. We call this temporal hour. This would render a dial with equidistant markers useless. There was something to remedy just that.

The hour markers were equidistant, but not straight lines. They were etched to slightly incline towards the middle marker, the noon line. This way, the gnomon's shadow would always account for the seasonal variation in the length of individual hours. There was another issue. The Sun wouldn't always shine on the same side of the slab. One side would face the Sun in winter, while the other would in summer. This was remedied by having two sets of hour markers, one on either edge of the inner surface.

Before we proceed from here, let's introduce something called declination. In simplest terms, it's the orientation of a celestial body expressed as an angle with the Earth's equatorial plane. It can be calculated for any celestial body and that includes the Sun. This angle changes from one day to the next, and for the Sun, ranges between -23.44° and +23.44°. Now, do recall that the marker lines are inclined toward the middle or noon line. So, the ends are farther apart on the outer edge than they are on the inside. Naturally, then, the outer edge corresponds to the longest hours (on equinoxes) and the inner, to the shortest (on solstices).

In other words, the distance between the centre line and the final marker on either side is half a day, but this length is more along the edge than along the centre. The longer one is half of an equinoctial day, while the shorter one is that of a solstitial day. The ratio of the two multiplied by six gives us a value that's called the hour angle of the Sun.

Solar hour angle is, in simplest terms, the angle the Sun makes with the local meridian at any given time. Due to the Earth's rotation, this changes by the hour. The value returned by the above calculation is the hour angle of the Sun when it just crosses the horizon. With this information, it's possible to calculate the latitude of the slab's installation. The formula is:

$\tan \theta = (\cos t \div \tan d)$, where θ is the latitude, *t* is the hour angle we just calculated, and *d* is the Sun's declination during the solstices.

When the slab was built, d was 23.9°. So the formula now reduces to:

$$\tan \theta = (\cos t \div \tan 23.9°)$$

When resolved, θ comes to 23.5°. In the northern hemisphere, we call this latitude the Tropic of Cancer. Finally, we know where the dial was meant to be installed.[20]

But the dial was found at Aï Khanūm, which lies on 37° N. That's a difference of over 13°. Which means the sundial wasn't meant to be installed where it was found; instead, it was transported there. But from where?

To find out, archaeologists surveyed all the routes Alexander followed on his campaigns. The southernmost point reached by Alexander turns out to be Patala, an ancient city near today's Hyderabad in Sindh. Patala sat on 25° N. The port city of Karachi being less than 100 miles from there, it was reasonable to assume Alexander planned on annexing it. Port cities were key to trade and having as many of those in one's inventory was a mercantile imperative. Whether Alexander managed to annex Karachi is unclear, but his navy certainly visited the port.[21]

This is sufficient grounds to assume that the Macedonian imperialist either conquered or planned to conquer Karachi, and develop it as a new maritime Alexandria of sorts. There were already Greek traders settled in the city and around those days. If that were the case, Patala could easily have been his planned local capital from where he'd mount his southward invasions. This implies that the sundial was initially meant to be installed in Patala, hence the corresponding latitude.

But everything so far, other than the derivation of 23.9°, is mere conjecture. Calculations are needed to improve plausibility. So further calculations were, indeed, done.

If you recall the slab's design we discussed above, it was meant to be on a tilt with the ground. This tilt was to keep the gnomon parallel to the Earth's axis and the dial to the equatorial plane, thus making it, in essence, an equatorial/equinoctial device. We also saw how that tilt ought to be the same as the latitude of installation.

Now here's the puzzling part: this angle of tilt was measured and it came to 37°, the latitude of Aï Khanūm![22] So the slab's tilt says it was for Aï Khanūm, but the calculation using solar hour angle says it was for Patala. And both are equally compelling maths! So what's the sorcery here?

None, actually. The discrepancy can easily be explained with a closer look at the slab's base plate. Here, one can clearly note signs of re-engineering. The base plate was originally carved for a 23.9° tilt, and then further chipped for a 37° tilt at a later point in time. In other words, it was first cut for Patala and then moved to Aï Khanūm and *re-carved* for the new latitude, which was 37° N. So, it can now be established with reasonable confidence that the dial was originally constructed and meant to be installed at Patala. This city sat where Thatta sits today, on or very close to the Tropic of Cancer. This latitude also runs through another ancient city—Ujjain.

As one would expect, this triggered a frenzy of speculation around the city's status as a timekeeping capital of the ancient world. Why else would a civilization as distant as the Greek one align its timekeeping devices with an Indian city? The sundial of Aï Khanūm and its tilt establishes with confidence that Ujjain indeed was the world's prime meridian, a role played by Greenwich in modern times.

Only one problem with this position: there is no textual evidence of Ujjain (then Avanti) having any timekeeping industry those days; nor did Alexander get anywhere close to the city. So it's absurd to assume this sundial has anything to do with it. Actually, there's a second problem too: Ujjain doesn't even have a sundial from antiquity. No sign of a timekeeping industry whatsoever from the period.

In fact, Ujjain only became the 'prime meridian' of the Indian subcontinent, as we've seen earlier, from Sūrya Siddhānta the earliest composition of which has been dated to at least half a millennium after Aï Khanūm was abandoned due to constant invasions from the north.

So that's the story of one of the most remarkable timekeeping devices ever built by man—only a single specimen of which has been discovered so far—and arguably the most compelling evidence in support of Ujjain's position as the ancient world's Greenwich. The device only came to light in 1975, more than 2,000 years after it was lost to time.

Key takeaways from this story? Several. That sundials are built to align with latitudes and not longitudes, for starters. That the first of those were Egyptian and Babylonian and came in the form of rock obelisks. That the first equatorial sundials, the kind we imagine when sundials are mentioned, were Greek. That the concept of longitudes was given by Eratosthenes of Alexandria in third century BCE. That the concept of local 'prime meridians' was also given by Greek cartographers after Eratosthenes. And that the concept of a global prime meridian was given by Ptolemy around 150 CE.

But these takeaways don't end there. We also learn that the concept of longitudes and the local prime meridian first appeared in India in 350 CE through the Sūrya Siddhānta, at least two centuries after Ptolemy. That's when Avanti, later Ujjain, became the timekeeping centre of ancient India due to it being situated on the middle longitude of the subcontinent. It's for this reason that Ujjain continues to be called the Greenwich of India and its meridian still remains the standard coordinate for Hindu time calculations.

As for the sundial of Aï Khanūm, we now know that it was built for the Tropic of Cancer but later moved to and re-shaped for Aï

Khanūm. The Tropic of Cancer passes through both Patala (today's Thatta, Sindh) and Ujjain. Alexander never got to Ujjain, so there's no way he could've transported the sundial from there to Aï Khanūm. But he did visit Patala, so it's fair to assume that that's where the sundial was initially installed. Another reason the sundial couldn't belong to Ujjain is that the city isn't known to have had any timekeeping industry before the common era. No ancient sundial installation has ever been found in Ujjain. And with that, we circle back to the first key takeaway from this whole discussion—that sundials are built to align with latitudes, not longitudes.

So, was Ujjain the timekeeping capital of the ancient world? In light of all material and historical evidence we currently have at our disposal, no.

How Homogeneous Is the Rajput Bloodline?

Rajputs are known for their valour, but more than that for their bloodline. Many of their clans, if not all, trace an unbroken lineage to antiquity, going all the way back to Vedic and other esoteric origins. Detractors, on the other hand, dismiss all such notions as mere forced retrofitting to establish ethnic superiority. So who's right? Not an easy controversy to settle, but let's try by examining the historical information at our disposal.

EVER NOTICED HOW ALMOST EVERY RELIGION attempts to usurp the historical lead-up to its origin and claims ownership of all history, even outside of its own life? This retrofitting isn't always exclusive to religion.

The longer one's lineage, the stronger one's claim on history. With history comes legitimacy, primacy and superiority. That's the driving force. Around the first century BCE, the Indian subcontinent witnessed a series of raids from the north. The most prominent among these raiders were the Scythians of the steppes. The Scythians were an Iranian people, known for their love of horses and their martial skills. Although they managed to spread as far south as Egypt, a branch called Indo-Scythian or Śaka crossed the Indus and floated the first Śaka domain.[1]

But even before the establishment of this domain, India was no stranger to this tribe. Nomadic as they were, the Scythians had moved to places as far as Persia and Greece long before India had its first Śaka king. Herodotus and other historians closer to the period have noted Scythian horsemen in the service of both Greeks and the Achaemenids. Many soldiers of this ethnicity would have crossed the Indus soon after Alexander's death in the early fourth century BCE.

Further affirming the notion is Śākyamuni or Śākamuni (lit. 'sage of the Śakas')—epithets assigned to Gautama Buddha in later Gāndhāra texts.[2] That pushes their chronology in India back by another four centuries. So the tribe may have started settling down in the north-western parts of the subcontinent around the fifth century BCE, if not earlier.

Some scholars, Sir Alexander Cunningham among them, push the chronology even further to as early as 1900 BCE. They hypothesize that a Scythian tribe—there were many—had invaded the Punjab region long before Alexander's time and founded the fabled city of Taxila. Cunningham calls these peoples early Turanians.[3]

Before we go any further, let's be clear that, at least in the context of this discourse, the names Scythian and Śaka are synonymous. That's because for a very long time, the two names were indeed used as such. The Achaemenids called the Scythians in their realm Śaka, and so did Herodotus in his records. And it's highly unlikely the Greeks of the time did otherwise.

Most scholars would baulk at the proposition that they are synonymous, though, and understandably so, as the difference between the two names is indicative of their origins rather than mere taxonomy. The Śakas originated in the Tarim Basin and, although a part of the wider Scythian culture, aren't the same as the Scythians of the Aral. In short, all Śakas are Scythians, but all Scythians are not Śakas. But in the context of this conversation, that's minor nit-picking, and the interchangeable usage is admissible.

So the Śakas managed to stay in business until as late as the fourth century CE[4] in the shape of two vassals or satrapies, the western and northern ones. The northern one ruled over Punjab and Mathura, while the Western over Sind, Gujarat and Malwa. Both continued to lose autonomy to emergent powers such as the Kuṣāṇas, the Guptas and the Sātavāhanas, until completely subsumed.

The Western Satrapy was the last surviving Śaka stronghold in the beginning of the fifth century when Chandragupta II of the Gupta dynasty got access to the Śaka chief dressed as a woman, murdered him and annexed the Satrapy into his dominion. This annexation officially ended Śaka rule in India.[5]

Now the Śakas, they weren't just kings and satraps. They were an entire people. Battle-hardened, highly resilient and great with horses. Those are useful qualities in the hostile environs of the Indian north-west. So it made sense, both politically and socially, to assimilate into the existing Hindu ecosystem as a useful part of the community. That's what the Indo-Scythian immigrants with no real 'homeland' to return to wound up doing. The hosts, in turn, got a whole community of martial peoples in a political windfall. Win-win for both.

Thus entered a Scythian people into the highly stratified Hindu totem as part of the Kshatriya varna, the one closest to their way of life. Suddenly, they weren't foreign invaders, but indigenous Kshatriyas. Members of this neo-Kshatriya community later called themselves Rajputs, which was indicative of their relationship with great rulers from antiquity. This is the position held most notably by the English Indologist James Tod in his nineteenth-century opus on Rajputana.[6]

But this idea doesn't concur with what the Rajputs themselves believe to be true. For one, various Rajput clans have a more-or-less unbroken genealogy all the way to remote antiquity. These genealogies establish them as descendants of either a celestial body—personified, of course—or one of several Vedic Kshatriya clans. There's also an Agnikula or Agnivaṃśa line that comes from fire. Blurring the line between history and mythology, the view challenges the notions of the community's heterogeneity and foreign origins.

So which one is it?

Before we proceed with a counterargument, it's important to note that the Rajputs would still be ethnically homogeneous if they were all Scythians, as Tod posited. But others have also added later tribes to the list, most notably the Hephthalites or Hūṇās. One such proponent attributed a Hūṇā origin to the Agnikula clans, mostly Gurjars, in a 1911 paper on India's ethnic composition.[7] This further negates the community's claims of racial homogeneity and indigeneity. Again, the theory is expressly rejected by the Rajputs themselves.

Now back to the counterarguments. One that vehemently rejects the Hūṇā angle theorizes that at the very foundation of this notion is the fallacy that two tribes collaborating for martial or political purposes and being noted together in the epics must also share an origin. For instance, just because the Gurjars and the Hūṇās were both allies in a campaign against a native king, doesn't mean they were both foreigners.[8]

Proponents of an unbroken, singular Vedic line of descent bolster their theories with multiple scriptural references. One such reference comes from the Mahābhārata itself. In fact, more than a dozen references can be found in this epic, the first two being right in the first book, the Adi Parva. Other references can be found in Sabha, Vana, and other Parvas.[9]

Interestingly, however, the word used here isn't rajput but *rājaputrā*. This changes things. Rājaputrā is actually a portmanteau of two words, rāja, meaning king, and putrā, meaning son. In other words, prince. Of any ethnicity, race or nationality. Thus, while Rajput is a proper noun today, referring to a very specific people, rājaputrā doesn't seem so.

At the very least, the term precludes any martial attribution focussing more on royalty. Especially given, with one exception, that the word consistently appears as part of a phrase—*rājāno rājaputrā*. The exception appears in *Drona Parva* as *brāhmaṇā rājaputrā*, which does little to establish the rājaputrā as a unitary race of martial clans, an idea that has been imputed to the Rajputs of today. Sure, it is possible that all kings back in the day happened to be from the Kshatriya class, but that doesn't *ipso facto* imply a collective ethnic cohesion. And even that bit isn't entirely true, because there have been many cases of non-Kshatriya ruling dynasties—the Nandas, where the founding king was born to a Shudra woman, being a notable example.[10]

To recap what we have so far, Rajputs don't seem to be doing terribly well on homogeneity, even if indigenous. The name Rajput finds abundant reference in the Hindu scriptures, the oldest one being in the Mahābhārata, but only as a generic term for princes and other members of the royalty, with no ethnic or racial connotation.

But that hasn't stopped people from seeking to antiquate the myths surrounding the community's vintage. One such exercise deals with the Chauhans, who subscribe to the Agnivaṃśa line and claim a Brahmin origin going back to the earliest Vedic times.

To understand this position, we need to visit Bhilwara in Rajasthan. Some fifty miles from the city is the census town of Bijolia Kalan. Here lies a reddish hunk of rock with thirty lines of verse inscribed on it. The inscription dates back to nearly nine centuries ago, when it was made on the order of a local king named Someśvara, father of the legendary Prithviraj Chauhan. The Chauhans (also called Cāhamānas) have always identified as Rajputs, Prithviraj being the poster child.

But why does the Bijolia inscription even matter to this discussion? Because, given that it's a most authentic record of the Cāhamāna genealogy up until Someśvara, much of import stands to be gleaned from it.

The earliest prince mentioned in this genealogy is one Vasudeva. After him comes Sāmantarāja. Now, Sāmantarāja has been noted here as a member of the Vatsa gotra, making him unambiguously Brahmin.[11]

Unfortunately, this far from settles the etiological dispute over Rajputs at large. All it does is offer an indication that one group, the royal dynasty of the Chauhans, is likely to have had Brahminical origins. Beyond that, the issues of how, say, the Chalukyas and the Parmars fit into the same ethnological template, or how the Guhilas of Medapata became 'suryavaṃśi', remain unresolved.

The latter is a case worth discussing. Today, all Guhila subscribers identify as solar dynasts or suryavaṃśi Rajputs. This, of course, does not mean they descended from the literal celestial body; the name is more metaphorical than indicative. Anyway, this accords the group a vintage that can be traced back to well within the Vedic era. In fact, the line of descent, if accepted at face value, links them directly with Ram, the suryavaṃśi hero of the eponymous Hindu epic.

But how do we know that? From inscriptions, of course. Kings back in the day had the habit of putting up glorious origin stories, tales of battlefield exploits and rich ancestral data as inscriptions at temples and other public places. Besides offering a considerable ego boost, this also served to establish and reinforce hegemony.

So there are inscriptions all over Mewar that declare the solar heritage of Guhila kings. These inscriptions relate them with Lord Ram, consequently lending them a measure of divine influence.

But the earliest such inscription only dates to the sixteenth century.[12] This makes one wonder, why shouldn't there be any earlier expression of the dynasty's ancestral clout? Perhaps they weren't aware of their lineage before? In that case, what happened in the sixteenth century? Whence the epiphany?

One word: Muslims.

Not just the Guhilas, but all western Indian fiefdoms felt the need to coalesce under a common hegemonic banner to counter a fresh incursive threat from outside the subcontinent. The Muslims had started invading India since as early as the tenth century. But the threat only grew with time. And with the advent of the Mughals in the sixteenth century, the Rajputs felt, for the first time in history, a civilizational threat. Remember, they were among the first to counter Bābur when he came.

The clans had to be brought together under a unifying force in order to mount any challenge against the overarching Mughal clout. And nothing brings together disparate peoples like a shared mythology. The Rajput identity was thus born. With time, it only grew more restrictive with new exclusions being added every now and then. Initially, it was a mere subset of the Kshatriya identity. Then they added a measure of aristocracy to the mix, restricting the nomenclature to just the royalties and their descendants: this circles back to the Rājaputrā of antiquity. Further down the line, a new layer was added to exclude similarly-identified peoples from outside of western India.[13] Thus, Rajputs of Bihar or the south were no longer considered 'true Rajputs'. It was a gradual process, but a synthetic one nonetheless.

This frenzy of 'descent fabrication' reached its peak under Akbar, when epics such as Pṛthvīrāj Rāso were composed and captured the collective imagination.[14] Romantic tales of Rajput valour against ungodly odds started going mainstream as a rally call against Agra's supposed tyranny.

From that point on, the Rajput story has further grown into a rich tapestry of royal intrigues, shifting loyalties, and disparate political imperatives driven by the changes in circumstances. Paradoxically, despite these changes, the community seems to have only grown closer on the question of ethnicity.

The myth of a shared origin dating back to remotest antiquity has become so entrenched in its genealogical narrative that ascertaining or denying it is no longer seen as a necessary exercise outside of scholarly endeavours.

Having said that, no, the Rajput community is not a unitary ethnic monolith, with or without the Scythians. All claims of fantastical origins and shared indigenous heritage are products of meticulous sixteenth-century hagiographic exaggerations.[15] The gene pool is a fascinating congeries of all kinds of peoples, from all kinds of places.

There's not just the Śākas or Hūṇās, but also the Aryans, the Vaishyas, the Brahmins, the Kshatriyas, and a whole continuum in between.[16] As expected of a community of this vintage, there's no one origin theory that fits all. It's as incorrect to call their progenitors foreign as it is to call them indigenous.

Diversity is a function of time, circumstances, and incentives, and far from exclusive to the Rajputs.

Did We Invent Our Script, or Import It?

There were cultures in existence long before ours that, to a remarkable degree, had perfected the art of writing. Many writing systems had been in place for millennia when the subcontinent's Brahmi script first emerged. What remains bitterly disputed, though, is whether they had a role in Brahmi's emergence. Some say it developed indigenously, others trace it to ancient Aramaic. Now both can't be right, can they?

A TWO-HOUR DRIVE FROM BETUL, IN MADHYA Pradesh, is an unremarkable little village called Tiwarkhed. Sometime in the mid-nineteenth century, a resident dug up a small parcel of land here to lay the foundation of a new home. During the process, he stumbled upon two copper plates and immediately handed them over to the authorities. With this began a frenzy of archaeological activities in the village and the unearthing of even more artefacts.

The plates were inscribed with what looks like a royal land grant to a brahmin named Mundibhatta in the year 631 CE.[1] The script in this inscription looks very similar to how we write Hindi today, and the language is Sanskrit. At the same time, several letters also look different from the modern script used for Hindi.

This is one of the earliest archaeological artefacts bearing what's called the Nāgarī script.

Just as it is with spoken language, scripts change over time. And so did Nāgarī. By the beginning of the second millennium,[2] it had changed to a form more familiar to us today and also acquired a new name—Devanāgarī. That's the script we write Hindi in today. Besides Devanāgarī, Nāgarī also gave us scripts for tongues such as Bengali, Oriya and Tibetan. Devanāgarī itself gave us the Gurumukhi script, one of the two used for Punjabi.

Back in the day, little homogeneity existed in the scripts used on the Indian subcontinent. Nāgarī was just one of the many that existed simultaneously but we won't get into those.

So where did Nāgarī come from?

As any decent epigraphist would attest, scripts do not suddenly emerge out of thin air. Nor do they just cease to exist abruptly. What happens is a gradual sequence of tiny unnoticeable changes over generations. These changes are hard to take note of in isolation, but over a period of time, they snowball into something recognizably new. In the interim, exists an amount of overlap where both parent and child scripts continue being used. For instance, the Latin script used for English today wrote *v* for *u* until fairly recently.

That's exactly what happened to a script called Siddhāṃ as it evolved into Nāgarī. It's not easy to put a finger on when exactly the shift happened, because there was a period when both remained in currency at once. For that reason, some epigraphists call the script early Nāgarī. This writing system was reported as early as the tenth century, a good three centuries after the Tiwarkhed inscriptions.

One contemporary with a first-hand experience of the Siddhāṃ script reported it as Siddhamātṛkā. His name is Al-Bīrunī.[3] Other names applied to the system, include Kuṭila and Vikaṭa. This script is understood to have developed in the late sixth century as some of the earliest extant specimens are from that period—the final decades of the three-century long Gupta era.

While Siddhāṃ itself did not have a very long run before completely turning into Nāgarī, its own development was just as organic as that of its successors.

As Siddhāṃ evolved during the Gupta era, the writing system it evolved from is referred to simply as the Gupta script. This is where things start getting undecipherable to the layman. While the average Hindi or Bengali reader today can still make sense of inscriptions made in Nāgarī, and even Siddhāṃ with some effort, the Gupta script would seem almost alien. Trained palaeographers and epigraphists, however, can and do read enough patterns to see a continuum from the Gupta script to Siddhāṃ.

Today, we have a wide assortment of scripts attributed to the Gupta era, and they are all considered different stylistic forms of the same writing system. Similar to its successors, this system wrote left to right and showed vowels as notations on the consonants they modified. The technical name for such a system is abugida. The Gupta script was of this kind, as are all its successors including Devanāgarī.

This Gupta script was a diverse but mutually readable family of scripts broadly classified into three evolutionary branches—eastern, western and the mainstream. From the western branch emerged the Śāradā script, the one used in the third-century Bakhshali manuscript. This script was the one of choice in the north-western parts of the subcontinent, particularly in Afghanistan and Kashmir, where it was used to write both Sanskrit and Kashmiri. Śāradā enjoyed a decent twelve-century run before finally giving into the Perso-Arabic scripts in which Kashmiri is written today. In some parts of Kashmir, Pandits still use it for liturgical purposes.[4]

The Gupta script itself was a rather seamless and organic improvement over an even earlier script called Brāhmī. In fact, the transition was so gradual that even the Gupta script is often referred to as Late Brāhmī or Gupta Brāhmī.

Before the Guptas came the Kuṣāṇas, a Yuezhi people that originated in China. They spoke Greek and Bactrian, and wrote in Greek and Brāhmī! Among this dynasty's better-known kings was Kanishka the Great, who expanded the empire to its largest extent, from Gandhara in the west to Patliputra in the east.

By Kanishka's time, writing had acquired a much wider range of applications than ever before. Earlier, it had been just royal edicts and administrative records. But now, common people were writing down all kinds of things that had nothing to do with governance.

When more hands get involved, more styles emerge. That's what happened with Brāhmī. Although everyone wrote the same script, they all started developing their own unique styles of writing the same letter. While at times a deliberate design choice for the sake of personalization, much of this was also a consequence of need—the need for speed. As many more started writing, more writable ideas emerged. And more needed to be done in lesser time. Consequently, as design, elegance and symmetry gave way to swiftness and ease, the cursive style grew in popularity.[5]

Just as the Gupta version, original Brāhmī is barely intelligible with modern Devanāgarī. To a layman, the two might as well be entirely unrelated scripts. Now, although the Kuṣāṇas were foreigners and they wrote in Brāhmī, along with Greek, they did not invent it. The script predates them by centuries.

The earliest known specimen of this script so far is a rock edict from the third century BCE, a date that will shortly become important to this discussion. These were made by an emperor from the Maurya dynasty, Aśoka. For this reason, the early forms found on these edicts are also sometimes called Aśokan Brāhmī.

Although some experts place at least one specimen in the pre-Mauryan times, the claim seems erroneous.[6] The item in question is a copper plate found in the Sohgaura village near UP's Gorakhpur. The inscription on this plate is in the Prakrit language, expressed using the Brāhmī script. But since it does not conclusively predate Aśoka, we'll keep that out of this conversation.

Aśoka's was an impressively cosmopolitan empire. And so, in order to make his laws readable to the maximum number of people, some of his inscriptions were made in not one but three different scripts. The language was still Aśokan Prakrit, but four different scripts—Greek, Aramaic, Brāhmī and Kharoṣṭhī—were used. Aramaic was among the primary tongues of the erstwhile Achaemenid territory, and Greek was the language of the Indo-Greeks that ruled much of India before the Mauryans. Aśoka's territory was still home to many who spoke and read those tongues.

Interestingly, Kharoṣṭhī was written right to left, as was Aramaic! This and several other similarities have led to a unanimous conclusion that the scripts are related, i.e., Kharoṣṭhī evolved from Aramaic.[7] But since it went extinct by the middle of the first millennium CE, we won't dwell on it. Of our interest is Brāhmī, the established mother of most Indian scripts in use today.

Now the question is, where did Brāhmī come from?

There are two schools of thought on this. One traces it to a foreign, likely Semitic, source. The other favours a more indigenous origin. We'll examine both.

The most common theory supporting the indigenous origin theory is that Brāhmī evolved from the script used in the Indus Valley Civilization. We don't have a formal name for the latter, so we just call it the Indus script. The first argument in favour of this theory is that the Indus script has 400 distinct symbols, which is very close to Brāhmī's 330. Another argument draws morphological similarities between certain consonants in the two systems.[8] The case seems compelling, except for one problem ... actually, two.

The first problem with the idea that Brāhmī developed from the Indus script is that the Indus Valley Civilization disappeared as early as 1500 BCE, while the earliest of Aśokan edicts show up only in the third century BCE. Even if we push Brāhmī further by another hundred years to account for the potsherds found in Sri Lanka (in 1988, the Archeological Survey of Sri Lanka excavated some half a dozen pieces that bore inscriptions in this script),[9] there still remains a gap of more than a thousand years between the latest Indus script specimen and the earliest Brāhmī specimen. That kind of gap is not easy to reconcile with; evolution warrants continuity, and a thousand years is just too big a break in the chain. For perspective, that's two-thirds the age of the English language!

Another problem with the Indus origin is the very fact that the script is yet to be deciphered. Although we have a fair amount of understanding when it comes to the Egyptian hieroglyphics and many other obscure ancient scripts, the one used by the Harappans remains a mystery. In the absence of such an understanding, it seems both premature and speculative to liken it to any later script purely based on chance morphological similarities.[10]

Some theorists also offer a third argument supporting the Indus origin—the direction in which the script is written. This argument is less in favour of the Indus origin and more in denial of Aramaic origins. Since Aramaic was written right to left and Brāhmī the other way, the argument is that it is unlikely that the latter came from the former.

That makes sense. For the most part. However, some Brāhmī specimens have also been noted as running right to left! In fact, one Aśokan edict found in Andhra Pradesh, called the Yerragudi edict, has it going in both directions alternately.[11] Some call this the boustrophedon style! Of course, it may be a sign of mere thoughtless scrawling, rather than a conscious effort to produce boustrophedon.

Now we come to the other side of the coin—foreign origin. While most advocates of this position seem unanimous on the source, one has gone against the grain and proposed Greek. We'll examine this first.

When Aśoka launched his edicts in the third century BCE, he also sent some to Gandhara, about a thousand miles from the Mauryan capital—in what's today Patna. At the time, Gandharans wrote and understood a different script that was quite different from the Brāhmī on Aśoka's edicts. That script was Kharoṣṭhī. Change always faces resistance, and so did this one. People initially weren't comfortable switching to a whole new script just to be able to read the royal edicts from a distant land. To make the transition easier, some of the major edicts were inscribed in multiple scripts, including Kharoṣṭhī.

Now, Aśoka had a very compelling reason to adopt or at least learn the Greek language. The Mauryans had enjoyed very close ties with the Greek-speaking Seleucid kings of Mesopotamia. The court in Patliputra was rarely without a Greek-speaking dignitary, the most well-known example being Megasthenes, the Seleucid ambassador to the Mauryan government.

Besides political, Aśoka also had close familial ties with the Seleucids. He was only one of the Mauryans to have married a Seleucid lady. Communication gaps between him and his Greek-speaking in-laws were another major motivation for him to learn Greek.

So, his subjects in the west knew Kharoṣṭhī, while his guests and in-laws from Mesopotamia knew Greek. Aśoka decided to create a whole new script drawing on both. This way, his edicts and scrolls would be readable to both with very little effort on their part. He could have just gone with Greek, but the latter doesn't have enough letters to represent all the sounds that made up his own native tongue, a dialect of eastern Prakrit called Magadhi. This was the birth of Brāhmī.[12]

But the hypothesis, at least for now, doesn't have many takers and sure leaves many questions unanswered. For example, the potsherds in Sri Lanka. Those carry inscriptions in Brāhmī, so if they predate Aśoka even slightly, the whole Greek-origin theory instantly falls apart. Also, this hypothesis does not explain how a new script would solve Aśoka's language barriers, given the final form of the new script differed drastically from Greek in appearance and ran mostly left to right, rather than right to left like Kharoṣṭhī. It'd seem the new script would be hard to read for both Kharoṣṭhī readers and Greek readers.

And that brings us to the single most popular hypothesis—Aramaic!

Aramaic was a north-western Semitic tongue, and its script is said to have derived from the even older Phoenician writing system, which itself owes it to Sumerian cuneiform. Now extinct, Aramaic was once the lingua franca of the Achaemenid Empire that ruled much of the Middle East for centuries before being driven out by the Greek-speaking Macedonian, Alexander the Great in the latter half of the fourth century BCE.

One of the arguments in favour of Brāhmī's foreign origin is the Sanskrit word for script, *lipi*. The word is first said to have been used by the noted Sanskrit grammarian Pāṇini, who likely came long before Aśoka. Pāṇini is said to have lived in the Achaemenian satrapy of Gandhara, which technically makes him a Persian subject. Although we don't know anything with certainty about Pāṇini's knowledge of Old Persian, one of the official languages of the Achaemenians (the other being Aramaic), we do know that the Old Persian word for script is *dipi*. And many Aśokan edicts use the words dipi and lipi interchangeably.[13]

The least this establishes is some form of etymological intercourse between the three tongues during or before Pāṇini's time. But this alone is not sufficient to establish a Semitic origin of a subcontinent script. We need more. Especially given the very big difference in the two script's writing directions.

A much older hypothesis, probably the oldest, attempts to further push back the script's vintage to around 800 BCE, besides connecting it to Phoenician, an ancestor of Aramaic. Phoenician is said to be the mother of most writing systems in use today, including Greek and Latin. Georg Bühler, the proponent of this hypothesis, refers to the Bāveru Jātaka to indicate that Indians and Mesopotamians had been trading and exchanging ideas for a long time. Supporting his position is the fact that the Jātaka in question speaks of the distant land of Bāveru—the Indian name for Babylon—routinely receiving peacocks from Indian seafaring merchants.

Bühler argues that, it's in the course of this exchange that Indians adopted a modified version of the Phoenician script for their purposes.[14] This became the Brāhmī script, although the name would not appear until centuries later.

Bühler goes on to argue that the north-western branch of the Semitic language to which Aramaic belongs, seems to bear the closest resemblance with Brāhmī. In his observation, all Aramaic symbols were found to be represented in the Brāhmī letter set, which had a few additional glyphs to represent sounds not found in the Semitic tongues. One major change the Semitic characters underwent upon being imported into India was their orientation. Indians held an aversion to top-heavy letters and a strong preference for symmetry. As a result, many Aramaic characters had to be turned upside down and resized in order to align them neatly under a top bar. Lastly, some letters also had to be flipped horizontally to facilitate a left-to-right orientation.[15]

At least for now, this hypothesis, along with all others, is just that—a hypothesis. The fact remains, we just cannot be entirely sure yet. There are just way too many missing links. For the indigenous origin, we need inscriptions to establish continuity between the Indus script and Brāhmī, and for the Aramaic origin, we need a more concrete explanation of the orientation switch.

All said and done, just taking into account all the epigraphical and linguistic evidence available right now, we can safely conclude that the script is more likely to be a foreign import than an indigenous innovation.

Is Roma the Only Medieval Diaspora from India?

The first time an Indian tribe is recorded to have ventured into Europe and Africa was before the Middle Ages. Today we call them Gypsies or Roma. It's generally taken for granted that these are the only premodern Indian peoples settled outside of the Indian subcontinent. Some, however, call them just one of many such groups that left India centuries ago either to escape persecution or for better opportunities. This, of course, remains a rather contentious take. So let's allow history to settle the dispute.

WHEN HITLER ASSUMED POWER IN GERMANY AND made ethnic cleansing a state policy, more than six million Jews ended up losing their lives in what we call the Holocaust. Everyone knows that term. What many don't know is *Porajmos*. This was another genocide from the Nazi era, which describes how upward of a million and a half lives were claimed.[1]

Despite the atrocious scale of suffering that was caused by the Porajmos, it failed to get much press attention.

The Porajmos saw the near-erasure of an entire community that sat, and mostly still sits, at the rock bottom of Europe's socioeconomic pyramid.

Who were these people?

Shrouded in a cloud of conflicting origin stories until fairly recently, the community today numbers around a fifth of a million in Germany alone. People call them different names, but for the most part, the standard term is *Sinti*. A few minor disagreements aside, there is a general consensus that the name belies the community's place of origin, Sind.

While Sinti may not sound very familiar, another term for the community certainly would—gypsy. But while all Sintis are gypsies, not all gypsies are Sintis. If there's one idea the word gypsy conjures up instantly, it's that of their non-sedentary lifestyle. Although most have settled down today, they really were itinerant for the longest time. It's this practice of being constantly on the move that brought them all the way from the Indian subcontinent to Europe in the first place.

If this sounds like the Roma, the other similarly itinerant community better known in and outside of Europe, that's for a good reason. The two groups share sufficient overlap in their ethnic trajectories. The Sinti are understood to have arrived in central Europe in the sixteenth century. Then they dispersed into different regions driven by the incentives and contingencies of the time. Two major sub-groups went south. One ended up in France and the Iberian peninsula and likely consisted of seven caravans, for that's what it eventually called itself—Eftavagarja (lit. 'Seven Caravans'). The other group called Extraxarja (lit. 'from Austria'), headed to Italy.[2]

The ones in France are also called *manouches*, and they speak a distinct language of their own, albeit with some Sinti remnants still intact. Those that remained in Austria and Germany continue as Sinti to this day. The name is also shared by their Italian brethren.

The umbrella term for these itinerant groups in Europe, for the most part, remains Romani or Roma. The idea that they originated from India centuries ago isn't subject to controversy. In fact, recent times have seen a vigorous shift in the official Indian attitude towards this community. Although yet to recognize them as part of the Indian diaspora, the Indian government is already warming up to the idea.[3] So first, we'll examine if the Roma people really did originate in India. That settled, we'll see if they are uniquely so.

Multiple genetic studies have confirmed that the groups now collectively referred to as Roma or Romani originated about 1,500 years ago in north-western India and travelled westward in multiple groups, settling down in multiple places. For the first six centuries, the Balkans remained the itinerants' western frontiers. It's only around the twelfth century that they ventured out of there and headed further west.[4]

Furthermore, linguistic and textual evidence also seems to indicate a similar trajectory. One of the earliest references to a group migrating out of the Indian subcontinent, for instance, is an epic poem written in the tenth century by a Persian poet in the court of Mahmud Ghaznavi. His name was Abul-Qâsem Ferdowsi Tusi, and the poem was titled 'Šāhnāme' (lit. 'Book of Kings'). Considered a seminal piece of Iranian literature, this epic has a story of a Zoroastrian Sassanid king named Bahram.

Firdowsi's account claims that Bahram had asked an Indian king for 10,000 Loris, a community of musicians. When they arrived, he gave them each an ox and a donkey along with some wheat so they could engage in agriculture. They, however, did no such thing and instead ate up the wheat as well as the animals. Infuriated, the king asked them to leave.

Of course, this is more legend than history and ought to be taken as such. But communities of Loris do live in parts of Iran and Baluchistan to this day. Many experts believe the Roma community of Europe to be an offshoot of these people, likely driven into Balkan after being banished by Bahram.

When they first arrived in Europe during the sixteenth century, almost everyone mistook them for Egyptians. And the reason was a

Biblical account of God scattering the Egyptians as punishment for not sheltering Jesus. The nomadic lifestyle of the new immigrants from the East were, thus, taken as the descendants of those cursed Egyptians. A most famous affirmation of this comes from Victor Hugo's 1840 classic, *The Hunchback or Bell-ringer of Notre Dame.*[5] And that's how we got to *gypsy* in English and *gitano* in Spanish. So, as we see, all these communities are just branches of the Roma community with varying levels of cultural and linguistic dissimilarities from each other.

Now the question is, are they the only non-Indian communities that trace their origins to India but have lived abroad since the earliest medieval times? There are people of Indian descent in places like Surinam and Fiji, but those are very recent and still maintain a relatively strong connect with India. Unlike the Roma who have diverged to unrecognizable extents over the 1,500 years since they left their original homeland. Are there others like them?

Remember the Loris of Iran and Baluchistan? We now know they came from India. That isn't the name they referred to themselves by, though, at least not originally. Later, when freshly Islamized Arabs snagged Persia from the Sassanids, they came in contact with these exotic musicians from India who called themselves Jats. The Arabs mispronounced the word as Zoṭṭ. With time, the new name assumed a much broader connotation and came to be used for anyone who came from India.[6] This included not just the itinerant musicians of Persia but also merchants and soldiers that later immigrated from India but were not necessarily Jats. Descendants of these early Jats continue to live in the Middle East with no cultural, religious, or linguistic ties left with the land they left behind a thousand years ago. Most of them are not even nomadic any more.

There are also scholars and ethnologists who relate the community of Zoṭṭs with the Meds of modern-day Baluchistan. Originally, the two tribes are said to have inhabited a vast territory on either side of the Iran–Pakistan border, mostly concentrated in parts of Sistan and Baluchistan, living side by side. Internal frictions and tribal rivalries are posited by these theorists as one of the motivations for the Zoṭṭ people's emigration.[7]

Despite their Hindu origins and India's Jats, the Zoṭṭ never really identify with India even remotely, which is perfectly expected given the hundreds of generations that have gone by since the last time they had anything to do with the subcontinent. Almost all members of the community today practise Islam and speak the language spoken in their immediate vicinity.

The same is the case with another community called the *Nawar*. These also originated in India. At this point, it's important to note that for the most part, 'gypsy' is used as a catch-all term for all itinerant communities that exhibit the general stereotypes earlier attributed just to the Roma in Europe. Even other names are sometimes used interchangeably, although in most cases that's incorrect even if they trace a common origin in the Indian subcontinent.

Now coming back to the Nawar. This is a coarsely applied, and often derisively so, term for a number of communities in Syria. Numbering around a quarter of a million, a vast majority of them are no longer nomadic and have completed their assimilation into the Syrian life. At the same time, they continue to maintain their heterogeneity.[8]

One of the sub-groups within the all-encompassing Nawar umbrella is the community of Dom, but we'll come to them a little later. First, some spotlight on Iraq.

The Iraqi political landscape has always been underscored by sectarian violence and state persecution of non-dominant groups. The most highlighted of these is, of course, the evergreen Sunni–Shia conflict. In the years leading up to the American invasion, this friction came to a head and caught even communities that have traditionally lived on the very fringes of Iraq's society.

One such incident occurred in the spring of 2004 when a Shia militant outfit called Jaysh al-Mahdī, now renamed as Sarayat al Salam, attacked a Sunni village in Sadr, killing many residents. This was no regular Iraqi village, it was a village of gypsies who had given up their nomadic ways to settle down and integrate.

This community of non-Arab ethnicity is variously called Kawliya, Qawliya, or Keche-Hjälp. As is the case with gypsies elsewhere, the Qawliya are known for dancing and performing at family events. That's how many still make a living. Their performance was once a highlight of the Tikrīt life.[9] This did not go down well with Islamic purists like Jaysh al-Mahdī who came to liken the Qawliya lifestyle to prostitution.[10]

And just like the Zoṭṭs, the Qawliya came from India! Although it's been over a thousand years since they arrived, and they have since assimilated to a great degree over the years, they still continue to maintain some of the uniqueness of their identity along with their dialect, which is more Persian than Arabic.

And this brings us to the community we placed on the back-burner a short while ago—the Ḍom.

The Hindu caste system is a totem pole of hierarchical identities, originally based on occupation but now almost entirely assigned by birth. Featuring at the top of this hierarchy are the Brahmins, and at the bottom, the Shudras. Among the latter is a community called Ḍom.[11] Society had traditionally assigned to them jobs considered taboo by others, scavenging and cremating the dead being the most notable of them all.[12] Being at the bottom of the hierarchy also meant being at the receiving end of all kinds of persecution and ostracism. And it was all much worse in the past. It's likely this sustained persecution and the lack of any avenue of upward mobility drove them out of India.[13]

Today, this community is scattered all over Central Asia and the Middle East, with some pockets even in Europe. The community remains largely homogenous thanks to its general reluctance to marry outsiders. Ḍom is also not the name they refer to themselves by, preferring, instead, other alternatives like Bani Murra in Jordan and Ben Souda in Morocco. In an attempt to better assimilate, they have also started to speak the local dialect, even though many can still understand their traditional Ḍomari tongue.

Unfortunately, the stigmatization that they intended to escape when they left their birthplace centuries ago, continues to haunt them to this day. Mostly stereotyped as thieves, prostitutes and practitioners of black magic, they are often shunned and treated as 'pariahs' (a term that itself comes from the caste system). Like other itinerant groups all over Europe and Asia, the Ḍom people remain on the bottom socioeconomic run in all societies. This is the biggest motivation behind many communities self-identifying as non-Ḍom and speaking Arabic, Georgian, and other regional languages instead of Ḍomari.

A similar nomadic group calls itself Lom and lives in and around the Caucasus. Major Lom populations can be found in countries like Armenia, Georgia and the Asian part of Turkey.

The Lom have assimilated better, thanks to their relatively relaxed attitude towards exogamy. But the economic disadvantages that plague other nomadic communities from India plague them too. Although the community self-identifies as Lom, others refer to them with names such as Bosha in Armenia, Boshebi in Georgia and Posha in Turkey.[14]

Just as their Ḍom counterparts, the Lom have also started adopting local culture and speaking the local tongue, such as Turkish, Armenian and Georgian. However, a tiny, constantly shrinking pocket of the older generation still continues to stay loyal to Lomavren, the native Lom tongue born as a creole between an Indian dialect and Armenian.

There are also historical attestations to the fact that the Loms and Armenians together fought against Ottoman persecution. Despite these attempts at integration, the community still endeavours to maintain its ethnic identity to the best extent possible. While exogamy isn't as frowned upon as it is among the Ḍom, it's not welcome either. Even when accepted, it's limited to situations where the groom is Lom and the bride Armenian, rather than the other way around.

For the longest time, historians have considered the three groups, Rom, Ḍom and Lom as members of the same migration wave. More recent studies, however, seem to contradict this notion and consider the three communities as parts of three independent waves.

While they all trace their origins to India and their names share a common Indian etymology, the three groups left India at different times. Even the languages spoken by them—Romani, Ḍomari and

Lomvaren—have been found to have split much earlier than hitherto assumed.

Of these, the Ḍom are posited to have been the first to leave. The biggest argument put in favour of this theory is the observation that Ḍomari grammar still has traces of the neuter gender, an element not found in Romani. This disappearance of gender was also featured in the earliest evolutionary stages of the Indo-Aryan tongues. Additionally, the dual number that existed in Sanskrit but doesn't in any of its descendants, is also part of Ḍomari but not Romani.

The Loms are now understood to be part of the second wave out of India. This, too, has linguistic and historical attestations. Even the circumstances of their exodus differ. While the Roma, the most recent emigrants, left as prisoners of war, military refugees and Ghaznavid conscripts, the Ḍom had more economic and social motivations.[15]

While these are the most commonly and instantly associated communities in any conversation about early Indian emigrants, many more exist throughout Eurasia and even Africa. This is interesting and certainly serves to shatter multiple myths. The first is that it's always been outsiders who have settled in the Indian subcontinent. The truth is, these journeys have been made in both directions, since hundreds upon hundreds of years.

The other myth is that all early nomads left in a single wave and with a single drive. But, as we have seen, people migrated in multiple waves spread over centuries and for a range of reasons. They were not even the same community or class. From the Jats who became Zoṭṭs to the untouchables who became Ḍoms, this pre-medieval diaspora exhibits a remarkable range of identities with little mutual overlap.

And lastly, the most interesting takeaway: while the Indians emigrating today make up *some* of the most, if not *the* most, prosperous minority communities abroad, there did exist a time when quite the opposite was the case. Members of those early communities continue to enjoy little in the way of prosperity.

Or social justice.

Are Sanskrit and Persian Related?

Sanskrit and Persian, given their distinct religious associations, are seen as disjoint, unrelated tongues. The two languages even sound very different and have different writing systems. But some linguists argue, contrary to popular belief, that the two have a common history, originating not too far back in time. Let's examine the science, the linguistics and the scholarship available on the subject, and settle the dispute once and for all.

In the early years of the eighteenth century, it was observed, for the first time ever, that there is a whole corpus of Indian words with cognates in Old Persian. The person behind the observation was a Benedictine historian and orientalist named Maturin Veyssière de la Croze. Whether he believed this finding was of some linguistic significance or just some amusing coincidence, we don't know; he certainly did not publish any further research on the subject. Nevertheless, this became the first time, on record anyway, such an observation was ever made.

Within years, another linguist, this time from Prussia, noted similarities in their counting systems too. But unlike Maturin, this man, Gottlieb Siegfried Bayer, dug deeper. In his quest to draw an etymological bridge, he also threw Greek into the mix. And concluded that the three languages could be traced to a common origin in some extinct Scythian tongue[1]!

Bayer's conclusions were not a novelty. Before him, similar Central Asian origin theories for the three number systems had been proposed by the celebrated German mathematician Gottfried Leibniz. And Jesuit scholar, Lorenzo Hervás y Panduro credited Leibnitz as one of the references in a later work, further establishing the link between Sanskrit and Persian.[2]

But before Leibnitz, the same idea was propounded by a Dutch scholar and linguist named Marcus Zuërius van Boxhorn. And as early as 1647, Boxhorn published, in three parts, an 'Indo-Scythian theory', which later linguists would further develop into the now-popular Proto-Indo-European hypothesis.

Boxhorn's paper was the first to suggest a Scythian origin for all non-Semitic tongues, including Persian and Sanskrit. The idea did not find unanimous acceptance during his lifetime, though; that would come much later.

While we've noted nearly half a dozen Europeans who took an interest in and studied the link between the two tongues, there's an Indian name we've missed so far. His name is Siraj-ud-Din Ali Khan, better known as Arzu. A noted poet in Shah Jahan's court, he was also a language enthusiast, proficient in both languages of our interest here.

Arzu's first work on the subject was an unpublished treatise on Persian lexicography and its relationship with Sanskrit, titled Muthmir. It was one of the most comprehensive texts on the subject of its time, and was later referenced even in many European works, such as those by Father Coeurdoux and John Richardson.[3]

At this point, even without getting deeper into the genetics of the Indo-European family ourselves, we can safely conclude that a link between the languages of India and those of Iran had already been appreciated and established by multiple experts well before the turn of the nineteenth century. But how grounded in science are those hypotheses really?

The relationship, if any, between two or more languages is established on two different levels—vocabulary and grammar. And both parameters must be satisfied. The mere presence of cognates cannot be taken as evidence of a relationship. Take Tamil and Korean, for instance. Over a thousand cognates, and yet, no evidence of a genetic link![4] That's not to say that lexical similarities don't matter. They just don't matter nearly as much in isolation. Which is where grammar comes in. The latter further has two aspects—morphology and syntax. We'll examine the relationship against all three metrics and see if the hype holds water.

Before we begin, a little insight into the two tongues' genetics is in order. Both Persian and Sanskrit emerged as evolutionary branches of a prehistoric Proto-Indo-Iranic tongue spoken during the third millennium BCE. From this ancestor came, roughly in the second millennium BCE, the earliest forms of two distinct languages in two different parts of the world—Sanskrit in north-western India and Avestan in north-eastern Iran. After another few centuries, a third evolved in south-western Iran, in what's today the province of Fars.

None of the three languages is the same today. Back then, Avestan was Old Avestan, Persian was Old Persian, and Sanskrit was Vedic Sanskrit. To untrained eyes, none of these ancient tongues looks anything like their modern offspring. Of these, only Persian remains in use as a language of communication, the other two being confined to liturgy and scripture.

So, given the genealogy of the languages in question, it shouldn't surprise us that their modern forms turn up a bunch of lexical parallels on a closer look. Let's see how many of those parallels, if any, have survived the millennia of separation.

The first case study in lexical parallels involves one of the most fundamental of civilizational imperatives—water. There's a reason all known civilizations sprouted and flourished around water bodies of one kind or another. Water was naturally crucial to our Indo-Iranian ancestors too. The first time a word for it emerges in Sanskrit is in the 49th hymn in the seventh book or *maṇḍala* of the Rigveda.[5] That word is *ápo*. Earlier, in the 35th hymn of the second maṇḍala, although not named explicitly, water has been alluded to as the progenitor of Indra, the Vedic creator of all things. The name used for Indra here is Apām Napād (lit. 'son of water'). Guess what? This deity also exists in Zoroastrianism, a pre-Islamic Persian religion! In the 19th Yašt of the Avesta, lies the Zoroastrian Supreme Creator named Apąm Napāt! Although no longer worshipped today and supplanted in that role by Ahura Mazdā, there was a time it was.

But this is about water and not water deities. Just as the Vedic Apām Napād came from ápo, the Avestan Apąm Napāt came from *āpō*. Ápo and āpō are what linguists call cognates. And since the words are similar in Avestan and Sanskrit, it's likely they are in Avestan and Persian too. And that's right; the word was borrowed nearly intact from Avestan into Old Persian—*āp*. By the time Old Persian became Middle Persian, āp had become *āb*. And that's how the word continues to this day. A most commonly used illustration of the word is in the name of Punjab. The word literally translates into five waters, a tribute to the five rivers washing through its territory.

Crucial as it sounds, just water isn't enough. We need more. How about clouds? No particular reason, just that they come from water.

The word in the reconstructed Proto-Indo-Iranian tongue was *ab*^{h}*rás*. How did we guess that? On the Iranian side, the word morphed into Proto-Iranian *abráh*, whence we get the Middle and Modern Persian *abr*. On the Indian side, the same Proto-Indo-Iranian ancestor became *abhrá*! And that's how we guessed that the etymological source of Persian abr and Sanskrit abhrá must be something like ab^{h}rás.

What's of import here is not that the two tongues share a common etymology, but that the similarities have still far from vanished. The only reason this seems incredible to the layman is the very different scripts the two tongues are written in. While Persian uses a modified form of the Arabic script, Sanskrit uses Devanagari. The former is written from right to left, and the latter from left to right. All of these differences make it rather difficult to accept that the two languages could have even the remotest familial link. But there's far more to a language than how it's written.

Scripts always come later, much later. And scripts are far more fickle than speech. Take Turkish and Uzbek, for instance. Turkish is written in the Latin hand while Uzbek takes Cyrillic. And yet, the two languages belong to the same Turkic family! Despite its Latin script, Turkish isn't related to English; and despite its Cyrillic, Uzbek isn't related to Russian. In fact, both were written in their respective forms of the Arabic script until fairly recently.

Even in writing, remnants of the past relationship between Persian and Sanskrit can still be unearthed. Persian wasn't always written right to left in the Arabic hand. The Arabic script only entered Iran in the ninth century during the Saffarid rule. Until that point, the dominant script was an Aramaic derivative called Pahlavi. This was the hand of Middle Persian. Old Persian was written in cuneiform, and it went left-to-right! As for Devanagari, there is some pretty reasonable speculation about a link between its progenitor Brāhmī and Aramaic.

Of course, these contrived epigraphic bridges do little to make the relationship between the two languages more palatable, simply because an appreciation thereof involves too much mental gymnastics. So let's get back to what makes more sense intuitively—to what actually matters to the subject at hand, etymology.

Ever noticed the suffix *-stan* in place names, especially the ones with sizable Muslim populations? Besides Islam, there's one more thing those places share—Persian. Many of these countries either speak, or have once spoken, Persian or a derivative thereof, such as Pashto, Dari or Tajik. There's a reason that's the case. The suffix -stan comes from Old Persian *stāna*, which means 'to stand' or 'be situated'. The verb shares its etymology with its English counterpart. Also sharing etymology with it are Avestan *stāna* and Sanskrit *stāna*, a word that literally means 'place' even today! This has got to be among the most enduring of lexical bridges between the two seemingly disjointed languages.

Another interesting word is hair. The term has multiple synonyms in both Sanskrit and Persian depending on the context and appearance of the hair in question. One of those in Sanskrit is *kéś*. Even Hindi speakers rarely use this word today, except when advertising hair oils; the preferred term now is *bāl*. But kéś seems to have a Persian cognate that still enjoys currency in Iran, along with other terms like *zolf*, of course. That cognate is *gêsu*, especially when referring to long hair on women. It comes from the Middle Persian *gēs*. Both gēs and kéś owe it to a common heritage in the Proto-Indo-European tongue.

What makes kéś and gēs interesting is the shift from *k* to *g* in the case of Persian. The phenomenon, it seems, isn't exclusive to gēs, and a whole repertoire of Persian words illustrates a comprehensive pattern.

Today, it is understood that the shift happened sometime before the Sassanian conquest of Parthia, as the Pahlavi script developed during the period did not have an exclusive letter to represent the /k/ sound. The letter *kaph* represented both /g/ and /k/. But that isn't all. This letter itself came from Aramaic where its pronunciation was exclusively /k/![6] This serves as a significant indicator of the shift from k to g.

Illustration of the shift can be seen in *-gar* words like *kârgar* and *bāzīgar*. *Kṛ* is a Sanskrit word meaning to do or to make. From this evolved *-kāra* as a suffix for people who do or make specific things. Added to śilp, Sanskrit for craft, the word became śilpakār, i.e., craftsman. With *suvarṇa* (lit. 'gold'), we got *suvarṇakār* (lit. 'goldsmith') and with *kumbh* (lit. 'pot'), we got *kumbhakār*. On the Persian side, the same suffix became *-gar*,[7] and we got words like *kârigar* (lit. 'craftsman') and *jādūgar* (lit. 'magician').

The Aryans have come to be seen as exclusively Indian in most generic contexts. That, however, isn't an accurate notion, and the tribe belongs as much to Iran as to India. The very name Iran goes back to

Old Persian *ariya,*[h] which comes from the same Proto-Indo-Iranian root that gave us ārya in Sanskrit, although the first instance of the word being written down is in a Sassanian inscription from the third century, which is nearly a millennium after the Rigvedic reference to ārya.

Iran's etymology is just one of the reasons we brought up the Aryans, though. Another reason is horses. Given their pastoral lifestyle, early Aryans placed a great deal of importance on horses. These were some of the most versatile beasts of the time, giving not just food and milk but also a quick, robust mode of transport. Its role in the growth of the Aryan civilization in both Iran and India can hardly be overstated. With that, it's natural for the name of this crucial asset to be at least somewhat similar in the two languages.

The Persian name for horse is *asp*, and the word has remained pretty much unchanged since as early as Old Persian. Before that, the word was *aspah* in Old Median. Remember how Avestan was born in the north-east and Persian in the south-west? Well, Median was a third dialect and was born in the north-west. Same family, of course. And this Old Median word just happens to have a cognate in Sanskrit—áśva! The word is far more interesting than that if we look at how it evolved elsewhere, but we won't get into that. For now, this asp-áśva parallel serves to further fortify the case for a Persian–Sanskrit parallel.

Another piece of evidence involves the Persian word for existence or being—*hasti*. What's the Sanskrit equivalent? Ástitva. The etymological relationship between the two words goes further. At the very root of ástitva lies ásti, meaning to be or to exist. And this root is now understood to have come from the Proto-Indo-European reconstruction, h_1*ésti*. Know what else comes from that reconstruction? Ancient Greek *estí*, Old Slavonic *estŭ*, Gothic *ist*, and most importantly, Old Persian *astiy*. Later, they slapped the /h/ sound to it and got hasti.

The list of cognates and near-cognates bridging the two lexicons runs in the hundreds, maybe thousands, many pairs being just slight variations in pronunciation, e.g., Persian dental versus Sanskrit cerebral or retroflex.[8] We're absolutely not going to examine all of them here for obvious reasons. Instead, let's now take a very quick look at some of the grammatical parallels.

The most immediate parallel can be seen in grammatical 'cases'. There are eight in both Persian and Sanskrit. But this isn't such a big deal. The big deal is that Sanskrit is an 'inflected' language. Here, nouns change their forms based on their grammatical case. Both Avestan and Old Persian followed this regime. With Modern Persian, however, the system changed from that of inflection to that of adpositional markers, i.e., prepositions and postpositions.[9]

Another key grammatical similarity appears in the case of gender. Again, Modern Persian has eschewed the whole idea in the interest of simplicity and become practically 'genderless', but this wasn't always the case. In fact, both Avestan and Old Persian had three genders—masculine, feminine and neuter.[10] And so does Sanskrit. The same goes for numbers. While Modern Persian has just singular and plural, both Avestan and Sanskrit have three, i.e., singular, dual, plural.

One may attribute much linguistic similarity between disparate tongues to natural contact, say, trade and commerce. When two peoples come in contact with each other, an amount of lexical diffusion is expected and happens all the time. Such exchanges, however, rarely go beyond lexical. Vocabulary is portable, grammar not so much. The similarities noted between Sanskrit and Avestan go far beyond mere etymology.

There are many other grammatical and syntactical similarities between Sanskrit and Avestan, some of which also carried into Old Persian, but just as we have seen with cases, numbers, and genders, much of it got lost in the move from Old to Modern Persian. So, do Sanskrit and Persian have enough grammatical overlap to even merit serious examination? No. At least not in the current form.

What cannot be dismissed in the face of overwhelming evidence is a common linguistic heritage shared by Persian and Sanskrit. Even if the two languages barely look or sound similar today.

Before we end this discussion, here's something amusing about the Persian script: Even though it runs right to left, like other Semitic scripts, numbers are still written left to write, as is done in Sanskrit and other Indo-European systems! Even among Semitic systems, Hebrew is the only one that writes its numbers right to left, not even Arabic.

Algebra Came from India ... or Did It?

Indians claim that algebra as an idea that was born here and later stolen by the Arabs. The West mostly credits the Arabs with its development. So it's basically Indians vs Arabs. But is there any truth behind that binary? What about the Babylonians and Egyptians—where do they fit in, if at all? To find the answers to these questions, let's dive deep into the history of algebra to see what the world really owes to Indian mathematicians of yore, like Brahmagupta.

IN 820 CE, A PERSIAN SCHOLAR AND POLYMATH NAMED Moḥammad bin Musā Khwārazmi, al-Khwārazmi for short, was appointed to Baghdad's famous Bait al-Hikma as its head librarian. Those days, Baghdad was the world's mecca of intellect and learning, thanks to the Abbasid penchant for arts and sciences. Bait al-Hikma, or House of Wisdom, was just one of Caliph al-Ma'mūn's initiatives. The idea was to bring the best minds from not just the Caliphate but all over the world under one roof.

The project proved successful and led to a frenzy of academic activities. All kinds of Greek and Sanskrit texts, many almost lost to time, were translated into Persian and given a whole new kind of exposure.

It's also here that al-Khwārazmi, either immediately before his appointment or right after, completed his most celebrated work, a treatise on mathematics titled *al-Kitāb al-Mukhtaṣar fī Ḥisāb al-Jabr wa'l-Muqābalah* (lit. 'The Compendious Book on Calculation by Completion and Balancing'), or al-Jabr for short.[1]

This was the birth of algebra. At least etymologically.

Later scholars translated this work into Latin as *Liber algebrae el almucabala*.

So how close to modern algebra is al-Khwārazmi's work anyway? Turns out, quite close. More than any such work from the period, for sure. The Latin translation, for instance, has the first seven chapters entirely committed to quadratic equations, one of the central topics in modern algebra. Of course, linear equations have also been dealt with.

The key concept of al-Khwārazmi's work was that of reduction and balancing. The idea of subtracting the given value from both sides of an equation, subsequently cancelling out like terms as a way to simplify and resolve the problem, is so fundamental to algebra that we don't even give it a second thought. Well, it's al-Khwārazmi who deserves the credit for inventing it. In fact, it's this concept that the term al-Jabr refers to.[2]

Thanks to this work, al-Khwārazmi is almost unanimously referred to as the 'father of algebra'. Why almost? Because, it turns out, the story of algebra has only just begun and the title has more contenders.

Just when the Abbasids were translating Greek and Sanskrit texts for their reference, another dynasty was doing the same with Prakrit texts in India—the Rashtrakutas. In this empire lived a Jain monk named Virasena. As is often the case with philosophers back in the day, Virasena was many things at once—orator, poet, theologian and, most importantly in the context of this discussion, mathematician.

Completely unbeknownst to al-Khwārazmi and just as unaware of his existence, this Indian mathematician propounded an idea he called *ardhaccheda*. The name referred to the number of times a given value must be halved in order to reduce it to one. In other words, the ninth-century equivalent of base-two logarithm. Later, he followed it up with a base-four version, *caturccheda*.

Besides these primitive forms of logarithm, Virasena also gave a formula to calculate the circumference of a circle, which indicates his knowledge of pi. And then came a handy formula to calculate the results of raising a number to its own power, something Indian mathematicians referred to as *vargita-samvargita*.

These calculations would not have been possible without a reasonable knowledge of what we consider algebraic operations today, at least in some primitive form. All of Virasena's works come from Dhavalā, a compendium of more than 70,000 verses that he composed about twenty years before al-Khwārazmi's al-Jabr. This text is considered seminal not only for its author but also for Jainism.[3]

So, can we call Virasena the father of algebra then? Some may, but do keep in mind that al-Khwārazmi's work was neither inspired nor aware of Virasena's. Also, while Virasena might have employed some algebraic principles in his calculations, his work on algebra was not as exhaustive and comprehensive as that of al-Khwārazmi. Therefore, the latter's title seems more or less secure for now.

This brings us to Brahmagupta. Some 170 years before Virasena and al-Khwārazmi, this man put together a landmark mathematical treatise in Sanskrit named Brāhmasphuṭasiddhānta. This is one of the earliest texts elaborating on concepts such as negative numbers and arithmetic operations using zero, although Brahmagupta was far from the first to imagine zero.

But that's all arithmetic. Brahmagupta also introduced, in his work, a range of algebraic novelties unheard of during his time. For instance, he elucidated his unique solutions to concepts like linear and quadratic equations,[4] the two cornerstones of modern algebra. This was at least a century before the Abbasids, let alone their House of Wisdom.

Note that Brahmagupta offered solutions to algebraic equations. That implies the problems must have already existed for him to work on. So there must be someone else before him who came up with ideas such as linear and quadratic equations. Who? Before we get into that, let's take a quick detour to China, where some interesting math was being done simultaneously with Brahmagupta's in India.

Wang Xiaotong was a writer, politician, mathematician, and a calendar aficionado who lived during the early years of the Tang dynasty. Of his works, the one that matters to us is named *Jigu Suanjing* (lit. 'Continuation of Ancient Mathematics'). Part biography, part mathematics, this book was among the Ten Computational Canons that made up the official math curriculum of the Tang dynasty's civil service exams. In short, it was a mighty important piece of work, and remained so for a long time.

While Wang did not exactly get into quadratic equations, he did introduce something similar—cubic equations. Quadratic equations are degree two polynomials, as the highest power of the unknown here is two. Cubic equations, as the name suggests, are degree three. Wang's solutions to cubic equations had lasting implications—many long after his time. They are said to have led to the development of Fibonacci's famous sequence more than 500 years after Wang's death.[5]

Going further back in time, we reach Āryabhaṭa, the internationally celebrated Indian mathematician who wrote *Āryabhaṭīya* and reintroduced us to zero. But this time, we're not discussing zero. We're discussing algebra and Āryabhaṭa's role in its story.

Āryabhaṭīya came out around 500 CE. That makes it over a hundred years older than Wang. This work may have been wrongly credited as the first to mention zero, but it is the first treatise to offer a solution to equations with two unknowns, i.e., Diophantine equations. Āryabhaṭa isn't very clear on how his algorithm really works, though, and it was only a hundred years after his death that another Indian mathematician named Bhāskara published a detailed study on it along with examples from astronomy. He named the algorithm *Kuṭṭaka*, Sanskrit for pulverization.

So, at least in some way, it should be fair to credit Āryabhaṭa with algebra, albeit without the name? Maybe, but we're only halfway through and several other contenders are still awaiting introduction.

Before we proceed, let's briefly dwell on the term Diophantine from Āryabhaṭa's story. We now know it's a polynomial with two unknowns, but doesn't it sound like something named after a person? That's because it is.

The name is Diophantus. While most scholars and mathematicians agree on al-Khwārazmi being the legitimate father of algebra, there are some that don't. The latter mostly consists of those who prefer this Alexandrian mathematician who lived and worked in the second or third century CE, long before Āryabhaṭa.

Diophantus is best known for his collection of over a hundred different algebraic equations and their solutions named *Arithmetica*. The collection is considered one of the earliest extant treatises on algebra, although of course, the word itself didn't exist back then. It's in response to these equations that Āryabhaṭa offered his own solutions. The equations include, among other things, quadratic equations.[6]

What makes Diophantus important to algebra is not just his departure from geometry, the otherwise mainstream field of mathematics at the time, but also his use of 'syncopated algebra'. His algebra looked remarkably similar to the one we know today. For instance, he's the first to start using symbols for the unknowns. The only way it differed was that he had no dedicated symbol for mathematical operators or exponents.[7]

Fun fact: not all of Diophantus' volumes survive to this day. Those that do, owe it to the Abbasids who had acquired and translated into Arabic whatever of his works they could get their hands on. Without their efforts, we probably would have never known about the Greek genius's existence.

Predating al-Khwārazmi by over five centuries and Āryabhaṭa by more than two, Diophantus sure seems to be a solid contender. But algebra, as we're going to see now, predates even him. Next up on our list is yet another Alexandrian, Heron. We commonly know him as Hero of Alexandria. Multiple theories exist around when he lived, the most widely accepted one arguing that it was around 60 CE. That places him at least a hundred years before Diophantus.

The name, by the way, is just a contraction of Heron and not a reference to some act of valour. Yet, since Hero, a champion of geometry and applied mechanics, was arguably one of the greatest inventors of antiquity, the title fit. The man invented so many gadgets still in use in the twenty-first century that a whole book could be filled with just reviews on them. Hero's list of firsts for the world ranges from a vending machine to a syringe, a wind-powered organ to a mechanical theatre show; his repertoire is as impressive as it is hard to fathom. Some historians also credit him with the first thermometer and a theory in optics that later developed into Fermat's principle of least time. In short, he was da Vinci over 1,400 years before da Vinci.

Among his works on geometry was a curious new formula for calculating the diameter of a circle using its circumference and area as inputs. Experts argue that this formula could only have been arrived at algebraically, and not geometrically. More specifically, by solving a quadratic equation. Hero called it geometry and did not even use algebraic symbols the way we do today, but his methods were undeniably algebraic,[8] which makes the discipline nearly 2,000 years old!

Jiŭzhāng Suànshù is the oldest extant text on Chinese mathematics. It is said to have been written by several authors over several decades, maybe even generations. Experts date it to anywhere between 150 BCE and 100 CE. So the work can be safely taken as contemporaneous with, if not predating, the Greek we just discussed.

The name of the book translates into 'Nine Chapters on the Mathematical Arts'. Amusing how just nine chapters took such a long time and so many authors to compile. Unfortunately, not all chapters remain to this day. Bamboo isn't as durable a writing medium as they once seem to have thought.

The penultimate chapter in the collection introduces an interesting algebraic concept relating to linear equations. The authors call it *fangcheng*. The word is made up of two components, *fang* meaning rectangle or square, and *cheng* meaning measurement. If this invokes images of a square or rectangle matrix, it's because that's what it is.

Fangcheng is nothing but a very primitive algorithm to solve a system of linear equations.[9] Remember, this is from a time when they were still counting with sticks and rods. The algorithm would take almost 2,000 years to achieve its now familiar sophistication as Gaussian elimination (thanks to Carl Friedrich Gauss, who devised a notation to represent it on paper in 1819).

The likes of Āryabhaṭa, Khwārazmi and Diophantus are all beyond the temporal horizon now. But can we go even further than this?

Remember the Jain mathematician we discussed earlier by the name Virasena? Well, looks like our next contender is once again a Jain like him.

Sthānāṅgasūtra is one of the earliest parts of the Jaina Canon and dates back to, according to some reckoning, about the second century BCE.[10] Others place it in more recent centuries, but we'll stick with BCE. One can only speculate about its authorship, and most speculations attribute it to Sudharmāsvāmī, one of the chief disciples of Mahāvīra himself.

Of particular interest here is the range of algebraic topics it covers. Not only simple and quadratic, the *sūtra* also goes on to discuss other equations such as cubic and biquadratic. Of course, the names are all Indian and would sound strange to Western ears. Simple equation, for instance, is yāvat-tāvat. Similarly, quadratic is *varga* and cubic is *ghana*. Besides the names and procedures, the algebra is unambiguous!

Now we're back to India, with a Jain monk at the helm of algebra. But we need to ask the same question again: can we push even further back in time? Was there anyone before Sudharmāsvāmī?

Of course there was, and it takes us back to Ancient Greece—to Alexandria. To Euclid. The man is best known for his geometry, but his thirteen-book treatise named *Stoikheîon*, better known as *Elements*, has quite a bit of algebra too. The second book in the collection is entirely dedicated to what mathematicians call geometric algebra. Herein, Euclid represented algebraic terms by sides of geometric objects and uses geometrical theorems to derive algebraic solutions. In fact, 'Proposition I' of this book uses a geometric theorem to propound one of the most fundamental items of modern algebra, the distributive law of binary operations.[11]

Euclid died in the third century BCE. That's almost early antiquity. But we can still push further.

Between the eighth and sixth centuries BCE, a collection of six texts, collectively called *Baudhāyana Sūtras*, emerged in India. Written in Vedic Sanskrit and belonging to the Krishna or dark Yajurveda school, these texts cover a diverse range of topics, including dharma, liturgy and mathematics.

The last of these six is titled Śulbasûtra and covers contemporary mathematics, in three chapters or adhyāyas. The mathematics addressed here pertains to geometry, useful in the construction of fire altars for yājñas, a central part of the early Vedic tradition. Of particular significance in this text is the reference to quadratic equations. The *Baudhāyana* proposed and then solved two kinds of quadratic equations for a very narrow geometrical use case.[12] Some experts still see it more as geometry than algebra, but the equations' presence cannot be denied.

Our next stop is a whole thousand years further back in time. This time, it's Ancient Egypt; enough of toggling between Ancient Greece and India.

Now we are so far back in time, we speak of texts not in terms of books but scrolls of papyrus. The ones in question come from around 1800 BCE and were first presented in a paper titled 'Der Berliner Papyrus 6619' by Hans Schack-Schackenburg in 1900.

What exists today, though, is just fragments of the original scroll, which means a whole lot is now forever lost to time. The fragments, though, still manage to offer a crucial glimpse into how mathematics worked back then. Here, two-term quadratic equations have been used to solve a geometric problem involving squares with sides in a very specific ratio.[13] As evident, some of the earliest applications of algebra, or mathematics in general, were understandably in the field of applied geometry. This was the case with India, and this was the case with Ancient Greece. And as the Berlin Papyrus shows, the same happened in Ancient Egypt too. (Or should we just say Ancient Egypt? After all, all the Ancient Greek innovations we've discussed so far have come from Alexandria, which is part of Egypt today.)

Unfortunately, given the fragments' extreme vintage, it's impossible to establish its authorship. We can't even say for sure if it was the work of a single individual or a team effort. But it sure takes the title of being one of the world's first introductions to algebra, in however primordial a form.

Wait, one of? Are there still others? Actually, many. For starters, there's a whole assortment of other Ancient Egyptian fragments with the same vintage as the Berlin Papyrus—Rhind Papyrus, Kahun Papyrus, Reisner Papyrus, Moscow Papyrus, and many more. And that's just Egypt. There's also cuneiform tablets from Ancient Babylon that offer concepts such as Pythagorean triplets and reciprocal pairs.[14] These may or may not predate the papyrus fragments of Egypt.

In conclusion, algebra is an enormous discipline, and it would be too reductive to assign all of it to a single culture, let alone an individual. While it's true al-Khwārazmi's al-Jabr gave it the name and form we recognize it by today, a whole body of work predates him, and it's impossible to pinpoint a time when the discipline itself came into existence.

Algebra does not have a father. It does not have an inventor. All it has is contributors, India being just one of them.

Is Hindu Atheist Really an Oxymoron?

We know Buddhism is atheistic, but what about Hinduism? Hinduism is hard to dissociate from its rituals and traditions, all of which centre on the Divine. There are hundreds of gods and hundreds of different ways to worship them. So much so that the idea of Hindu atheism is seen as a contradiction in terms. But many do identify as Hindu atheists. So let's examine whether it is possible to be a Hindu and also dismiss its gods. And if the term is just another new-age fad?

IT ALL GOES BACK TO ROUGHLY 1500 BCE WHEN THE FIRST of the Vedas, the Rigveda, was composed.[1] This piece of scripture formed the primary scaffolding for a school of thought we now identify as Hinduism. Although reduced to mostly a liturgical blueprint barely referred to outside of rituals today, the Rigveda remains the most identifiable source of the Hindu philosophy.

Thus, any discussion on Hinduism and its tenets ought to start with this book.

The religion followed today, contrary to popular assumption, is very different from the religion followed by the authors of the Vedas. It wouldn't be totally unfair to distinguish the Vedic religion from modern Hinduism, even though several similarities persist. Arguably, the biggest shift has happened in the context of gods.

The Rigveda, given its sheer expanse, is rather confused on the question of God. There's little consistency in its identification of what we understand as the Supreme Creator. At the same time, it's not polytheistic like Greek mythology. In the Vedic scheme of things, different deities acquire absolute supremacy in different contexts. At times, the idea of absolute supremacy for a single deity is entirely missing.[2] In other words, Vedic deities are mostly dependent on and subservient to nature as well as each other. Early Aryans, being a nomadic people, were highly dependent on fire. From cooking to protection from the elements, fire was indispensable to nearly every aspect of their lifestyle. It's therefore natural that it also became a subject of reverence. Most early hymns of the Rigveda are odes to the 'fire god'.

Later, other forces of nature were deified. With time, as the pastorals began settling down and agriculture took over, rain became far more important. That's how Indra, the god of rain, came to acquire dominance over the pantheon. Today, Indra is barely worshipped.

Throughout the scripture, the position of supremacy has shifted from one deity to another.[3] The epithet 'Prajapati' (lit. 'lord of all beings') has been accorded to multiple deities as convenient. This is unique to the Vedic religion. Max Müller calls this system Henotheism.

The Rigveda also maintains a measured amount of mystery on the question of a Creator God. It's only in the last chapter or mandala that the idea of a creator starts taking shape as an unborn, unseen deity called Vishwakarma.[4] Towards the end of the Vedic period, though, came the Upaniṣads. Considered part of the Yajurveda, the last of the four, these texts introduce and expound upon the concepts of *ātma* (self) and *brāhmaṇa* (universe). It's here that we are first introduced to the idea of the universe or Brahma as the creator. The first reference is made in the Kutsayana Hymn of the Maitrayaniya Upaniṣad. Here, the creator Brahma and the 'created' ātma have been shown as indistinguishable from each other. In other words, Brahma is the Supreme Creator God—not in an independent capacity but as part of everything in existence.[5] This is certainly a move in the general direction of monotheism, but with the pantheon of deities still intact.

The latter half of the first millennium BCE saw the emergence of two philosophies so different from the Vedic thought that they came to be identified separately from the prevailing theology. These were Buddhism and Jainism.

The emergence of these new religions also coincided with several other philosophical experiments that departed from the original Vedic ideals in varying degrees. Some survived, many died. Among the earliest such experiments was Sāṁkhya.

But before we get into these post-Vedic developments, an understanding of atheism in the Hindu context will help. Generally, we translate the word theist as *āstika* and atheist as *nāstika*. But that parallel isn't accurate. Truth be told, a true Hindu equivalent just doesn't exist. While the theist–atheist distinction hinges on God, the āstika–nāstika distinction is about the Vedas and the soul or 'ātma', depending on who one asks. An āstika isn't one who submits to God, he's one who submits to the Vedas.[6] A nāstika doesn't necessarily reject God, he rejects the authority of the Vedas or the existence of soul. This is a crucial distinction to make in order to fully appreciate the idea of Hindu theism.

The post-Vedic era saw a frenzy of ambitious philosophical innovations, some that adhered to the Vedas and others that didn't. Although there were many—most lost to time—ten of them remain the most studied and recognized in the modern world. Six of these schools of thought are orthodox or āstika, i.e., they adhere to the Vedic creed. The remaining four don't and are nāstika or heterodox.

Among the earliest āstika philosophies is Sāṁkhya. All that we know of this school of thought today comes from a third-century work by Iśvarakṛṣṇa, Sāṁkhyakārikā. The school itself is generally attributed to Kapila, a Vedic sage said to have lived between the sixth and seventh centuries BCE.

The Sāṁkhyakārikā expressly rejects the notion of a perpetual, self-caused Creator God. In Sāṁkhya, karma is central to the affairs of Creation. While Western philosophies divide the world between Man and God, Sāṁkhya posits Puruṣa (man) and Prakṛti (nature). Prakṛti is independent and eternal and the source of all creation. But it isn't God. Even in Kapila's original thought, it's all karma, an eternal chain of causes and effects that govern the world and rejects the need for, and thereby the existence of, a Creator Deity.[7] Having said that, it still does not eschew the rituals and practices outlined in the Vedas. Instead, it interprets the Vedic idea of the 'all-knower Creator' as merely people who have attained perfection through meditation and other forms of abstinence,[8] thus rejecting God while still adhering to the Vedas. In other words, Sāṁkhya is āstika, but atheistic.

If this sounds similar to much of the Buddhist philosophy, that's because it is. Sāṁkhya is said to have informed some of the most fundamental aspects of not only Yoga[9] but also Buddhism and Jainism.[10]

Concurrent to Sāṁkhya emerged the Mīmāṃsās. There were two—Pūrva and Uttara. Both came about as critical investigations of certain Vedic positions; *mīmāṃsā* is Sanskrit for reflection of investigation. While Pūrva and Uttara translate into early and later, respectively, they don't necessarily reflect a chronology of the Mīmāṃsās themselves.[11] Instead, they refer to the parts or kāṇḍas of the Vedas the two systems deal with—Karma Kāṇḍa and Jñāna Kāṇḍa. Karma Kāṇḍa speaks of actions, i.e., sacrifices and rituals, and is the first section. This is what Pūrva Mīmāṃsā studies. Jñāna Kāṇḍa, on the other hand, is the later section consisting of the Upaniṣads and expounds on speculative knowledge. This is the subject of Uttara Mīmāṃsā. There is a third too; it's called Upāsanā Kāṇḍa, but the Mīmāṃsās don't discuss that.

Mīmāṃsā Sūtras, a 200 BCE text by Rishi Jaimini, is accepted as the foundational scripture for Pūrva Mīmāṃsā.[12] The Uttara schools of thought, on the other hand, find expression in texts composed much later, Badarayana's *Brahma Sutrās* from around 400 CE being one of the earliest. Earlier works have unfortunately been lost to time.

While the two Mīmāṃsās may seem similar at first glance, they do diverge on one key item, the question of God. Pūrva Mīmāṃsā sees existence as perpetual. Just like Sāṁkhya, Pūrva Mīmāṃsā places much import on karma; rituals and sacrifices are said to create good karma, which helps with spiritual elevation. Devas, in this philosophy, are just beings that have attained this elevated existence through good karma. Thus, both devas and humans are subservient to the same rules. There's no room for a Creator or a Destroyer, as everything is handled by karma, and the perpetuity of material existence renders Creation and Destruction moot.[13]

As a study of later Vedic texts, Uttara Mīmāṃsā is also known as Vedānta. The Vedānta hermeneutics is thought to have crystallized with Badarayana's *Brahma Sūtras* from about 200 BCE, although the philosophy had been in development for over half a millennium by then. This is the second time God shows up as a higher entity separate from, and above, both ātma and brāhmaṇa. In other words, Uttara Mīmāṃsā is unambiguously theistic, and this is what sets it apart from not only the other Mīmāṃsā but also almost all other schools of Hindu philosophy.

Sometime in the sixth century BCE, a sage named Kaṇāda Kashyapa established what one could call India's first treatise on Physics—Vaiśeṣika. Kashyapa's Vaiśeṣika Sūtra is the central literature and several later commentaries exist thereof. What makes this a cornerstone of Hindu scientific inquiry is its most sincere attempt at explaining the nature and composition of matter. It's here that we first learn about the smallest building blocks of the universe, *kaṇa*. Kaṇāda wasn't the first to postulate a fundamental particle, though. The same was postulated by Leucippus and his pupil Democritus in Ancient Greece around the same time. They called it atomos or 'the uncuttable'. Leucippus and Kaṇāda never shared notes. It, however, took a good 2,200 years for a John Dalton to come up with empirical evidence of such a particle. He called them atoms. Besides kaṇa, Vaiśeṣika Sūtra also proposes the concept of earth, water, light and air as the four fundamental types of matter.

Returning to the question of God, Vaiśeṣika Sūtra maintains a bit of a mystery. While there are two verses[14] that allude to some kind of a 'Higher Being', there's little else to clarify its stance on the nature and even the existence of God. A direct mention of God is missing in the entire text. Sure, there's soul in chapter 3 and virtue and sin in chapter 6, but no God anywhere. It can thus be said that the Vaiśeṣika philosophy either eschews God entirely or maintains the existence of one with limited authority.[15]

Before discussing the remaining orthodox philosophies, let's take a quick break and check out a heterodox system for a change. It's called Ājīvika. Along with Buddhism, Jainism and Cārvāka, Ājīvika forms what we call the nāstika schools of thought. As the name suggests, these are some mighty radical ideas, rejecting not only God but also the Vedas.

Ājīvika started with Manthaliputra Goshalak, a contemporary of Gautam Buddha and Mahavira. Its original literature has all been lost to time, so much of what we know comes from later commentaries. Depending on the commentary in question, the Ājīvika idea of divinity is limited to yakṣas and other demigods. No Supreme Creator whatsoever. The Bhagavatī Sūtra, where Ājīvika finds much overlap with Jainism, mentions two yakṣas by the names Pūrṇabhadra and Maṇibhadra.[16] Neither have the omnipotence and omniscience of a Creator Deity.

Ājīvika peaked under the Mauryan emperor Bindusara around the fourth century BCE and had a decent 2,000-year run lasting well into the fourteenth century CE. Towards the end of its life, the movement found itself confined to regions in Karnataka and Tamil Nadu, and accrued many ideas from the later Vaishnavite movements. In essence, though, Ājīvika tilted more towards a universe without God.

Empiricism, scepticism and materialism—these replace the supernatural and divine in the nāstika creed called Cārvāka. Also known as Lokāyata, this one is a major coup, arguably, the 'Marxist' face of Hinduism. Many place it before other nāstika schools, seeing it as the first to expressly reject the Vedas. *Barhaspatya Sutrās*, the foundational text, is said to have been composed around 600 BCE, predating both Buddhism and Jainism. Unfortunately, this text exists today only as fragmented references in later commentaries. This rebel of a creed must've created quite the stir in its time, for it rejected not just the Vedas, which it dismisses as works of 'buffoons, knaves and demons', but also karma, afterlife, soul and God itself.[17] No room for metaphysics! It deviated from the Vedas as well as other nāstika traditions of its time. Unfortunately, the fad didn't stand the test of time and died a quiet death.

That leaves us with Yoga and Nyāya, both within the āstika framework of Vedic tradition. Yoga builds upon the Puruṣa–Prakṛti dualism of Sāṁkhya and can be read as an offshoot thereof. Several disparate texts make up the scripture for this philosophy, but the most authoritative piece remains the one by Patañjali called *Yoga Sūtra*.

Yoga is a bit dicey on God. While it doesn't exactly reject the idea, it doesn't embrace it in the way traditional theologies define it either. Instead, Yoga posits a 'personal God' it calls Īṣvara.[18] Thus, it can be seen as the theistic update to Sāṁkhya or, as some say, Sāṁkhya with God. That said, the Īṣvara here isn't a qualified entity, much less anthropomorphic. It's, at best, a state of higher consciousness where Puruṣa becomes one with Prakṛti through meditation. In fact, Yoga Sūtra in book 1, verse 24 defines God or Īṣvara as just a spiritual man who has, through meditation and discipline, conquered sorrow.[19]

Nyāya Sūtras, composed between 600 BCE and 100 CE, possibly by multiple authors over multiple generations, forms the central text of the Nyāya philosophy. The corpus largely deals with epistemology and metaphysics in a little over 500 aphorisms across five books. Just as Yoga builds upon Sāṁkhya, Nyāya builds upon Vaiśeṣika. Of its 530 aphorisms or sūtras, particularly important are 19, 20 and 21 from book 4, chapter 1. Therein lies a terse aphoristic argument to establish the redundancy of God, saying all events are simply results of human actions.[20]

These three sutrās are generally interpreted as the Nyāya school's outright rejection of God. At least they were, until later interpreters such as Vatsāyana and Udayana tried retrofitting theistic elements into its epistemology. If not atheistic, Nyāya was certainly agnostic.

Both Buddhism and Jainism are widely accepted as atheistic, and although independent faiths today, both branched out as nāstika schools of Hindu thought. The name Hindu itself is a misnomer in this context, though, because there was no concept of a single named collection of faiths at the time. That happened only with the advent of the Greeks and Muslims.

So, what we're left with here is ten major Hindu philosophies, six āstika and four nāstika. Of these ten, only one is truly theistic and makes the case for a Supreme Creator God unambiguously, and that is Uttara Mīmāṃsā or Vedānta. Yoga accepts God but not as a Higher Absolute: Nyāya is, at best, ambivalent on the question. That still leaves us with seven atheistic forms of Hinduism. As for the Vedas, we've already noted how a Creator Supreme doesn't even show up until Yajurveda.

In short, more than 70 per cent of what constitutes Hindu philosophy is atheistic! So, is the term 'Hindu atheist' really an oxymoron? Turns out, not necessarily. Far from an anomaly, atheism is a rather established feature of Hinduism.

Was There Ever a River Named Sarasvatī?

Ganga exists, and so does the Yamuna. But the two rivers are often spoken of as parts of a 'holy trinity' of Hinduism, the third member being Sarasvatī. But no river by that name exists today. The most dominant explanation offered is that it did in the distant past but dried up long before we came about. This is where we examine the geographical and historical substance, if any, in this theory.

VERSE 41.16 OF RIGVEDA'S SECOND BOOK OR MAṆḌALA venerates a river as the best of mothers, best of rivers and the best of goddesses. The river in question is not the Ganga. It's Sarasvatī.

In fact, Ganga doesn't show up at all in the first five books of the Veda. The first time it finds a mention is in the forty-fifth hymn of Book 6. In all, the entire scripture mentions the Ganga a mere four times, including two references to Jahnavi, another name for Ganga.

Sarasvatī, on the other hand, finds no fewer than fifty references. Which clearly indicates that it was mighty important, with far more social and religious clout than even the Ganga!

But the question is, did it exist? If so, where and until when? Much ethnopolitical incentive lies on either side of the debate, because this isn't a debate on just a river that may or may not be mythological but also on the elephant in the room—the Aryans. We won't get into the latter part of the debate here, but let's try to address the former.

The Shivalik Hills of Himachal Pradesh is the birthplace of many intermittent rivers, most of them fed by the monsoons as there's little snow to offer meltwater. Ghaggar is one such river. Sarasvatī may or may not be mythical, but Ghaggar isn't. It flows through Punjab and most of Haryana before hitting a dam near Sirsa where it loses much of its payload to a couple of irrigation canals. Whatever remains, weakly snakes through the Thar Desert before crossing into Pakistan. Once in Pakistan, the river tapers into a mostly dry paleochannel named Hakra. The course of this river, especially the Hakra section, is home to a large number of Harappan sites until as far south as Bahawalpur. And that's why we're bringing this river to a discussion on Sarasvatī.

A significant number of experts see the Ghaggar-Hakra as a remnant of Sarasvatī. They present a multitude of compelling arguments making a case for this theory. Let's examine them as we ask: could today's Ghaggar-Hakra be yesterday's Sarasvatī?

The Rigveda, as we've already established, makes dozens of references to Sarasvatī, most of those as a river. This makes it a very good starting point for any investigation into the existence, nature and vintage of the water body. Of course, many of those references are merely reverential in nature, offering little insight other than the fact that the river—mythical or otherwise—was deified and worshipped when the book was composed. But there are some that do bring useable pieces of the puzzle to the table.

As we've already noted, the first time the Rigveda speaks of Sarasvatī as a deified, personified river is in 2.XLI.16. Later, in 3.XXIII.4, the river is mentioned alongside yet another whose existence remains just as contested as that of Sarasvatī but is far less spoken of—Dṛṣadvatī. The latter also finds mention as a river marking the frontiers of the Vedic state of Brahmavarta, along with Sarasvatī. Any attestation that establishes the existence of Dṛṣadvatī, therefore, should also help strengthen the case for Sarasvatī.

One such attestation comes from a Samavedic book of chants called Tandya Mahabrāhmaṅa, better known as the Pañcaviṃśa Brāhmaṅa. Verses XV.10.13–15 of this text describe in ample detail a site at the confluence of Dṛṣadvatī and Sarasvatī where a sacrifice of boiled rice is offered to the deities before crossing over to the other side.[1] This account serves to further affirm Rigveda 3.XXIII.4.

The next Rigvedic nod comes from the verse 6.LII.6, wherein Sarasvatī is said to be teeming with waters from other rivers and rain, implying a distributary status with multiple lesser streams pouring into it. Although the verse doesn't mention rain explicitly, it does mention a lesser-known entity called Parjánya—one that scholars have variously interpreted as a minor god of rain, thunder, clouds (particularly in the context of rain), or water, likely subservient to greater deities such as Bṛhaspati and Váruṇa,[2] and certainly to Indra.

In the following book, verse XXXVI.6 brings up Sarasvatī again, this time as *síndhumātā* or a 'roaring mother of the river Síndhu'. The verse could be interpreted in one of two ways, depending on how one translates the word Síndhu. As a common noun, it can mean flood or just a very large water body. This interpretation makes Sarasvatī a great river with a highly fluvial character. As a proper noun, though, Síndhu is the Indus River. This interpretation makes the Indus a tributary of Sarasvatī. Either way, Sarasvatī does seem to have a mighty important position in the Rigvedic scheme of things.

So far, all scriptural references seem consistent with not only there being a river named Sarasvatī, but also it being a highly voluminous water body in the general vicinity of the Indus. But that's not all. The same book that describes Sarasvatī as síndhumātā also has an entire hymn (sūkta XCV) dedicated to this mystery river. Here, the second verse even lays out the course of this river, saying it originates in the mountains and pours into the *samudrá*, today interpreted as the ocean. Ghaggar-Hakra, too, originates in the Shivaliks and, discounting the dried-up status of its Hakra section, runs into the Arabian Sea, already having merged with the Indus along the way.

A final Rigvedic reference to the river comes in a river hymn from its tenth book, sūkta LXXV. Here, in the fifth verse, the five most important rivers of the time have been enumerated, likely in the order of location from west to east, or vice versa. Although the highlight of this hymn seems to be Indus, Sarasvatī does find a mention among the big five. Assuming the enumeration really follows an order, Sarasvatī seems to be located between *Yamune* and Śutudri, i.e., Yamuna and Sutlej. And that's the course Ghaggar follows today. Further fortifying this position is Sarsutī. That's the name of an ephemeral stream that feeds into the upper reaches of Ghaggar.[3] Sarsutī and Sarasvatī—the similarity could be purely coincidental. Or, read alongside the numerous Vedic attestations, an indicator that Ghaggar-Hakra and Sarasvatī are one and the same, Sarsutī just being a linguistic remnant thereof.

While many early Indologists agree with this notion, some modern experts do so too. In those circles, the generally accepted theory is that back in the day, Sarasvatī originated in the Shivaliks and drained the Thar before emptying into the Arabian Sea. The drying up was a consequence of Late Harappan seismic events that disturbed its watershed and caused much of its payload to divert into other rivers.[4]

But not everyone agrees. One of the biggest objections to the Ghaggar–Sarasvatī equivalence comes from the fact that the river, as described in RV 7.XCV.2, originates in the mountains and empties into the sea. While Ghaggar fits the description, there is another candidate that seems to fit better.

About 25 miles west of Kabul, on the western fringes of the Hindu Kush, originates the largest in Afghanistan—Helmand. Having received water from five tributaries along its upper reaches, the river snakes through 800 miles of Perso-Afghanistan territory before pouring into the Sistān marshlands as Daryā-ye Sistān or the

Sistān River. A secondary branch named Pariān follows the Iran–Afghanistan border for some distance before running into *Hāmun-e Helmand*, the largest freshwater lake in the Iranian Plateau.[5]

A sizable portion of contemporary scholarship considers this river a better fit against the Vedic description of Sarasvatī's course. The Hindu Kush range certainly seems more 'mountain-like' than the Shivaliks. Having said that, the Sanskrit word girí, the term used in RV 7.XCV.2, does not have to strictly mean mountains and can also be applied to hills or other lesser elevations.[6]

Just as girí can mean more than one thing, so can samudrá. Although in modern usage, it exclusively refers to the ocean, the Sanskrit term was less stringent in its interpretation. The word came about as a combination of *sam*, Sanskrit for together, and *udán*, Sanskrit for water. Thus, it could refer to any rendezvous of two or more rivers. While mostly such a body of water happens to be an ocean, it could also be a more inland reservoir, such as a lake. Hāmun-e Helmand easily qualifies as a Rigvedic samudrá under this definition, making the case for Helmand as Sarasvatī.

Of course, such lexical manoeuvres alone cannot be enough to establish a definitive link between the two rivers; we need more. For that, let's take a look at Helmand's five tributaries. But before that, a bit of etymology. Helmand wasn't always Helmand. Once upon a time, the name used to be *Haetumant*. This is how the Zoroastrian scripture refers to it. The Helmand basin is understood to be one of the earliest centres of the faith, a notion that may shock many as Afghanistan is rarely, if at all, spoken of in any conversation about Zoroastrianism. The reference appears in the fourteenth verse of the first chapter, or *fargard*, in *Vendidad*. Here, Ahura Mazda is quoted as having created the 'bright and glorious' Haetumant.[7]

Another verse that comes right before gives us Harahvaiti,[8] sometimes spelt as Haraxvaiti, which bears a remarkable similarity with Sarasvatī!

This changes things. Or at least comes close. Helmand originates in the mountains, drains into a lake, and at least a part of it was originally called Harahvaiti, which sounds almost like Sarasvatī, just as Hindu sounds almost like Sindhu. There's little to dismiss it as a viable candidate now.

We are, however, still left with one bit unresolved—that of reverence. While the Rigveda deifies Sarasvatī in no uncertain terms, the Haraxvaiti enjoys no such reverence in Avesta. In fact, the name received a grand total of one mention in the entire text of the *Vendidad*, that too as a creation of Ahura Mazda (one of the two discussants in the verse). That's it. No further discussion, no personification, no special treatment.

But that alone cannot be grounds for elevating Ghaggar to stardom as the river hasn't been deified in living memory either. Any attempt to deify Ghaggar now would merely amount to retrofitting.

Coming back to the Indian subcontinent, there exists a third hypothesis that invokes neither Helmand, nor any of its tributaries. This hypothesis traces a paleochannel from the point where the Yamuna emerges from the hills to the meeting point of the Ghaggar-Hakra system, someplace in Punjab. Proponents of this idea examine the topography between the two rivers to establish that at some point in the distant past, the Yamuna flowed west to feed the Ghaggar.[9] Then some dramatic seismic activity caused it to change course to its present-day trajectory, leaving its original channel at the mercy of the monsoons. This now-defunct channel is what they see as remnants of the legendary Sarasvatī.

This hypothesis has found several advocates in recent times, especially after a 1972 satellite image of western India showing what appears to be a wide paleochannel running from Suratgarh in northern Rajasthan to Fort Abbas in Pakistan's Bahawalnagar. Researchers have identified that wells along the alleged channel hold water better than those further away. They have also found vegetation to be richer along the channel as compared to adjoining areas, although the channel itself is far from contiguous.[10]

Proponents of this hypothesis explain that the channel's death was tectonic. Large-scale geological events are known to have caused dramatic hydrological changes all over the world, so the theory does hold water.

And then comes a whole array of unanswered questions that defy all theories thus far.

The first such question—the most obvious of the lot—is why only Sarasvatī? Why not any of the other mighty rivers mentioned in the Vedas? Beas, Indus, Sutlej, Yamuna—all are doing just fine, flooding their basins just as bad as they probably did thousands of years ago. Rivers have also changed course over time, and that's an established geological fact. But then there's this river that the Vedas never tire of revering as the mightiest of them all that suddenly ceases to exist? Something seems off. Clearly, this was the most voluminous of rivers in the area when the Rigveda was composed, more than even today's Indus and Yamuna. And it's already inconceivable that these rivers would vanish within a matter of millennia.

For a water body the size of the Rigveda's Sarasvatī to dry up, it would take an enormous, if not cataclysmic geological upheaval. No major event capable of something that drastic has been recorded, at least in the last 10,000 years. So if the Sarasvatī existed and the Rigveda recorded it without gross exaggeration, it must have been more than a hundred centuries ago. Things are already beginning to sound absurd at this point, but there's more. Let's dwell on the tectonic aspect a bit longer to be sure we haven't overlooked anything.

One of the earliest papers making a case for Sarasvatī using satellite imagery came out in 1979. It's this study that theorized the relative abundance of water and vegetation along the supposed paleochannel as evidence of a long-dead river. This paper also attempts to answer the tectonic question.

In it, the proponents support their argument with a rather recent occurrence in Kutch—the M8 temblor of 1918. This earthquake had effected one of the most dramatic topographical changes in recent times—the Allah Bund.[11] The force was so great that it raised land, creating a ridge about twenty feet high, effectively damming a small local river named Puran. This geological 'dam' came to be known as Allah Bund (lit. 'God's dam').

As bad as it was, the ridge that appeared was merely twenty feet high. In comparison, the Indus delta runs an average of 75 feet. And Sarasvatī was described practically as the 'mother of Indus' in the Veda.

The same paper also offers a clue as to how long ago a 'mild tectonic activity' that could have altered the river's course might have occurred, if it did—sometime in the Quaternary period.[12] That period corresponds to the most recent segment of the Cenozoic Era and spans more than 2.5 million years! That means the earliest of Vedas could have been composed any time during that period—an absurd idea indeed.

Furthermore, the idea of a river this big vanishing into the desert due to climate change and earthquakes becomes more untenable when applied to other similarly great rivers charting more or less similar terrains in other parts of the world.

The biggest illustration is the Nile. The river has survived thousands of years, charting more than a thousand miles through one of the most hostile and arid landscapes on Earth, the Sahara. Similarly, the Colorado River hasn't given in to either the Mojave or the Sonora, both bone-dry deserts with little vegetation.[13] It's hard for rivers that big, to evaporate away or dam out of existence. They just continue to cut their way through rocks and mountains. And yet, Sarasvatī vanished?

Isn't that strange? It's possible that further studies could throw more light on the matter and bring out hitherto unexamined pieces of evidence. But the way things stand now, there is little to establish that a physical river named Sarasvatī, greater than the Ganges and the Indus, ever washed through the Indian subcontinent.

Trojan Horse, but Trojan Elephant?

We know that pre-Medieval literature from our subcontinent was rich. But could it have been influenced by foreign cultures such as the Greek one? And did one of the most iconic figures in Indian literary history draw inspiration from what remains the single most enduring part of Greek Mythology? Many disagree, not just about this but also about the scale of Greece's influence on our overall culture. Let's see if they should.

HELEN WAS IN TROY. SOME SAY IT WAS WILLINGLY, others claim abduction. Either way, it was trouble, for she belonged in Sparta, as its queen, wife of its king, Menelaus. Troy's king was Priam. Among his kids were Cassandra, the chief Apollonian priestess and prophetess, and Paris. The latter had abducted Helen in the hope of marrying her.

Naturally, Menelaus wasn't happy. But the only way to bring his wife back was to subdue Troy militarily. This was easier said than done, so he rallied for support and successfully put together a formidable confederacy of all Achaean armies to take on his wife's kidnappers.

Troy's fortification was the subject of legends. Virtually impermeable. The confederacy mounted an airtight siege upon the fort and patiently made it last. But nothing moved. That's when a Spartan named Odysseus came up with a workaround—a gift horse that would be used to deceitfully gain entry.

A giant wooden horse was quickly built within three days and wheeled over to the city gates with one solitary Spartan soldier. Everyone else retreated. When someone enquired about the horse, the Spartan announced the confederacy's surrender and retreat. He said that the horse was being offered as a token of apology for the desecration of their temple. Why horse and not, say, elephant? Because horse was on Troy's official sigil.

The ploy worked, and the horse was let in. Cassandra, the prophetess, didn't like this. She could see what nobody else could. She protested. But nobody heeded. That was her curse; she would always tell the truth but never be taken seriously.

Later that night, as Troy slept in peace after a long evening of celebrations for their victory, a hatch on the side of the wooden horse popped open. And from it emerged three to four dozen armed Spartan soldiers. The first step was to open the city gates, to let in the rest of the contingent that lay in ambush. Caught unaware, Troy had little time to mount a defence. What happened next is anyone's guess.

Thus a city with the most impenetrable fortification finally fell. All it took was one good actor and one realistic decoy. This was the story of the Trojan Horse—now a metaphor for anything that purports to be friendly but is actually a backdoor to attacks.

The story recounted above is just that, a story. Part of the overarching Greek Mythology. There's no material evidence suggesting the events ever took place. But that's inconsequential to this discussion. The main point for us to note is that the contraption first made its appearance sometime in the eighth century BCE, most likely in Homer's *Odyssey* as *douráteos híppos* (lit. 'wooden horse'). While an amount of uncertainty still hangs on the exact decade, a few suggest it was a later century.

Also, the *Odyssey* isn't the only ancient work that speaks of the wooden horse; it's just one of at least three. The other two are *Ilias mikra* (lit. 'Little Iliad') and *Iliou persis* (lit. 'Sack of Ilium'), both sharing roughly the same vintage. *Ilium* here is just an ancient name for Troy. Various dates have been offered for their composition, but the maximum deviation remains less than two centuries. At the latest, we could place these works in the later decades of the seventh century BCE, no later than that. So the Trojan Horse is very old.

Fast forward about a thousand years. This is when something similar shows up more than 2,500 miles away from what used to be Troy—in a place called Gandhāra or Kandahar in today's Afghanistan.

The British Museum has an impressive collection of artefacts from this time and region, almost all of them Buddhist. Part of the collection is a metamorphic tablet, about 6 inches high and 13 inches wide, with a rather interesting depiction. Dating back to the second century, the relief shows a mechanical horse being wheeled towards a doorway guarded by what appears to be a topless girl. There are three men in the panel, two wheeling the contraption and a third attempting to stop them with a spear.[1] Interestingly, the tunics they're clad in look less Indian and more Roman.

Theories abound on the question of this schist's true origins. The first time it was discovered, they suggested Mardān near Peshawar. A subsequent theory changed the place of origin to nearby Hund. Yet another theory placed it in Chārsadda.[2] All these sites are within miles of Peshawar. Somewhere along the way, then, the site further moved west—to Kandahar. While the site has remained in dispute, the depiction hasn't. Nor has the Roman–Greek influence.

The depiction looks remarkably like Homer's Trojan Horse—soldiers in Greek-Roman attire, a mechanical horse with wheels, a spear, the doorway. Even the girl in the doorway reminds one of Cassandra! So what's a Greek artefact from the seventh century BCE doing on a Buddhist stupa in the second century CE? Before we answer that, let's fast forward another 300 years or so and meet some more surprises.

Buddhaghoṣa was a mighty well-known Theravāda thinker, theologian, and evangelist from the fifth century CE. Although born and raised in what's today Bihar, the man spent most of his time writing and teaching at the Great Monastery of Anurādhapura in Sri Lanka. Buddhaghoṣa's enormous body of work includes at least fourteen Aṭṭhakathā or commentaries on the Pāli Canon that makes up the Buddhist scripture. Much of his work involves short esoteric stories meant to drive home one or more moral lessons, much like the Gospels of the Holy Bible. We call them Buddhaghoṣa's parables.

One such parable involves a queen by the name Sāmavatī. But she comes later in the tale. The story opens with another, unnamed queen. Once, carried by an evil bird as prey, the queen of Vatsa landed in the woods. Rescued by a hermit, she was unable to return to Kosambī, her capital. The queen eventually decided to stay back with the hermit as his wife. Meanwhile, she'd also given birth to a child whom she named Udena.

One day, news came from Kosambī. The king, her first husband, was dead. To console her, the hermit granted her boy an enchanted lute named Hatthikanta. When the right notes were played, Hatthikanta had the power to subdue elephants. It would help Udena regain his father's kingdom, the hermit said to her.

In possession of the lute, the boy rode an elephant and headed to Kosambī to reclaim his throne. At first, nobody would believe him, but once he showed them his mother's ring and cloak, they did. Udena was now the king of Vatsa.

This is where Sāmavatī makes her entry. Driven by famine and pestilence, the beautiful girl from Bhaddavatī showed up outside Udena's palace. It was love at first sight, and Udena immediately took her as his queen. Her name was Sāmavatī.

The lute had made Udena a very powerful king, thanks to all the elephants in his army. This made his neighbours a tad insecure. One such neighbour was Kandapaggota, king of Uggenī, Pali for Ujjain.

When told about Hatthikanta, Kandapaggota decided to capture both Udena and his magical lute by deception. He ordered his men to build him a large wooden elephant carefully painted and finished to make it look lifelike. Inside the contraption was a system of ropes and pulleys to help move the animal mechanically. The belly was made big enough to hold up to sixty soldiers.

This elephant was then placed in Udena's territory. When Udena learnt of the new animal, he struck his magical lute. The animal, however, began to drive away instead of towards the lute. The king gave it a chase, playing his lute harder. The animal kept accelerating, moving further and further away. Eventually, Udena found himself isolated, his army left far behind. That's when the elephant's belly flung open, and out came the soldiers. Cornered and without backup, Udena was helpless and soon in Kandapaggota's custody.[3]

Interestingly, this story follows a path very different from that of Homer's *Odyssey*. However, the similarity in decoys cannot be overruled. Both 'Kosambīan Elephant' and the Trojan Horse share the same operation and the same construction, and to an extent, the same purpose. Yet, 300 years apart!

But Buddhaghoṣa's story may or may not have been inspired by an older work with some literary licence. This brings us to the third century, about 200 years before the parable of Sāmavatī.

In the context of great Sanskrit playwrights from Indian antiquity, Śūdraka is a lesser-known name. But this man wrote plays more than a hundred years before Kālidāsa, the star everyone recognizes, was even born.

Śūdraka only penned three plays in his entire lifetime, at least that's what we know so far. That could very well be the reason he isn't as well-known as Kālidāsa. Among the three is one that interests us the most—Vīṇā-Vāsavadattā.

The manuscript, unfortunately, does not exist in its entirety today, and the last few acts seem to have been lost forever. What does remain gives us a fair bit of insight into the plot, which involves a mix of romance and drama and a helping of magic and fantasy.

Vīṇā-Vāsavadattā is about a princess named Vāsavadattā who falls for her music teacher, seemingly against her father's will. The twist in this otherwise banal story is that the music teacher is actually king Udayana of Vatsa. Udayana had been secretly hired by the girl's father, Chaṇḍapradyota of Avanti, to woo her on the pretext of teaching her the vīṇā. Why? Because he really liked the guy but was too proud to admit it to her. The portion of interest to this discussion, though, is about how the father discovered the music teacher in the first place.

It so happened that by the time she came of age, Vāsavadattā had acquired all life skills and arts from the best of teachers in the realm. Only one remained—music. So Chaṇḍapradyota launches a headhunt.

After a long and frustrating search, his minister finally found someone eligible. That someone was Udayana of Vatsa. The man's biggest flex was that he could lull wild elephants into submission with his music. But capturing Udayana himself wasn't going to be easy, so the king and his minister planned a decoy.

A giant wooden elephant was built and planted in the forest. It could be moved mechanically and looked remarkably similar to a real animal. As Udayana began singing, this elephant moved closer—as if lulled by the music. Once close enough, a hatch fell open in the animal's belly, and a large group of armed men sprang forth. Before Udayana could process what was happening, he was in the custody of Chaṇḍapradyota's soldiers, ready to be taken to Ujjain, the capital.[4]

This is thus the story of a mechanical wooden elephant that served as a decoy to get armed men as close to their target as possible by deception. Which is exactly what the Trojan Horse did. Ujjain is a world away, not just far from Troy, but also from Kandahar!

But the intrigue doesn't end here. In fact, it's just the beginning. About two centuries down the line, in the fifth century, the story makes a comeback in another work, this time a parable.

While Buddhaghoṣa's parable seems to be a mere retelling of Śūdraka play, it is also, apparently, an inspiration for a still later work—*Bāṇabhaṭṭa's Harṣacarīta*. The latter was composed in the seventh century, a good two hundred years after the Buddhaghoṣa.

The *Harṣacarīta*'s claim to fame is its status as the first biographical work from the Indian subcontinent. The text follows King

Harshavardhana, a mighty well-known character from Early Medieval India who reigned over an impressive territory spanning all of northern India as far south as the Narmada River. Best recognized for his sharp sense of justice and the general prosperity that characterized his reign, Harsha is one of the most favourably noted emperors in all of Indian history.

Harṣacarīta is generally counted as a seminal work not only for its author but all of Sanskrit literature. Born in today's Bihar, Bāṇabhaṭṭa was referred to Harsha by one of the latter's cousins, Krishna. Those days, Bāṇa was a penniless orphan who excelled in poetry and prosody but lacked a job. Krishna felt he could make a good fit as one of Harṣha's court poets.

The idea worked, and impressed with Bāṇa's mettle, the emperor hired him to his court in Kannauj. This is where Bāṇabhaṭṭa composed his most recognized work along with a few others. Of our interest here is this work, *Harṣacarīta* (lit. 'Harṣa's deeds'). Among the anecdotes making up the book are various exploits of both emperor Harsha as well as other rulers, mostly legendary. Some are elaborated at length, while others get little more than fleeting references. A number of such anecdotes serve to impress upon the emperor the perils of unchecked transparency.

There is, for instance, one that talks about a certain Çrutavarman. His glory faded after a parrot eavesdropped on his secrets, probably revealing them to a bad actor at a later point. Another speaks of a contender to the Nāga throne by the name Nāgasena who was done in by a çārikā bird. In yet another illustration, one Suvarṇacūḍa ended up losing his life because he said something in his sleep that he shouldn't have. In the same vein comes up a story that involves something familiar—elephants.

A man named Vataspati was hiding in an elephant forest while fleeing from his king or Mahāsena, we don't know why. All seemed to be going fine when one fine day, he came across an elephant that looked quite convincing. As he drew closer, Bāṇa writes, the elephant turned out to be a mere decoy, as the belly was sheltering a number of

Mahāsena's soldiers. As soon as Vataspati drew close enough, the belly opened up, and the soldiers spilt out, immediately taking the startled fugitive in custody.[5]

The same mechanical elephant leitmotif recurs in a bunch of other Indian works, too—some earlier, others later. The question is, why?

The clue lies in the very same work that speaks of Mahāsena's sham elephant. Among the numerous one-line anecdotes Bāṇa offers as warnings against too much trust, is one that involves the fall of a king brought about by an attendant who read a rather crucial bit of information off an inscription on the king's golden fly-swatter. Bāṇa identifies this king as a Yavana. There are several other references to the Yavanas throughout not only his work but those of many others from centuries ago. The name also finds mention in the Mahābhārata! So who are these people?

The term Yavana, it turns out, was just an Indian corruption of the more familiar word, Ionian. Ionia was back in the day a region on the western coast of Anatolia, part of present-day Turkey. Those days, the whole region was under Greek influence, both politically and socially. When Alexander launched his eastward campaigns, Ionian soldiers made up the bulk of his cavalry. As his juggernaut overran the Achaemenid territories, the Ionians became Yunanis in the local Persian tongues. Ionia was already known to these people as Yunan.

When this army came in contact with India, the name was further corrupted to Yavana. From that point on, although Alexander could not complete his Indian campaign successfully, it was only a matter of time before other Greek rulers followed, and much of India was subjected to Indo-Greek rule.

Since a majority of these first-wave Greeks that entered Persia and India were ethnic Ionians, Yunani and Yavana came to be used for all Greeks in general, in the respective cultures. In fact, according to some experts, the names even predate Alexander and were first used by none other than the Achaemenid king Darius I in an inscription dating back to the sixth century BCE![6]

So this is the story of how in a thousand years, an implement from Greek Mythology entered and assimilated into its Indian counterpart without anyone batting an eyelid. And this is just one such example, out of many. The Greeks have influenced India in far more ways than many historians care to acknowledge, in an area few other entities have touched—mythology!

How Akhand Was Bharat Anyway?

Some say India was once several times larger than it is today and encompassed everything from Afghanistan and Indonesia. Others argue it didn't even exist as an entity until the British made it one. Both sides find the other side's argument preposterous. But only one is. Which one? At least we know there was a Bharat well before the common era. So why the contention?

We'll start with Aurangzeb, loop through the British Raj, and then work our way backwards. Not because Bharat was Akhand under Aurangzeb or the British, but because it's there that the idea began its journey as a political trope.

AURANGZEB DIED IN 1707 AND LEFT BEHIND A THRONE that switched seven occupants in the space of forty years. His was a reign marked with the most pronounced communal animosity in a long time. The power vacuum his death triggered allowed a powerful Hindu empire to gain prominence for the first time in centuries. The change alarmed the subcontinent's Muslim population. To the extent that a Muslim theologian had to seek foreign help in restoring Mughal glory.

In a letter to a foreign Emir, Shah Walīullāh Dehlawī wrote, 'If, God forbid, domination by infidels continues, Muslims will forget Islam and within a short time become such a nation that there will be nothing left to distinguish them from non-Muslims.'[1]

That Emir was Ahmad Shah Abdali, who went on to raid India eight times over the following twenty years. With this letter, Walīullāh became the first known Indian to propound, in its most primitive form, a 'two-nation theory.' Centuries later, the idea found resonance with the Hindus when Savarkar, a pioneer of Hindu nationalism, proposed it at a Hindu Mahasabha meet in 1937.[2]

Interestingly, though, neither Savarkar nor Walīullāh meant nation in a geographical sense, although Allama Iqbal had come pretty close in a 1930 address. Until that point, the term merely referred to communities. Thus, Savarkar's two nations were two communities of Indians living within the same political entity—Akhand Bharat (Undivided India). It was only three years after this address that the idea finally crystallized into Sir Syed Ahmed Khan's Pakistan Movement.

Savarkar's 1937 speech is also a landmark because that's where the idea of Akhand Bharat showed up for the first time. Subsequently, the term has gradually acquired different definitions at different times. Roughly, it can safely be understood as referring to the territories of present-day Afghanistan, Pakistan, Nepal, Tibet, Bhutan, Bangladesh, Sri Lanka, and of course, India. But Savarkar's definition was far narrower and included only Pakistan, India, and Bangladesh, even left out Baluchistan.[3]

This complicates the answer to the question at hand—was India ever truly *akhand*? Going by Savarkar's narrow definition, it almost was until the Partition. Why almost? We'll come to that a little later. But first, let's examine the idea in currency today, one that includes Afghanistan, Burma, Bhutan, Tibet, Nepal, and Sri Lanka too.

Three years before Savarkar's birth, the vicar of St. Mary's hospital in Ilford, also known as Ilford Hospital Chapel, published a Geography textbook for middle school kids. His name was John Richardson. In this book, he defined India or, as he called it, Hindustan as the peninsula bounded by the Himalayas on the north, Tripura on the north-east, and an offshoot of the Hindu Kush called Suleiman Mountains on the north-west. His definition excluded not only Burma but also Baluchistan, Tibet, Nepal, and even the Andaman and Nicobar Islands.[4] That doesn't seem to jive with the modern idea of akhand. But we can go further back.

Just before the British, the largest entity on the subcontinent was the Mughal Empire. The territorial apogee of this empire came towards the end of Aurangzeb's reign, around 1700. At this point, it included parts of Afghanistan, such as Kandahar and Kabul, but excluded Baluchistan, which was under the Safavids of Iran. It did not include Nepal either; the entity was a sovereign Hindu kingdom in its own right. Down south, parts of Tamil Nadu and Kerala were, again, independent kingdoms with no allegiance to the Mughals. Burma? Tibet? Also independent.

The largest Indian entity to have ever existed was Mauryan. Now we're going ancient, as the Mauryan dynasty ended even before the common era. Its high point was around 250 BCE under none other than Aśoka, India's first empire builder in the truest sense of the term. This was shortly after the devastating Kalinga War. His empire covered a gargantuan two million square miles, as big as Alexander's. For perspective, today's India falls short by over 7,00,000 square miles.

And yet, it did not include Nepal or Burma. Nor the south, which was under sovereign Chera, Pandya and Chola rulers. It did not include Tibet or even Ladakh. This is the largest India has ever been—territorially.

Now, notionally is a different matter altogether. When the Aryans first crossed the mountains, they saw something in abundance—rivers. In their tongue, the word for river was *sindhu*. Eventually, the term became a proper noun, and the largest sindhu in the region came to be known as the Sindhu.

Not all Aryans came to India, though. Some branched into Iran as well. The two branches evolved into two distinct religious systems—Vedic in India and Zoroastrianism in Iran. Later when a Zoroastrian Achaemenid king decided to expand eastward, he ran into a problem, the Sindhu river. The locals called it Sindhu, but he took it as Hidūš.

Contrary to what many believe, this S-to-H switch didn't happen due to there not being an S letter in Old Persian. Old Persian very much had the letter, but the change happened anyway. This isn't uncommon. English very much has an H, and yet hour and honour are pronounced without it. Languages evolve in complex ways. The first time Hidūš appeared in a written form was in a 500 BCE edict by Darius I. The script used was cuneiform. Later, when the Greeks arrived, the H too vanished, and Hidūš became Indoi. Both Persians and Greeks used the term loosely.

To them, everything east of the river that is today called Indus was India, and everybody inhabiting the region, Hindu. Could this be called Akhand Bhārat? Depends. Was it a single political monolith? If so, it certainly qualifies. But turns out, it wasn't.

Much of the subcontinent remained uncharted and off limits to the Aryans for the longest time. The south, for instance, had its own thing going on. As did the north-east. And the islands were not even part of the fold until the common era!

Let's now examine the Bhārat in Akhand Bhārat. The natives never really called it India; the Aryans never called themselves Hindu. In fact, there was no all-encompassing name for the religion at the time. There were Brahmans, Buddhists, Jains, Charvakas, Vaiśeṣikas and so on, but no Hindu. Similarly, there was no India in the native vocabulary but Bhārat.

There are several theories on what the name encompassed, let's examine some of them. We'll start with Amara-siṃha, a fourth-century Sanskrit scholar and a contemporary of Chandragupta II. Among his dozen-odd works is a thesaurus of the Sanskrit language titled *Nāmaliṅgānuśāsanam*, better recognized as *Amarakōśaḥ*. Two names find mention in this work. One is Bhāratavarṣa and the other is Aryavarta. While Bhāratavarṣa isn't clearly defined here, Aryavarta is. Both words are today used synonymously with Akhand Bhārat, so Aryavarta's definition is key. *Amarakōśaḥ* posits it as the landmass between the Himalayas and the Vindhyas.[5] No eastern boundary is defined. That's less than half of today's India.

The Rigveda makes no mention of Bhārat or Bhāratavarṣa as a geographical or political unit, although it does speak of a tribe by that name. The first mention is in the seventh maṇḍala or book. Here, three hymns describe a 'Battle of the Ten Kings,' where one of the kings belongs to the Bhārata tribe. The site of this battle is by the river Ravi, which should then be seen as the easternmost frontier of their territory.[6] As for the name of this territory, the best we get in the Rigveda is Sapta Sindhu (lit. 'land of seven rivers') in Book VIII, hymn 24, verse 27. Today, we instantly recognize that as an appellation for Punjab and its vicinity.

So when does Bhārat show up as a political unit? Good question. More than a thousand years after the Rigveda.

Towards the end of the first century BCE, Kalinga (today's Orissa) was under a rather ambitious Jain king named Khārabēḷa. Those days, the only way to relay important pieces of information—new laws, royal exploits, administrative plans and so on—was through edicts carved into big rocks. One such edict was made by Khārabēḷa on Udayagiri Hills near today's Bhubaneshwar. It's called the Hathigumpha inscription.

This Prakrit-language edict speaks of a successful military campaign Khārabēḷa had just concluded against a rival territory named Bhāradavasa, Prakrit for Bhāratavarṣa.[7] This is by far the earliest reference to the name in a political context. What this implies is that far from the 'akhand' trans-national entity imagined today, Bhārat did not include even Kalinga more than a thousand years after the first Veda!

Bhāratavarṣa also finds mention in several post-Vedic works, including the well-recognized Mārkaṇḍeya Purāṇa. But the description therein is as vague as it gets. Many other Purāṇas, attempt describing the geography but fail to offer anything resembling reality. They generally explain Bhārat as an archipelago of mutually inaccessible islands, which is obviously not what India is in reality.[8] But there's one exception.

The *Viṣṅu Purāṇa*.

This one not just mentions Bhāratavarṣa but even goes on to elaborate its geographical frontiers in the most detailed fashion possible. The third *adhyāya* or chapter of the second *aṃśa* (part), defines Bhārat as the land between the ocean and the snow-clad mountains inhabited by the descendants of Bhārata. This is the closest a scriptural description gets to the modern notion of India. As for the east–west extent, instead of clearly establishing a boundary, it just says that to the west are the Yavanas and to the east, the Kirátas or the barbarians.

Now, this seems to lend clear antiquity to the idea of an Akhand Bhārat—antiquity, which comes with a measure of historical authority. So, India was a monolithic nation-state back in the day after all!

But here's a twist. All that hinges on the *Viṣṅu Purāṇa*'s date of composition. While the purāṇa in *Viṣṅu Purāṇa* makes it sound prehistoric, almost as old as the later Vedas, that doesn't seem to be the case with this one. Right off the bat, it's the reference to the Yavanas. That's the Sanskrit name for the Ionians (and, by extension, Greeks and Macedonians) who invaded India with Alexander the Great. So can we say that whoever composed this text, probably came after the first Greek invasion? That would be 327 BCE, the year of Alexander's first raid.

Although experts have offered widely varying theories ranging from Ramachandra Dikshitar's 700 BCE to Horace Hayman Wilson's 1045 CE,[9] more evidence seems to support the latter than the former.[10] At this point, it'd be unfair to not appreciate just how remarkable it is for the authors to have known India's geography even in 1045 CE.

In short, the idea of Bhārat as a territorial entity with a unitary, cohesive regime is fuzzy at best. There has never been a time in recorded Indian history that the entire domain purported to be part of Akhand Bhārat was under a single political system or rule. It has all been different empires at different times, with different territorial imperatives.

So, it's really all down to what we mean by Akhand. If we mean everything that an Indian ruler has ever conquered, then Rajendra Chola went as far out as Indonesia. But it would, of course, be absurd to include it as part of Indian antiquity.

Let's quickly examine each non-Indian component of this Akhand Bhārat and assess their cultural association with the centrepiece of this entity, India.

First up, Burma or Myanmar as we know it today. Here, the earliest extant evidence of an Indian influence comes from Pali fragments found in the ancient Pyu capital of Śrī Kṣetra on the Irrawaddy river. These only go back to 500 CE, which is far more recent than one would have thought. The Pyu are understood to be one of Burma's earliest inhabitants.[11] But Tagaung legends indicate Buddhist influences as early as Buddha's lifetime. This places Burma firmly under the Indian sphere of influence. But was Burma ever ruled by an Indian king, or was it ever part of an Indian empire? It was not—at least not until 1834, when the British added it to their Indian possessions, that too for a mere thirteen years!

Bhutan is Buddhist today. But that wasn't always the case. Even its name is said to be from Sanskrit originally. Buddhism only reached the country when a Tibetan king annexed it and imposed the religion on it in the first half of the seventh century.[12] Before that, the region was a Bön pagan one that had nothing to do with any Vedic tradition. Despite the eventual Buddhist predominance, the nation was never under an Indian kingdom. It did rule over Cooch Behar and parts of Assam for a brief window until the British changed that, but never became part of British India or any of its predecessors.

Nepal, on the other hand, has experienced Hinduism since at least the time of the epics, as is evident by many RāmāyanaRāmāyana-related sites being located within its territory. Politically speaking, the closest this country ever got to India was during the Licchavi-era, between the fifth and the eighth centuries CE. The first Licchavi king is said to be from India, who arrived in Kathmandu and built himself an independent kingdom there, but he had left India for good. This is not unlike Babur, who left Samarkand and built an empire in India. There do exist theories that place Nepal under the Indian Gupta rule, but none has ever been proven conclusively.[13]

Now, remember how Buddhism came to Bhutan when a Tibetan king annexed it in the seventh century? That king was Songtsen Gampo, and before Bhutan, he had also introduced the religion to an otherwise Shamanic Tibet. His reign is marked by several contacts with India, and it's in India that the Tibetan script is said to have developed. But at no point was the nation under Hindu rule, nor was it ever part of an Indian polity.

What about Sri Lanka? It sure had a cultural and social kinship with the Indian mainland throughout its prehistory, but it has maintained its own independent trajectory for centuries now. The first documented account begins with Prince Vijaya, the first Sinhalese king. Mahāvaṃsa, a fifth century Pali text, introduces him as an erstwhile prince from Kalinga who established an independent kingdom in Sri Lanka while in exile.[14] But just like the Licchavis of Nepal, Vijaya's dynasty never ruled India and Sri Lanka simultaneously. Even Aśoka, who sent Buddhist missions to Sri Lanka, did not rule it at any point.

Afghanistan sure had been part of multiple Indian empires including, for a brief while, that of the Mughals. In fact, historically, it had the longest unbroken Indian influence outside of Pakistan and Bangladesh. But that ended with the emergence of the Sassanians around the third century CE. This date could push further back if the preceding Kushans were to be considered non-Indian, given their Central Asian origins. In that case, India can be ruled out of Afghan history until as far back as 250 BCE when the Mauryan Empire began its decline.

This brings us back to the question, exactly how Akhand was Bhārat?

If we mean every region ever inhabited or influenced by Hinduism, or offshoots thereof, then we can start seeing Akhand Bhārat as a legitimate idea. However, that quickly becomes problematic if extrapolated to other polities. Should the Roman Empire enjoy a similar privilege? An Akhand Rome? How about Genghis Khan's, which spanned continents? Akhand Mongolia? At this point, it's very tempting to claim the primacy of Akhand Bhārat over Akhand anything-else, because they were all multicultural imperialistic empires whereas India had always been culturally a Hindu hegemony.

The problem with that thought is its reductive presumption. For the longest time, what we call Hinduism today, was just a large assortment of traditions and practices with widely varying levels of overlap. Some shared between them the pantheon, either fully or in parts. But others didn't. There were different tribes with different deities that were later subsumed into the larger Aryan hegemony. Some didn't even follow the Vedas! The Indian subcontinent of yore was just as multicultural as the Europe of today. Which means that sure can't be grounds for an Akhand Bhārat.

So where does that leave us? Right here in India—a Bhārat that was never truly akhand.

Did bin Qasim Introduce India to Islam?

It is widely accepted that Muhammad bin Qasim invaded the subcontinent for the Umayyads in the early eighth century. But there are some who dispute that and claim that the faith reached India far less violently and much earlier. This debate ties in with the larger debate around Islam's penchant for muscular expansionism. Settling it is one of the biggest socio-political imperatives today.

IN THE YEAR 709, HAJJAJ BIN YŪSUF, THE UMAYYAD governor of Basra assigned to his teenage nephew his first military mission—the conquest of Fars, a region then under Kurdish influence. The teenager proved to be a good bet and quickly brought the whole region under Umayyad rule.[1]

Two years later, emboldened by this success, the nephew, still a teenager, landed his next big mission. This time, he was to go east—to a place called Sind. The region was then under a Hindu king named

Raja Dahir Sen. The campaign ended, just like the last time, in Fars, with Muslim victory. The seventeen-year-old is said to have ordered the dead Raja's beheading. The head was then sent to his uncle back home as a token of the conquest. Sind would never have a Hindu ruler again. Over the following years, many Hindu residents converted to Islam either to evade persecution or to enjoy special privileges. The unremittingly zealous teenager from Iraq had successfully and conclusively managed to 'Islamize' Sind.

That teenager was Muḥammad bin al-Qāsim al-Thaqafī, bin Qasim for short.

At least one contemporary account reasons that the raid was more political than religious and the Umayyads were merely responding to provocations. Sind, at the time of the raid, was a melting pot of many eastern cultures. The territory was inhabited by Hindus as well as Buddhists, Jains and other independent creeds, including the Meds. The latter, a Baloch-speaking community, claims to be the first inhabitants of the region—sons of soil, if you will. They mostly lived around the coast and made a living off raiding Arab merchant ships en route to their eastern destinations. These Sindhi pirates were quite the menace, and the Umayyads had suffered great losses at their hands.

According to the contemporary account in question, one such raid involved a ship being raided and looted by Med pirates off the coast of Debal, an ancient port city not far from Karachi. This ship was sailing from Serendib (today's Sri Lanka) and carrying gifts for the Caliph. This was the last straw, and the governor of Basra was ordered to put an end to the nuisance once and for all.

The problem with this 'contemporary' account is, it isn't exactly as contemporary as it pretends to be. While bin Qasim lived in the eighth century, the *Tareekh al-Hind wa a'S-Sind*, *Chach Nama* for short, was only penned in the thirteenth—a good half a millennium later—as a Persian translation of an earlier work in Arabic.[2] While some scholars dismiss the existence of any such Arabic work, others question *Chach Nama*'s credibility and believe it to be 'influenced' literature.[3]

So, did bin Qasim conquer Sind to expand the Caliphate? Or was it done to avenge material losses to Med piracy? Be that as it may, conquer Sind he did, and with this conquest came the first comprehensive and irreversible Islamization of the region. But the story of Islam in the Sind goes a little further back in time.

Thanks to its commercial significance and proximity to Iran, Sind was known to the Arabs since even before Islam. When bin Qasim began his ascent, the Umayyad Caliphate was still a nascent entity, albeit one that experienced a stellar ascent. The period was of immense turbulence in the Islamic world. Only fourteen years had passed since the Battle of Karbala, an event that crystallized the Sunni–Shia schism, when bin Qasim was born. Sunni Umayyads themselves were barely four decades old and had already switched five caliphs in that span. Spreading Islam was as much a political imperative as a theological one.

One of the earliest Shia evangelists was a man named Atiyah ibn Saʿd ibn Junādah al-ʿAwfi. We'll just call him Atiyah. When bin Qasim's uncle Hajjaj bin Yūsuf was elevated to the governorship of Basra, a rift began to appear between him and an old friend and relative named Ibn al-Ashʿath.[4] Within years, this rift, compounded by a few other events, burgeoned into open rivalry.

By the beginning of the eighth century, al-Ashʿath had launched an all-out rebellion against Hajjaj and, by extension, the Umayyads. When the rebellion proved unsuccessful, al-Ashʿath fled to Fars where he received, at least for a while, safe harbour among the Kurds. Accompanying him was his closest disciple, Atiyah. This is where we circle back to bin Qasim's first campaign. When his uncle sent him to Fars, the mandate was to subjugate the Kurds, capture the fugitives and bring the region under the Caliphate.

Fars fell and al-Ashʿath died. Some records say he was killed, while others claim it was suicide. But his disciple survived. And to ensure his longevity, he fled to a place further east. That was Sind.

While *Chach Nama* attributes bin Qasim's Sind campaign to piracy, others attribute it to this rebel refugee. According to those, the whole Sind mission was to capture Atiyah and bring him to justice in order to prevent him from revitalizing the now-dead revolt.

So that's at least one Muslim who was in Sind before bin Qasim arrived. Curiosity among the natives around his strange new faith cannot be ruled out. But there is no record of him actively engaging in any proselytization at the time. He was just a Shia fugitive fleeing from Sunni persecution.

This pushes India's acquaintance with Islam, however cursory, further back by about a decade.

Before the Umayyads, the Caliphate belonged to the Rashiduns, a rather short-lived dynasty that ended with the First Fitna in 661 CE. The third in this line of five Caliphs was Prophet Muhammad's own son-in-law, Uthman. Another son-in-law, Ali, would later succeed him as the fourth Rashidun Caliph. One of the Prophet's companions was al-Ḥukaym ibn Jabalah al-ʿAbdī. Some half a century before bin Qasim, this man had paid a visit to Mokrān, a semi-arid part of Baluchistan, connecting Sind with the Gulf of Oman. Some historians call it a visit, others prefer the term 'raid'. Upon return, al-Ḥukaym presented Caliph Uthman with a detailed account of his exploits in Mokrān. The region at the time was mostly inhabited by Brahmins, Buddhists and several other communities sharing varying degrees of affinity to either group. Among them was the community of Jats.

Uthman died in 656 CE after a reign that was marked by widespread corruption and unrest. His death only accentuated the unrest as two camps emerged—one loyal to the Prophet's youngest widow Aisha, the other to his son-in-law Ali. This struggle for succession finally culminated in the 656 CE Battle of the Camel. In this battle, al-Ḥukaym sided with Ali. And lending a helping hand were a number of Jats from Sind![5]

Although al-Ḥukaym died fighting, the presence of Jat soldiers in his army establishes their acquaintance with Islam beyond doubt. From this point on, many Jats joined the Islamic forces under Ali's influence.

Arab writers of the time chronicled them as a community of Zuṭṭs, a name still shared by a gypsy community of Oman today, although some historians see Zuṭṭ as a collective Arab name given to all inhabitants of Sind and not just the Jats.[6] Now the question is, was Sind unaware of Islam when al-Ḥukaym visited?

The fact is, Muslim raids in Sind were not a new phenomenon during al-Ḥukaym's time. Arab raids were rather frequent in the region, given Sind's proximity to the Caliphate's territory. Their primary objective, though, was to gain tributes and slaves rather than proselytize.[7] Sind's acquaintance with Islam, thus, gets further pushed back to the very beginning of the Rashidun Caliphate, nearly seventy years ahead of bin Qasim's emergence. In fact, given how early these raids started, the Jats of Sind should be some of the earliest converts to Islam in the northern Indian subcontinent, regardless of whether or not conversion was on top of the raiders' agenda.

It's understandable why Sind experienced so many cross-cultural contacts, both peaceful as well as military. After all, it was the Indian subcontinent's frontier to the Muslim world. And India wasn't exactly unknown to either the Muslims or the Europeans.

But Sind wasn't the only region that enjoyed that unique position. Let's venture south now. India has a coastline stretching thousands of miles and straddling two seas on either side. Since antiquity, the western world has sought to do business with India, and the reason, besides other things, is its location.

Greek and Roman merchants had sailed to India in search of trade since centuries before Prophet Muhammad. And so had the Arabs. But we're talking Islam here, so we won't go that far back in time.

One reason why Sind witnessed so many violent invasions from the Arab world despite India having such a long coastline open to foreign contact is the Caliphs' general preference for terrestrial campaigns over maritime. But that's just the Caliphs whose campaigns were mostly military. Arab traders were still peacefully interacting with the subcontinent independently of the goings-on in Sind.[8] Remember the justification *Chach Nama* gave for bin Qasim's raid—the Med pirates of Karachi? Remember the most immediate trigger, the plunder of a ship from Serendib headed to Arabia? So yes, Arab ships were already sailing all around the Indian peninsula long before Islam. The Sassanians, who were a multi-ethnic, multicultural polity ruling most of the Middle East before Islam, had enjoyed a healthy amount of cultural intercourse for centuries. That's when Indian texts such as Panchatantra and board games such as chaturanga found their way into Persia and, later, the rest of the world.

It then naturally follows that when Islam emerged, it should have travelled to India on board one of those mercantile ships. Unless those merchants had somehow avoided conversion, which they hadn't, so the idea seems all the more plausible.

Back in the day, some of the biggest trading hubs of the Indian subcontinent were on the west coast, more specifically in Kerala. One such hub was not far from Kochi near Kodungallur—Muziris. The Arabs held monopoly over all Indian Ocean trades, and Muziris was their first port of call on the peninsula.[9]

These Arab traders were generally received with much warmth and grace by local Hindu families, and the local rulers gave them the choice of settling down and conducting business. This treatment wasn't exclusive to the Arabs; Muziris was a thriving metropolis of all seafaring nationalities, including Chinese, Africans and even Romans. As a result, trade flourished and culture got enriched. The Arabs maintained a non-aggressive stance here, given their non-military motivations. Over time, Muziris and the surrounding region became home to several Arab enclaves as more and more visitors chose to give up seafaring to settle down with a native wife.

The native Malayalam word for son-in-law was *māppiḷa*. Multiple theories exist around its etymology. One traces it to *pillai*, Tamil for son, while another gives it a Sanskrit and Pali origin (*marga pilla*).[10] A detailed analysis of this etymology is beyond the scope of this conversation but the word itself isn't. The matrilineal societies of Malabar, at some point, began applying the term to foreigners who settled down in Kerala having taken local wives.

With time, as Arab settlers started outnumbering non-Arabs, the term was narrowed down further to mean Arab Muslims and descendants thereof. Today, we know them as the Moplahs.[11]

Māppiḷa, a term of endearment and respect, being assigned to Muslim settlers is a testament to the peaceful interaction, unlike the experience of their counterparts up north.

There is little in the way of epigraphical evidence to support Kerala's claim as a jumping board for Islam in India. Sure, several coins from the early Umayyad period have been recovered from Kothamangalam, but these merely prove trade, not settlement. But there are a remarkable number of folk legends that corroborate the theory. For instance, there's this mosque in Kodungallur called Cheramaan Juma Masjid. This mosque makes a rather bold claim—that of being the first anywhere in India.

The legend of this mosque is interesting and still serves as a template for interfaith harmony, if not history. The region was under the Cheras back in the day. One Chera king, the legend goes, made a trip to Mecca and, impressed, embraced Islam. When he returned, Cheraman Perumal had become Thiāj-ud-Dīn. The first thing the now-Muslim Chera ruler did was to convert an existing Hindu temple into a mosque.[12] This became the Cheraman Juma Masjid. Legend even claims he met the Prophet himself while in Mecca. The year of construction is believed to be 629.

Prophet Muhammad died in the year 732. So, if the legend of the mosque is true, Islam in India is almost as old as Islam itself, as the first mosque came up when Muhammad was still alive!

At least two other versions of the above legend exist in circulation today, but they remain just that—legends. There is just no historical evidence to corroborate either the date or the circumstances of the king's conversion. That said, the one piece that cannot be ruled out is Malabar's acquaintance with Islam well before the Umayyad expansion in Sind.

So, coming back to the original question, did bin Qasim introduce India to Islam? Turns out, no, even if one discounts the legend of

Cheraman. At least one pocket of Muslim settlers and local converts was already thriving in the Malabar region well before bin Qasim was even born. Even Sind and Baluchistan were not complete strangers to the religion when he arrived.

Why, then, is bin Qasim so widely believed to be the person behind the spread of Islam? Because he was the first to introduce Islam to India, at least a part thereof, as a political system. Before him, Islam was just a cultural idea that some liked while others didn't. With his conquest of Sind, Islam became a political imperative. Probably for the first time, people were coerced into conversion and at scale, because Sind became part of the Umayyad hegemony. This is what lends bin Qasim the erroneous credit of bringing the faith to the subcontinent.

The fact remains that some of the earliest introductions to Islam for the Indian subcontinent were both peaceful and unchallenged. It sure spread by the sword, but not in the beginning.

Was Urdu Always a 'Muslim' Tongue?

Hindi is mistakenly seen as a national language for India. But more than that, it is seen as a Hindu tongue, distinct from Urdu, which is believed to be Muslim. But how far are these associations true, and how old are the two languages? There are those who claim that both originated as one, with no communal baggage, and there are those who argue otherwise. Is this just another debate fuelled by linguistic chauvinism, or is there more to it than meets the eye?

Once upon a time, the Indian subcontinent had five divisions, with Madhyadeśa or the 'Middle Country' being one of them. Manu identified it roughly as the stretch between the Himalayas and the Vindhyas. Within Madhyadeśa was Śūrasena, one of its sixteen Mahajanapadas or oligarchies, corresponding to today's Braj. People here spoke a vernacular that is said to be the closest to Sanskrit. *Prākṛta* (lit. 'nature') is Sanskrit for vernacular, and the one spoken in this region came to be called Śaurasenī Prākṛta. Some say it derived from Sanskrit, while others say

Sanskrit derived from it.[1] Either way, the association between the two is indisputable.

By the end of the tenth century, Śauraseni Prākṛta had started corrupting into regional dialects such as Braj Bhasha, Awadhi and Khaṛībolī. The 'corruption' didn't really stop there, though. With time, most of those dialects evolved into independent languages in their own right, many mutually unintelligible today. Of these, Khaṛībolī makes up the primary register of the type of Hindi spoken in and around Delhi today.

In the north-west, Prākṛta evolved a bit differently, and Punjabi was born. Needless to say, this Punjabi was nothing like the one spoken today. Just as the tenth-century Khaṛībolī would be barely intelligible to the average Khaṛībolī or Hindi speaker today.

Interestingly, the same Khaṛībolī that today forms the official register of Hindi was considered rustic and unrefined in its early days. Back then, Awadhi and Braj Bhasha were tongues of prestige in most courts across north India.

And then came the Muslims. It was the beginning of the thirteenth century. Some of the first invaders had a Turko-Afghan heritage. From there began a series of dynasties, starting with the Ghurids and culminating with the Lodhis, collectively known as the Delhi Sultanate. Sometime during this period, Persian found its way into the Sultan's court and slowly spread downwards to become the language of the Indian Muslim aristocracy. Concurrently, in and around Delhi, Khaṛībolī started absorbing Persian words and evolved into a new-ish register. Amīr Khusrau named it Hindavī or Dehlavī.[2]

But Persian had already lost its shine in India by the time the Mughals showed up. Amīr Khusrau died in 1325, followed a decade later by Amīr Hasan Sijzī, the inventor of ghazal. These were just two of many Persian poets who produced a rich body of work between the twelfth and fourteenth centuries. From that point on, the language experienced a steady decline in influence as Hindavī grew stronger. So much so that the Lodhis even started adding Persian into the Devanagari script![3]

With the Mughals came a whole new language alien to not just Delhi but the entire subcontinent—Chagatai. This Turkic tongue would eventually go extinct, but at one point, it was the language of authority. Things began to change with Humāyūn's exile after a defeat by the Suris of Afghanistan. That's because the exile was in Iran. When he returned, many Persians accompanied him and even lent a hand in recovering lost territory. This Persian-Mughal symbiosis would become a running theme of the dynasty's military and political success throughout its existence.

Ironically, many Persians also came to India as refugees fleeing religious persecution. When Babur settled in India, Persia was already almost three decades into the Safavid rule. The Safavids were Shia and didn't like the Sunnis very much. In fact, they were the first in the world to make Twelver Shiʿism the official state religion. Many Sunnis saw this as a threat to their way of life and decided to leave; they headed east—to Hindustan. Although there was no active large-scale state persecution of the Sunnis, the overt Safavid preference for the Shia community dried up nearly all opportunities for Sunni poets and artists.[4]

By the time of Akbar, Persian's conquest of the Mughal court was officially complete. So far, it had just been a subject of preference and prestige. Now it became the language of administration. Akbar named Persian the only language of business at all levels of government—a first on the Indian subcontinent. This prompted a substantial number of Hindus, primarily Khatris and Kayasthas, to learn the language in the hope of better employment prospects. They were soon working as clerks, munshis and in other important positions of authority in government offices all over the empire. Har Karan Ibn Mathuradas Kamboh of Multan was the first such munshi in the Mughal court. He wielded great clout not only as a government official but also as an exponent of Persian poetry.

Many upper caste Hindus were even teaching Persian in madrasas! Akbar also floated an active outreach for Persian dissidents and intellectuals seeking royal patronage no longer available in Persia.

While this made India a fertile ground for Persian literary activities, many Hindus also made significant contributions to the language. Lexical works such as Anand Ram's *Mir'aat ul-Istilah* and Lala Tek Chand's *Bahār-i 'Ajam* were well received by both Hindus and Muslims.[5]

One more thing going for Persian was its foreign image. Chagatai, throughout its reign, remained confined to the courts and came to be seen as a 'Muslim tongue'. Dehlavī, on the other hand, remained the language of the masses, overwhelming Hindi. This left open the need for a more 'secular' tongue with no ethnic encumbrance. Persian became that tongue. Despite its association with an Islamic Iran, it became the language of the elite, thanks to enthusiastic Mughal patronage. It became the 'English' of its time.

In the same vein, Persian also acted as the bridge tongue while the Mughal Empire assimilated new territories with new, at times mutually unintelligible, regional tongues.

Meanwhile, Dehlavī continued to grow outside the bureaucracy and nobility, among the middle-order Hindu populations around Delhi. As the Mughal Dynasty progressed, something interesting happened. Dehlavī itself started Persianizing! Hundreds of Persian loanwords made their way into common parlance, lending the local tongue a distinct Persian character.

This syncretism birthed a new language—Hindustani. Okay, that's a bit of an exaggeration as the language had been a work in progress since as early as the twelfth century. But it's only this time around, towards the close of the seventeenth century, that it came to be called Hindustani for the first time.[6] As its influence grew outside the capital, Hindustani even started replacing Braj Bhasha and other erstwhile 'prestige tongues'.

But this was, again, a very organic development. For the longest time, Persian, Hindustani, Braj, Awadhi and a multitude of vernaculars existed and thrived side by side with varying degrees of overlap. An impressive amount of Sufi literature was produced in Awadhi and Braj, even as many Hindu storytellers wrote in Persian.

In 1648, Shahjahan completed the walled city of Shahjahanabad. And just outside those walls were settlements of defending armies along with a vibrant marketplace for them. The space rapidly grew into a hub of economic activities and cross-cultural exchange.

One of the English words for a large number of fighters or wandering troops is 'horde'. This word has a curious etymology. It comes from the Russian орда (/ɐrˈda/) via Polish *horda* and German *Horde*. The Russian word itself goes back to Turkic *orda*. They all mean more or less the same thing—a clan or tribe of wanderers looking for plunder or war. Since a large number of senior officers in the Mughal army were of Turkish descent—remember, the Mughals themselves traced a partially Turkic bloodline—or influence, they referred to the army by the Turkic name, orda. Consequently, the army camps right outside the Red Fort came to be called Ordu Bazaar.

The military register had experienced a great deal of Persian influence over the years, and by the end of the seventeenth century, Zaban-e-Ordu (lit. 'language of the horde') was born.[7] For writing, a cursive form of the Perso-Arabic script called Nasta'līq was adopted. By the end of the eighteenth century, Zaban-e-Ordu had started replacing Persian among Delhi's elite. Some such as Meer and Sauda had already started calling it Hindi, as a derivative of Hindavī. By 1780, Zaban-e-Ordu had become just Urdu, and the credit for it goes to a man named Ghulam Hamdani.

Hamdani was a seminal ghazal writer who lived and worked in Lucknow when the region was ruled by Nawab Asaf-ud-Daula. He wrote entirely in Zaban-e-Ordu under the pen name Maṣʿḥafī. His affinity for shorter names wasn't limited to his own; it extended to the language he wrote in. Thus Maṣʿḥafī became the first to shorten Zaban-e-Ordu to just Urdu—a name that caught on and quickly became the only way to refer to the language.

Parallel to this, another Hindustani register with a relatively heavier Persian influence was born for poetry. Since poetry called for cadence and profundity, adding a generous amount of Persian to an already Persianized language became a new fad. They called this new register

Rekhta. Why not just use Persian? Because poetry had to be accessible to the masses too. Rekhta offered just the right mix of literary flourish and mass accessibility.

Hindustani came to be used as a catch-all term for all these 'dialects' that emerged in different parts of the country with varying proportions of Persian and vernaculars. Slowly, what started as a pidgin of Persian, became the first language of a whole empire. Persian, meanwhile, remained the language of the government.

Throughout the period, Hindustani remained one language common to both Hindus and Muslims. Sure, the proportion of Persian varied, but there was no communal assignment of its forms. This changed in 1837 when the East India Company inadvertently added a communal colour to India's linguistic landscape.

Thus far, nobody had a problem with Persian, much less with Hindustani (or Urdu, as it was referred to in some circles). In 1837, the Company decided to do away with Persian as India's language of administration. They replaced it with English for higher echelons of the government, and Hindustani written in the Nasta'līq script for the rest.[8] This move triggered many Hindus.

Urdu wasn't all that different from Hindustani, but the difference in writing systems was too big. Hindus wrote in Devanagari, Muslims in Nasta'līq. Even though Persian words remained acceptable to both, the script wasn't. But this was not always so.

In fact, even as late as the turn of the twentieth century, celebrated Hindu writers such as Premchand, who were fluent in Persian, were never ostracized for it. There were also Muslim scholars that wrote in impeccable Braj Bhasha and studied Sanskrit without any backlash. There were Brahmins who taught Persian and Muslims who taught Sanskrit.

The decision to replace Persian with Urdu—Hindustani written in Nasta'līq and with a large Persian vocabulary—for administrative business triggered Hindus, who saw Urdu as distinctly Muslim even if rather open to Persian. Their reservation? Hindustani ought to be in Devanagari and not Nasta'līq. This is when 'Modern' Hindi was born.

By 1850, Hindi and Urdu had both acquired identities independent of one another. There was no Hindustani any more; the same language became Urdu when written in Nasta'līq and Hindi when written in Devanagari.

How did this come to be? The first real seeds of Hindi chauvinism were sown in 1866 by a man from Surat. His name was Narmadashankar Dave, but he went by Narmad. A renowned Gujarati poet of the late-nineteenth century, he wrote what was the first-ever autobiography in the Gujarati language. It was titled *Mari Hakikat* (lit. 'My Reality'). In it, he made a very unambiguous case for Hindi as the national language on the ground that Hindustan had twelve times as many Hindus as Muslims.[9] Earlier, in the same book, he also explained his reasoning behind his Hindi–Hindu association. Given their proximity to Sanskrit, he argued, Hindi and Gujarati were 'purer' than other, more Persianized registers such as Urdu.[10]

In 1870, Shardha Phillauri wrote the first devotional song in Hindi, *Om Jai Jagdish*. The following decades saw Hindi and Urdu accelerate along divergent paths. As Urdu started absorbing more and more Persian words, Hindi cozied up to Sanskrit. This divergence was as synthetic as it gets. By 1881, Hindi was the official language in Bihar—a first.

The list of later Hindi chauvinists includes a surprising name—Mahatma Gandhi. With the idea of 'gently imposing' Hindi in the south, he and Annie Besant floated the Dakshin Bharat Hindi Prachar Sabha in 1918. The exercise didn't prove very successful.

By Independence, Hindi for Hindus and Urdu for Muslims had acquired irreversible socio-political undertones with little in the way of reversal. The carnage of Partition didn't help matters much either. At least at first, both India and Pakistan resisted the temptation to name an official 'national language'. This changed in 1950 when Nehru legislated that Hindi would be an official language, one out of many. In Central Government offices, it became the only acceptable language besides English. Two years later, Pakistan followed and upped the ante with Urdu, a move that would later cost the nation its eastern part.[11] There, Urdu became not just an official but a national language—the only national language—although Bangla did get some official status a few episodes of violence later.

But it's unfair to pin this irreconcilable rift singularly on Hindi chauvinism. The story of Urdu nationalism is at least as old as the story of Hindi nationalism. Our man of interest in this regard is Sir Syed Ahmed Taqvi bin Syed Muhammad Muttaqi—Syed Ahmed Khan for short. Born in Mughal India, educated in Scotland, and later employed in the East India Company, Khan was quite the bridge between the East and the West. The man remained hard to decipher throughout his life. Having sided with the British in the 1857 mutiny, he was also a bitter critic of their imperialism. During his earlier years, Khan was a vocal advocate of Western-style scientific curricula, Islamic reformation and other progressive ideas. He even read Darwin and partially agreed with evolution. Then came the Aligarh movement, and things started changing.

Khan's advocacy of reformation and modern education expectedly earned him criticism from Muslims at large. It also earned him fatwas from the clergy, especially the Deobandis.[12] Yet, none of that could discourage him from his objectives. But the Aligarh movement added another dimension to his activism—Urdu.

In 1857, India made a concerted bid to oust the British in what came to be known as the Sepoy Mutiny or India's first war of independence. Unfortunately, the British prevailed and the revolt died. But the event did manage to bring about some landmark changes in the relationship between Britain and India. It also marked the official end of the Mughal Rule with the emperor's exile to Burma. The revolt left India devastated, and some of the worst affected were Muslims. Khan lamented this sorry state of affairs and decided that only modern education could emancipate the community. He thus decided to open up the community to opportunities for economic progress. This was the germ behind the Aligarh Movement, a frenzy of initiatives to modernize Muslim education spearheaded by Khan and centred on Aligarh.

The first bottleneck he had to address was that of language. Khan picked a simplified, more accessible form of Urdu for the job. He soon emerged as the champion of Urdu hegemony, being fully drawn into the general Hindi–Urdu controversy playing out all over North India at the time. Once, he is said to have exclaimed, 'Urdu was the language of the gentry and Hindi that of the vulgar,' triggering massive backlash.[13]

In 1869, Khan embarked on a tour of England, where he was deeply influenced by the grandeur of Cambridge. This influence fructified upon his return in 1875 in the shape of the Mohammedan Anglo-Oriental College, today's Aligarh Muslim University. By then, Sir Syed Ahmed Khan was already a full-blown Urdu nationalist.

His influence travelled as far as Hyderabad, where Urdu became the official State language and the medium of instruction at Osmania University. This was a state where the majority of Muslims spoke Telugu and Dakhani—as they do even today.[14]

As calls for an independent Muslim homeland intensified, Khan began active advocacy of that cause as well. Soon, he was enjoying support from the same Deobandi and Wahhabi clerics who had once issued fatwas calling him a *kafir* (infidel) for his reformative ideas.

Khan died in 1898, but his Urdu nationalism didn't. The baton passed on to the likes of Jinnah and Iqbal, who championed the notion of Urdu as a language of Muslim identity. This association persisted despite many non-Muslims making their mark as Urdu scholars.

Today, 'Hindu Hindi and Muslim Urdu' seems to be a norm hard to argue against. But does it hold water in the face of linguistic and historical realities? From what we've understood so far, the whole controversy is no older than 200 years and only started gathering significant steam in the lead up to Partition. Urdu as a secular composite of Persian and Hindavī emerged as early as the mid-seventeenth century. It was a common tongue devoid of any communal baggage. Some called it Hindi, while some called it Urdu—the names used interchangeably without a thought.[15] This state of affairs had already existed for way over 200 years before the language was given communal colour.

So, again, is Urdu Muslim and Hindi Hindu? Historically and empirically speaking, doesn't seem so. Not in literary circles, and not in the vernacular. At least not until fairly recently. As many would say, they're both the same language, just in different scripts, and that language is Hindustani. Take out the scripts, and the line between the two becomes impossible to draw.

The religious assignment is synthetic. It's political. And unfortunately, it's here to stay.

How Many Temples Did Tipu Destroy?

Tipu Sultan is one of the most polarizing figures in India's history. People either love him for his resistance against the British or hate him for his anti-Hindu actions, which included the destruction of several Hindu temples within his territory. While his anti-British stance remains the subject of unanimous agreement, bitter disputes continue to rage over his religious fanaticism or a lack thereof.

THE YEAR IS 1791. TIPU IS NINE YEARS INTO HIS REIGN and Mysore, a year into its penultimate conflict with the British—the Third Anglo-Mysore War. The contest could not have been more lopsided.

While Tipu had a couple of tiny potentates in Gujarat and Kerala on his team, his adversary was a formidable axis of the East India Company and Travancore, along with two military behemoths of the time—Hyderabad and the Marathas. Theoretically, Mysore had

France on its side too, but when push came to shove, this alliance proved rather inconsequential. It did work in the Second Anglo-Mysore War, but the Revolution back home and temporary peace with Britain drove the French into withdrawing all overt support, choosing neutrality instead.[1]

So, back to 1791.

Actually, let's make it 1783. Because that's when the Marathas began cosying up to the British, a key aspect of this story. Some may find this friendship amusing as the two parties had faced each other on the battlefield barely a year earlier.

What also happened in 1783 was Hyder Ali's death. That's Tipu Sultan's father. At the time, his territory spanned all of Kanara and vast swathes of Baramahal, Malabar and Coorg. Part of this territory was a place called Nargund. Now, Nargund had been a Peshwa protectorate until just five years ago when Hyder snagged it, along with the rest of Krishna–Tungabhadra Doab, and made it an autonomous vassal under the existing Brahmin governor, Venkat Rao Bhave.[2]

Despite the rare autonomy and peace, Bhave remained instinctively affiliated with the Marathas, and Hyder Ali's death made him see opportunity. So he wrote to the Maratha court in Poona requesting collaboration to take advantage of a power vacuum in Mysore. No response.

This lack of response did not imply a lack of covert support, though, and Bhave's secret intrigues with the Peshwas continued unaffected.

Next up were the British, so another note to the Bombay Presidency. This is funny because the First Anglo-Maratha War was not even a year ago at the time. Bombay ignored him too. The East India Company was trying to close the ruinous Second Anglo-Mysore War and negotiate a peaceful deal with Tipu, and any misadventure could hurt their objectives.

When both calls to action went unanswered, Bhave elected to take matters into his own hands and launched a series of acts in open defiance of Hyder's son and successor, Tipu. First, he stopped paying tributes. Then he began plundering Mysore's villages. Again, Tipu was too busy negotiating with the English to bother. A peaceful and advantageous end to all hostilities with them was a more pressing imperative.

So he continued to ignore Bhave's intrigues.

Then came 11 March 1784.

Tipu and the Company finally reached a deal—the Treaty of Mangalore. Both parties agreed to return to the pre-war status quo. Now he was free to focus on internal affairs.

First things first, an envoy was dispatched to Poona. The message was for Nana Fadnavis, head of the Barabhai regency council in Pune and the most influential Maratha statesman of the time, to desist from secretly helping Bhave as the act amounted to interference in Mysore's sovereignty.

Nana refused. His grounds were financial rather than territorial. The tribute being demanded of Bhave was just too high and thus unfair, he reasoned. Tipu, on the other hand, refused to relent as he viewed Nana as a foreign entity with no *locus standi* in the matter. Moreover, he could not afford to make an exception for Nargund as it would trigger similar defiance among other vassals. So he communicated the same to Nana in a correspondence to Mahommed Ghâyas, his envoy or *wakil* in Poona dated 21 February.[3]

Another envoy was then sent to Bhave himself. Again, no success. Even at this point, a likely worn-out Tipu was willing to let go and forgive Nargund's treason should the latter agree to end all hostilities and pay up his dues. But then came a relative of Bhave named Parashuram Bhau who, although not yet in Nargund, promised his support and headed to the troubled fort with his own army right away.

Meanwhile, Tipu sent an envoy to Nargund, who wrote back reporting an increase in hostilities. At his minister's instigation, Bhave had prepared for unilateral military action. Seeing things come to a head, Tipu sent a 5,000-strong military reinforcement to settle the debate. A brief skirmish outside the fortification followed, and Bhave's men were compelled to retreat, while Tipu's cavalry remained encamped right outside. Nargund was now under siege. In response,

Nana green-lit military reinforcements for Nargund and dispatched one Ganesh Pant Behre with a large contingent. But he did add a rider that the reinforcement was only to be deployed for defence and nothing more. Bhau was almost there, happy that Nana was finally taking a firm stand against Nargund's Muslim oppressors.

Still, anxious to avoid any further escalation with the Marathas and preserve his resources to later take on the British, Tipu ordered his general to relax the siege. There are grounds to believe this was inspired by an acute shortage of water in the encampment, rather than a desire for peace; summer being harsh in the region, water-shortages can become debilitating in the lead up to the monsoons. Bhave and his men noted the retreat and further mobilized for offensive action, despite Nana's rider. Parallel to this, Tipu's envoys in Pune continued to bargain with Nana.

Just as talks seemed to be making headway, Tipu learnt of Nana's designs. The Maratha plan was to somehow drag these talks through the monsoons and then, once the rains were gone, launch a comprehensive campaign against Mysore. Nana was just buying time. His ambition was to retake all territories south of the Krishna River earlier annexed by Hyder Ali. But he could not take on Mysore on his own; he needed strategic reinforcements and political backing. From other powerful parties. And this is when efforts to build a Maratha-English-Nizam confederacy take root for the first time. Reaching out to the English must have been a bitter pill to swallow, but politics warrants such retreats.

Tipu could not afford to enter another war so early in his reign, but it was unavoidable. Everything hinged on the rains. And the fort at Nargund.

Nargund sat on the very frontiers of Tipu's kingdom, and the border with the Marathas almost ran through it. That's what made this fort so crucial to Mysore's integrity. Should it fall, little would stand between the Marathas and Seringapatam. Securing it was the mother of all priorities for Tipu. And currently, it was housing rebels. One big problem with this fortification was that heavy rains didn't much favour the occupants; seasonal flooding was common in the region. With such weakened defences, Nargund was almost a sitting duck during the wet season. Which is why Nana was so keen on avoiding any skirmish until the end of the season. For the exact same reason, Tipu wanted to complete the siege before the end of rains. Once the monsoons were gone, the fort would be nearly impossible to take.

Parashuram Bhau, on the other hand, was a less patient man. Keen on making an impression on Poona, he decided to go solo. In defiance of Nana's diktat, Bhau launched an attack on Tipu's retreating contingent outside Nargund.

And lost miserably.

This misadventure pushed the entire garrison into despair and left its occupants in Mysore's custody. The sieging party returned, this time with massive reinforcements from neighbouring vassals. Nargund's defences could not keep up, and within months, the fort fell. Now, the whole town was captive. Later, Tipu ordered them all released in batches, except for Venkat Rao Bhave and his minister Kalopant Pethe.

And a girl.

It was Bhave's daughter. Burhan, Tipu's general, knew of the girl and chose to take a look at her. A girl, especially if good looking, was quite the prize. A high-ranking adversary's daughter, even more so. One look and Burhan made up his mind. Instead of releasing her, he would gift her to the Sultan![4] This episode is also corroborated by nineteenth-century authors Dattatray Balwant Parasnis and Charles Augustus Kincaid[5] in their seminal three-volume work on the Maratha history.

Having taken Nargund, Tipu's general proceeded to discipline other adjoining principalities in varying states of rebellion, pinning hopes on a strong Maratha backup. By the end of the year, Kittur, Hoskote and many other places were already part of Tipu's realm.

Tipu, however, continued to maintain restraint and avoided any official military action against the Marathas. All he'd done so far was the disciplining of errant vassals back into submission. But Nana was determined to use this as a pretext to invade Mysore.

The stage was set. The Nizam had also offered his allegiance to the Marathas for two and a half million rupees. The Confederacy was finally united against a common adversary.

The following year, Coorg rebelled. The region had just been made a Mysore protectorate in 1765 after a bloody campaign led by Hyder Ali. Many ugly palace intrigues down the line, Coorg was now in open rebellion, perhaps seeing opportunity in Hyder's death.

When Tipu heard of the commotion, he stormed into the region with cavalry and crushed it with an iron fist.[6] This was carnage, and on an enormous scale for a place as small as Coorg. Hundreds were killed and thousands were taken to Seringapatam as prisoners of war. Once there, all adult men were forcibly circumcised and conscripted into Tipu's army. Depending on whom we ask, the number of those forced is anywhere between 40,000 and 80,000.[7] Tipu himself brags about having converted 70,000 Coorg residents in his autobiography, *Tarikh-i-Khudadadi,*[8] which is further corroborated by his overt sympathizer and contemporary, Husain Ali Khan Kirmani, in his hagiographical work titled *Nishan-i-Haidari.*[9]

And now we can finally fast forward to 1791.

Some 150 miles from Mysore, on the banks of the Tunga River, is the ancient temple town of Śṛngēri. Here sits a rather important Hindu monastery that traces its roots to the eighth century when the great Hindu theologian and Advaita thinker Ādi Śaṅkarācārya established four such monasteries or *math*s in four corners of the Indian subcontinent. Back in the day, the temple, along with nearby Mangalore, was part of Tipu's territory.

One fine day that year, at the height of Maratha–Mysore hostilities, Śṛngēri was visited by the kind of pilgrims no temple would desire. A cavalry of armed horsemen thundered through. What followed was sacrilege. The temple was sacked, its occupants maimed if not killed. Such was the plunder that the priest, or *swami*, was stripped of even his pitcher and walking stick. Women were molested, and some wound up dead. In short, Śṛngēri was looted down to its bones.

The Swami identified the raiders. Well, not exactly the raiders but their banner. It was a familiar ochre standard. Not Mysorean, for sure. The horsemen were irregulars attached to a bigger contingent led by two men. Importantly, Brahmins. More importantly, from the Maratha Empire. They were Raghunath Rao Patwardhan and Parashuram Bhau!

Unable to reconcile with the fact that a Brahmin-led band would conduct such desecration of a supremely holy Hindu site, the Swami threw himself into an indefinite hunger strike, having written to Nana requesting for justice.[10]

Nana responded with little more than lip service, and Raghunathrao disavowed the incident in a letter later that year, blaming it all on the Lamans.[11] It's true these were merely hired mercenaries with enough autonomy to afford them liberties like this. The Marathas had little oversight here and really were helpless, at least to a degree. What they could have done, at the very least, though, is offer to rebuild. But there's no record of Nana offering anything like that. Frustrated, the Swami turned to Tipu. Besides Śṛngēri falling in Tipu's domain, the priest had another reason to turn to Mysore.

The monastery enjoyed much royal patronage, and Tipu is said to have routinely sought the Swami's blessings. Given its religious and cultural significance, and being one of just four like it, Śṛngēri was a mighty wealthy temple. High-profile pilgrims and princes visited from all over the subcontinent and brought with them enormous tributes for the monastery. This also made it a raid magnet. Naturally, protecting an institution this rich comes with its own socio-political incentives. Tipu, like most Indian rulers, understood this too well to ignore Swami's—Tipu called him Jagadguru—call for help.

The priest's letter filled the Sultan with rage. 'People do evil deeds smiling, but will suffer the consequences weeping,' he's said to have quoted in his reply.[12] Enclosed with the letter was a pledge of monetary and material help to consecrate a new image of goddess Sharada, as the raiders had stolen the one before.

Needless to say, the consecration was duly carried out, and Tipu personally sponsored a '*sahasra chandi japa*' at the monastery, for Mysore's welfare. Throughout the duration of the ceremony, a thousand brahmins were hosted and offered gifts each day.[13]

At this point, it may be argued that Tipu was merely responding to his own political imperatives, for a vast majority of his subjects were Hindus, and so were his adversaries. Religious appeasement has been the order of the day in such circumstances since forever.

Possible.

But this wasn't the first time he attempted such 'appeasement'. Earlier, in 1785, he'd gifted a dozen elephants to the Cheluvanarayana Swami temple at Melkote. Earlier still, he sent silver utensils to the Lakshmikanta temple in Nanjangud. These may or may not have been political imperatives. Having said that, a pattern is hard to dismiss here.

So, how Hinduphobic was Tipu anyway? Before we attempt to answer that question, let's revisit the Coorg episode and examine a small but crucial piece of the puzzle that we forgot to mention earlier. Shortly before the attack, Tipu had issued a warning to the rebels.

In the letter dated 3 December, he warned them that should they continue to rebel, for they'd be uprooted from their native lands and Islamized. To add insult to injury, he used some mighty disrespectful words while describing Hindu traditions in his letter, being particularly derisive of fraternal polygamy. He clearly considered them less than civilized, going by the tone of this letter. Even so, he promised he wouldn't hurt or molest anyone.[14] The condition of conversion is of consequence here. Clearly, Tipu used it as a punishment for sedition, not a matter of religious zeal. But this one small corroboration doesn't suffice.

There were thousands of captives from Coorg—that much is beyond debate. Tipu seems to have converted all of them, at least so he claims in his autobiography. But how unassailable is that source to begin with? Turns out, the 'autobiography' isn't really an autobiography but just another book of tales written in the first person. How do we know that? Because its entire text is an exact copy of another work titled *Sultan-ut-Tawarikh*! It makes no reference to Tipu's personal life—something an autobiography would surely have focussed on—and is packed with chronological, factual and historical inconsistencies.[15]

One final case against the big number comes from none other than one of Tipu's Maratha contemporaries, Ram Chandra Rao. In his four-volume work on Hyder Ali and his son, Rao categorically acknowledges mass conversions but pegs the number at an underwhelming 500.[16] This only serves to further bolster the notion that conversions were used as tools of punishment rather than vehicles of Islamization, for a zealot fundamentalist would endeavour to convert (or kill) the entire population instead of just a minuscule section thereof. So it's safe to assume, in light of these additional materials, that a great deal of exaggeration and misrepresentation has dictated the narrative around Tipu and his conducts. But Coorg alone isn't enough to draw all conclusions. We need more.

Remember Venkat Rao's daughter, whom Burhan had taken hostage in Nargund for his Sultan's harem? While there are sources that claim it happened, one calls the episode a later-day fabrication based on gossip and populist rhetoric. It'd be easy to dismiss the latter as a face-saver had it come from, say, a Muslim source or one with obvious sympathies for the Sultan. Interestingly, the source at hand is not only Brahmin but a Maharashtrian! In his enormous multi-volume Marathi-language compendium of historical essays, celebrated litterateur and scholar Vasudev Vaman Khare dismissed the episode saying everybody was released with the exception of Venkat Rao Bhave and his minister—both of whom were released separately at a later date. He categorically rejects the abduction story as political grapevine and confirms that no official or contemporary Maratha records note this episode.[17]

What we're still left to reconcile with is Tipu's burning desire to bathe his sword in Maratha blood. But that's exactly how a ruler would feel about an adversary during an active military engagement. At best, it proves that Tipu hated the Marathas. Was that contempt an expression of Hinduphobia?

Unlikely.

Let's not forget that it was a Brahmin general under whose watch raiders desecrated Śṛngēri and went unpunished. And that it was Tipu who helped restore it to former glory while also ordering and sponsoring a highly ritualistic event marking Sharada's consecration.

And this is where history refuses to play in the binaries.

We still cannot conclude with certainty that he wasn't Hinduphobic. Nor can we conclude that he was. What we can say, though, is that most of his actions were mere responses to immediate political imperatives rather than religious zealotry, as is the case with any ruler with territorial aspirations. The general who directed Seringapatam's defence against Cornwallis was, at the end of the day, a Brahmin. Not a Muslim.

So again, how many temples did Tipu destroy? We don't know. But we do know that the Kote Venkataramana Temple that stands outside his summer palace in Bangalore to this day once saved him from cannon fire and received the Sultan's patronage for the remainder of his life. That the Navasara Hanuman Temple on the Mysore–Bangalore highway was built by the same Sultan who forced thousands of Coorg rebels into Islam.[18] That the Kollur Mookambika Temple of Udupi still performs a Salam Mangalarati every evening in recognition of the day, more than 250 years ago, when Tipu had dropped in, along with his entourage, just to offer prayers and partake in the prasad.[19] That a Karnataka Tourism plaque outside the Yoga Narasimha Temple in Melkote commemorates a 'huge drum and a bell' it received as donation from Tipu. And that a jade linga sitting next to Goddess Parvati in Nanjangud's Shrikanteshwara Temple was a gift from a practising Muslim Sultan.[20]

Did Rajputs Always Stand Up to Aurangzeb?

Aurangzeb was an Islamist tyrant; his Hindu contemporaries, the persecuted majority; and Rajputs, the force of resistance. That's the dominant position many take today. Over the years, the narrative has come to cover not only Aurangzeb, but also the entirety of his lineage. In this narrative, the fact that Akbar had a Rajput wife is often cited as an exception. But was she?

There are some who argue that the relationship between the Hindus (Rajputs) and the Muslims (Mughals) was a symbiotic one and Akbar marrying a Rajput woman was an example of that. Is that correct? And if so, what changed with Aurangzeb and why?

LET'S START FROM THE VERY BEGINNING. BECAUSE TO understand the Rajput community's relationship with the Mughals (and subsequently, Aurangzeb), it's important to understand how they came about.

There've been several Rajput clans and dynasties throughout history. Only one is of significance in the context of this discussion. So, we'll quickly examine how they showed up. Jaipur, the capital of Rajasthan today, was Amber or Amer, the capital of Dhundhar, once. The area belonged to a non-Rajput tribe native to the land—the Meenas. Towards the later years of the eleventh century, a man named Dulha Rai left Gwalior to marry into Ajmer's royal family and floated a kingdom of his own. This is the genesis of the Kachwaha dynasty.[1]

All this, of course, comes from oral accounts that were primarily etiological myths retrofitted to the clan's story around the sixteenth century to lend it an imperial aura. It's only with the advent of the Mughals that the Rajput story shows up in clear contemporary records, shedding many of the bardic embellishments that came with oral accounts.[2]

By the mid-1200s, Ajmer was already home to an extremely popular Muslim shrine, a *dargah*. Fast forward a few centuries, and we come to the era of the Mughals. The dargah has by now been firmly established as a pilgrim staple to the subcontinent's Muslims—which is why the Mughals are willing to pull out all the stops in securing a free passage between Delhi and Ajmer. And the latter happened to be deep in Rajputana heartland. This led to much conflict.

The pilgrim trail cut right through Kachwaha territory. Amer those days swore allegiance to another Rajput dynasty ruling over neighbouring Mewar. Before we go further, a quick note on Ajmer's curious location in this scheme of things. It's a triangular pocket of prime Rajputana real estate spanning about 2,700 square miles between three small but feisty principalities—Marwar on the west, Mewar on the south, and Dhundhar on the east.[3]

Now, although the Mughal-held Delhi–Ajmer corridor did not touch either Mewar or Marwar, it did bother both. Marwar, in particular. As Ajmer's next-door neighbours on the west, they had reason to be wary of Mughal presence close to their frontiers. And they protested. Needless to say, this was as unequal as a fight could get, because Marwar had little going for it against a military and political leviathan like Akbar.

The friction over the pilgrim route resulted in Akbar's near-complete suzerainty over Rajputana in general and Marwar in particular.[4]

Let's take a few steps back to understand this friction better. In 1503, Prithviraj Singh I took the Kachwaha throne. Twenty-four years later, he found himself in Khanwa fighting off Bābur as part of a military coalition led by Rana Sanga of Mewar.[5] Before the end of the year, he was dead.

Now the throne went to one of his sons, Puranmal. Not because he was the first in line, but due to the fact that his mom was the dead king's favourite. This was problematic.

Puranmal's coronation was bitterly opposed by many, including some of his own siblings. Dynastic infighting is always an opportunity for enemies. Interestingly, in this case, those enemies weren't the Mughals but fellow Rajputs from the neighbourhood. That's when, some say, a saviour appeared.

This saviour, without whose help the dynasty wouldn't have survived the decade, was none other than Bābur's son, Humāyūn![6] This marked the beginning of a friendship between Amer and the Mughals—one that could potentially transcend both Puranmal and Humāyūn. Just to reiterate here, Amer was also subordinate to neighbouring Mewar at the time.[7]

Khanwa had proven disastrous, not only for Amer but also its liege, Mewar. Both states lost their heads in the battle, and the reins had gone into not-so-experienced hands. While Amer went to Puranmal, Mewar went to Ratan Singh II, then Vikramaditya Singh, and then Vanvir Singh—all in less than a decade.

By now, Mewar's fragile political situation was public knowledge. Practically an open invitation to anyone opportune enough.

And there were many.

Meanwhile, Marwar, too, got a new king in 1532—Maldev Rathore. This man had taken over a kingdom on the verge of extinction. Once almost nine large districts, they were now down to just two. Maldev was determined to reverse this. Mewar presented an excellent opportunity in Vanvir Singh, whose own men were desperate to cut him loose. So, Maldev teamed up with the dissidents and invaded Mewar.[8]

Up north, things weren't looking great for the Mughals either. Bābur had died shortly after Khanwa, and his son, Humāyūn, was on the throne, soon being presented with a formidable adversary from Haryana—Sher Shah Suri. Ethnically Afghan, the Suris had started off as small-time horse traders and risen up the ranks with acumen and cunning to finally become rulers of serious reckoning.

This threatened Humāyūn for obvious reasons, but it also threatened the fast-burgeoning Marwar. Why? Because in 1542, Sher Shah Suri took a territory dangerously close to Marwar and Mewar—Malwa. To make things worse, Puranmal, too, joined hands with the Suris, technically betraying Humāyūn.[9]

Desperate to counter any potential threat, Maldev allied himself with Humāyūn. This may sound strange given that the very same parties had faced each other at Khanwa a mere fifteen years ago, but desperate times call for desperate compromises.

The alliance, however, didn't last as Humāyūn had to eventually flee to Iran as Sher Shah Suri took over his empire. Some historians say Maldev had betrayed him; others disagree. Either way, one chapter of Mughal–Rajput amity ends here. Others would begin shortly.

To recap what we have so far, there are three Rajput entities—Marwar, Amer and Mewar. Marwar doesn't like the Mughals, Mewar doesn't like Marwar, and Amer has little say in matters, as it is struggling to get its own house in order. As for the Mughals, they're out of the picture for at least a decade and a half now.

Now let's finally return to Amer. In just seven quick years, Puranmal had been tossed aside by one of his brothers, Bhim Singh. Being the eldest in the family, Bhim Singh actually was the rightful heir. Puranmal's story doesn't end here, though. He left behind a son who would surface later. Bhim didn't last long; he died three years into his reign. Some sources even claim he aided in his own father's death, but that remains unverified. After Bhim came Ratan Singh, who ran a crumbling Amer for a little over a decade. Ratan's reign was underscored by two things—family feuds and the loss of sovereignty to the Suris.[10]

Ratan Singh had a major drinking problem,[11] not the best of traits, especially for a weak ruler. We saw what happens to such rulers, in the case of Mewar's Vikramaditya Singh. Just over a decade into his reign, the unfortunate Vikramaditya was poisoned to death by his own half-brother, Askaran, who then quickly ascended the throne. An understanding of these intra-clan intrigues in the Rajput courts is key to appreciating the role played by the Mughals, both positive and detrimental.

Askaran didn't last either. A mere two weeks in, the same uncle who had helped him against Ratan helped himself to the throne with the help of local feudal lords. This uncle was Bharmal.[12] But we'll come to him a little later. Let's dwell on the deposed raja for a minute.

Having lost his throne, Askaran had nowhere left to go. In desperation, he sought help from the only family ally he could count on—the Mughals, who, by the way, had pulled off an impressive comeback with Humāyūn's return in 1555. On the Mughal throne those days was Akbar. But the latter, being emperor, didn't intervene directly. Instead, he appointed a local governor named Haji Khan to mediate between the uncle and the nephew.[13]

The mediation worked, and Ratan Singh ended up with a tiny principality of his own in Narwar in today's Madhya Pradesh. Under Mughal suzerainty, of course.[14]

Ratan Singh went on to marry a Rathore princess from Marwar with whom he had, among other kids, a daughter named Manrang Devi. The daughter, in turn, married a man from Marwar, in keeping with what now looked like a family tradition. This man was Raja Udai Singh. Marwar and Amer were now firmly family.

Manrang Devi and Uday Singh together had a daughter—Manavati Baiji Lall Sahiba, later known as Jagat Gosain. But not for long. By the time she was twelve, her father gave her away in marriage to a sixteen-year-old Jahangir, after which she was known as Jodhabai.[15] This Jodhabai must not be confused with the other one who married Akbar. Soon after marriage, Jodhabai gave birth to a healthy boy—Khurram, later called Shah Jahan.

Now let's go back to Bharmal. Bharmal had just replaced Askaran on the throne, and a Mughal general had helped with reconciliations between the uncle and the nephew. Bharmal's story is incomplete without a discussion of his relationship with the Mughals, especially with a specific one.

Bharmal had at least eight children, including a girl named Hira Kunwari. In 1562, Akbar appointed a new governor to Mewat. (We'll get to him in a bit.)

Now you may recall, Bharmal, Bhim Singh and Puranmal were all siblings. Remember we said Puramal had a son who'd surface later? Well, now's the time. There are several theories on how Puranmal died. Some say he died fighting for Humāyūn. Some that it was against one Tatar Khan, while others peg it on Humāyūn's brother, Hindal.[16] Yet others say he was ousted by elder brother Bhim. And some even allege fratricide—that Bhim Singh didn't just oust him, but had him killed.[17] Whatever the case, Puranmal had a son.

In the Mahābhārata, Pandu was elder but Dhritrashtra was king, because of which when the newer generation came of age, there was a dilemma around succession. The Pandavas staked claim because their father ought to have been the king. But Kauravas wouldn't relent because their father was the reigning king.

The Puranmal–Bharmal story was the exact same situation. Bharmal was the king now. But Puranmal was the ruler once. And after Puranmal, the throne ought to have gone to his son, Sujamal. It didn't only because he was still a minor at the time. Now that Sujamal was a grown man, he naturally wanted what was rightfully his.

But things aren't so simple here. Bharmal, in his defence, didn't consider Sujamal the rightful heir after Puranmal because the latter was not the rightful heir to Prithviraj.[18]

Finally, Sujamal plotted to overthrow Bharmal.

And now we come to the new governor Akbar had appointed to Mewat—Mirza Muhammad Sharaf-ud-din Hussain. Sujamal reached out to Hussain and discussed his plan.[19] It worked. Hussain marched on Amer and, seeing his troops, Bharmal surrendered without a fight.[20] In fact, he also agreed to pay tribute to the Mughal governor. As collateral, he offered his own son.[21] But the Mughal governor wasn't done yet.

Word of a second invasion reached Bharmal. This time, he reached out to the emperor in Agra, who agreed to help and had a little talk with his governor, the same Mirza we were just introduced to. Amer was restored to Bharmal.[22] As was his son. Bharmal returned the favour—and it was a massive favour—by offering his daughter to the emperor in marriage. This was none other than Hira Kunwari, popularly and erroneously known as Jodhabai (erroneously so, because she had nothing to do with Jodhpur or Marwar).

Bharmal was succeeded in 1574 by his son, Bhagwant Das. Besides being the king of Amer, Bhagwant Das was also one of Akbar's most trusted generals. He served in campaigns in places such as Afghanistan, Punjab, and even Kashmir. His loyalty and bravery earned him the title *Amir-ul-Umra*.[23]

He, too, had a daughter, Manbhawati Bai. In 1585, when she was only fifteen, Manbhawati was married to Prince Salim, later known as Emperor Jahangir. She came to be called Shah Begum, as the young prince's first Rajput wife.[24] The following year, she was joined by a second, Jagat Gosain. Bhagwant Das was succeeded by Man Singh I, who was also a trusted general in Akbar's service, just like his dad. Man Singh even went on to become one of the Mughal court's *Navaratnas*. Akbar conferred upon him the title Mirza right after the latter's coronation. As you can see, familial as well as diplomatic alliances were often used to ensure territorial integrity.

Man Singh further crystallized his esteem in the Mughal court by leading his troops against Maharana Pratap in the Battle of Haldighati.[25] Pratap managed to escape, but the battle ended in a decisive Mughal victory. Mewar, if you remember, was Amer's suzerain until not very long ago. That equation now stood changed. Haldighati brought Mewar into Akbar's fold.

Upon Man Singh's death in 1614, the throne went to his younger son, Bhau Singh. It ought to have gone to Jagat Singh, but he was dead. Even then, Hindu primogeniture dictated that the title then go to Jagat Singh's son, Maha Singh. But that was overruled by Jahangir. After Jahangir's endorsement of Bhau Singh,[26] the Kachwahas had no choice but to accept him on the throne, even though it ran against their customs. The problem with Bhau Singh was his alcohol addiction, short life, and lack of heir.[27] This was illustrated by the fact that Jahangir sent him on an expedition against Malik Ambar. Malik Ambar was a Muslim ruler in the Deccan who had, in a remarkable career leap, graduated from being a hopeless slave import from Africa to being the biggest pain in the neck for the Mughal Empire.

Jahangir hoped a Rajput force led by the Kachwaha king would end the problem once and for all. But that didn't happen. Bhau Singh's military prowess proved no match for the slave-king's guerrilla acumen. This failure cost him a lot of esteem in the Mughal court, which, in turn, drove him into depression and alcoholism.[28] He'd never recover from this. After Bhau Singh's premature death, Jahangir appointed a ten-year-old Jai Singh I to the throne. He was not the direct heir, but since the dead king hadn't left any, Jai Singh was the one. The boy's tenure spanned the entirety of Shah Jahan's reign and further. The power struggle that followed Shah Jahan's descent into infirmity saw the emergence of two key players: Dara Shikoh and Aurangzeb.

The struggle was a bloody one which sent one to the grave and the other to the throne. Jai Singh happened to be loyal to the latter.[29] Wise call.

Jai Singh's successor was Ram Singh, the only highlight of whose career was being sent by Aurangzeb to invade the Ahom king of Assam. What followed was a humiliating defeat, and subsequent disgrace in the Mughal Emperor's books.[30] After Ram Singh came Jai Singh II, with a rather unremarkable Bishen Singh in between. This man made quite the impression on the Mughals.

Aurangzeb, impressed by both his military prowess as well as his wit, conferred upon him the title of *Sawai*, equivalent to a king and a quarter.[31] And that's how Jai Singh II became Sawai Jai Singh; his descendants would carry the title for generations. In 1727, he established a new township close to Amer as his new capital, and named it Jaipur.

Coming back to the original question, did the Rajputs always stand up to Aurangzeb's tyranny? Going by the case of Amer, they did not, as the royal title of Sawai establishes. In the case of Mewar and Marwar, on the other hand, they firmly were. Starting off as vassals to the Mughals, the latter only turned on Aurangzeb after his alleged misadventure, where he poisoned Marwar's king and his son with the intention of usurping the state.[32] Also, Aurangzeb's role in the assassinations remains in dispute to this day, as the poisoning story only comes from folklore and not scholarly works. The raja in question was known for his bitter opposition to Aurangzeb's hegemony.

In Marwar's case, things only went from bad to worse after the assassination. Aurangzeb offered to coronate Ajit Singh Rathore on the condition that he'd be raised as a Muslim.[33] Foolish move, because what followed was an all-out war between the Rajputs and the Mughals, one we hadn't seen since Haldighati. The entirely avoidable misadventure went down in history as the Rajput War of Independence. The result was disastrous for the Mughals and cost them not only Marwar but also lives, money and reputation on an unprecedented scale. The empire would never recover from this.

Aurangzeb died within months of this disaster.

So yes, the Rajputs did stand up to Aurangzeb and quite aggressively so. But not until fairly late in his tenure.

Did Hindus Ever Desecrate Hindu Temples?

Any Hindu temple being desecrated or vandalized is usually made out to be the work of Muslim perpetrators, including the Mughals. Even if not Muslims, it has been other non-Hindus, such as in the case of Goa. Or at least non-Indians. A section of scholarship, however, suggests that Hindus have been responsible for such acts too. But why would a Hindu vandalize a Hindu temple? Or is it all just academic propaganda?

About fifty miles inland from Chennai sits an imposing Pallava-era rock temple dedicated to Lord Shiva. The Kailāśanātha Temple is among the oldest in the region, which is littered with such structures in varying stages of ruin. Although still retaining much of its original grandeur, the temple was quite the marvel of civil engineering back in the day. The entire structure was carved into sandstone boulders sitting atop a granite foundation.

The question is, why was it built at all? Just the need to worship one deity, or even multiple, could not have motivated a project of this scale. Was something else at play here?

Rajasimha, the ninth Pallava ruler who was officially known as Narasimha Varma II, is the man who commissioned this temple.

The temple has another name too, likely more common back in the day—Rajasimhēśvara Temple. Temples, as a rule of thumb, are named after the deity they are meant to house. Therefore, the Kailāśanātha Temple today is meant for the worship of Lord Kailāśa, i.e., Śiva. Similarly, the Rajasimhēśvara Temple is used to worship Lord Rajasimhēśvara. The latter is a portmanteau of Rajasimha and *ēśvara*, Sanskrit for lord. And Rajasimha, the king, is also Śiva, the lord.[1]

In other words, the king was, or was at least expected to be, indistinguishable from the gods. Translated into material expressions, the patron deity (every kingdom, every household had one) was often named after the king himself. Lending a measure of divinity to the king has been a time-tested way of securing their subjects' loyalty and adversaries' awe. Think Egypt.

While Rajasimhēśvara was among the first such expressions, the model became a Pallava leitmotif from that point on, and a frenzy of royal temple complexes ensued. As the Pallavas gave way to the resurgent Cholas, the frenzy only gained steam.

In the eleventh century, one Chola king built the Bṛihádīśvara Temple of Thanjavur. An alternate name for this temple was Rajarājēśvaram. Where does that name come from?

Raja Raja Chola I.

Both Rajarājēśvaram and Bṛihádīśvara are alternative names of Śiva. Further down the line came Rajendra Chola I, who openly identified as a Śiva incarnate, if not Śiva himself.

Clearly, the earlier century of the second millennium witnessed vigorous temple activity; the temples themselves underwent an unequivocal shift—from being mere places of worship to ambitious political icons. What does all of this mean, though? For starters, the obvious—that the king and the deity were almost shared sovereignty.

So an attack on the temple would translate into one on the king. While on the upside, this was a huge morale boost for the king's subjects, the converse was just as true—destroying a temple could be the quickest way to break their spirit.

This was a precarious landscape. One that would produce some of the biggest architectural marvels the world has ever known, but also unleash a wave of sectarian vandalism that easily surpasses the ones we witness today in longevity.

But did Hindus really desecrate each other's temples as a matter of practice, or are we just reading too much into stray incidents? Let's see.

Some sixty miles north-west of Nellore lies Udayagiri, named after a small hill crowned by the ruins of a fort that goes back more than half a millennium. In its heyday, the fort was among the most impregnable in all of India. Clearly, the builders—local chieftains called Gajapatis—were obsessed with security. This obsession had two reasons—a Muslim Sultanate on the west and a Hindu kingdom on the south.

By the time, Pratāparudra ascended the Udayagiri throne, a third joined the mix from the north. So now there were the Bahmani Sultanate, the Vijayanagar Empire, and the Husain Shahis of Bengal. In the year 1512, the fort came under a siege that lasted eighteen months. Neither Pratāparudra nor his general was prepared for something this persistent. Udayagiri fell. The invading army came with three times as many men as the Gajapati had in his defence. And 800 war elephants. The fort stood no chance.[2]

With the conquest concluded, the adversary dealt one final blow to seal the deal: it looted something more precious to the losing king than even his crown, his patron deity. It was a dark granite Kṛṣṇa about three feet tall with a ball of butter in one hand. They called it Bālakṛṣṇa or baby Kṛṣṇa. To any Hindu ruler, loss of the royal deity was, as we learnt, an absolute sign of capitulation. The ultimate humiliation, if you will.

To the victor, Bālakṛṣṇa was a war trophy and, thus, a prized possession that deserved to be flaunted as much as treasured. So a new temple was built just to house it. Outside the temple came up an inscription detailing the conquest and a marketplace to draw maximum attention.

This victor was none other than Kṛṣṇadevaraya of Vijayanagar. The conquest of Udayagiri and the acquisition of Bālakṛṣṇa was the highlight of his tenure. Does robbing a temple of its deity amount to desecration if the latter is then duly consecrated with full rituals and honours in another? Opinions exist on either side of the argument.

To settle this, let's return to our 'Śiva incarnates', the Cholas. In the middle years of the eleventh century, Rājādhiraja and his successor waged a series of assaults against the Chalukyas. Although the Chola–Chalukya feud predates Rājādhiraja by generations, this one was particularly bloody. One that cost the Chola patriarch his life. Besides life, what this battle also claimed was temples. A lot of temples.

As the Chola army stormed towards the Chalukyan capital in Kalyani, it burnt every temple along the way, down to a crisp. This account comes from a contemporary Chalukyan inscription at Karnataka's Annigeri, dated to within three decades of the episode. The inscription offers detailed insight into the invading Chola infantry's exploits in the lead up to up to Rājādhiraja's fall. The account relates to a particular incident in the Beḷvola province of the Chalukyan territory where the invading horde consigned to flames several temples in the region, many of them later rebuilt.[3] Although this may not qualify as a Hindu-on-Hindu assault as the temples were all Jaina, warring Hindu kings weren't exactly above doing the same to Hindu temples either. For there are other inscriptions offering glimpses of atrocities committed by Hindu kings far worse than vandalism.

One inscription on the walls of the Rajagopala–Perumal Temple near Chennai, for instance, recounts Rājādhiraja's campaigns in Ceylon where he's said to have killed a king and abducted the women in his household, including his sister and daughter. If that weren't enough, the Chola also cut off the defeated king's mother's nose. The episode, with slight variation, is also corroborated in the Pali epic Mahāvaṃsa.[4]

Let's step out of south India for a while now, and see if the practice transcends geography. A few miles south of Jabalpur in Madhya Pradesh is the village of Bilhari. Here was once found a grey sandstone monolith, dating to the tenth century, with mostly extant Sanskrit inscriptions in thirty-three lines.[5]

This inscription, among other things, speaks of a Kalachuri king named Lakshmaṇarāja II who, on a trip to Somnāth, made a gift to the famous temple. It was a bejewelled gold figure of Kāliya, the mythological Nāga from Vṛndāvana. This figure, the inscription goes on to say, hadn't always been in Lakshmaṇarāja's possession, though. The king had obtained it as a war spoil after beating another ruler in Orissa,[6] conclusively implying a temple's desecration at the hands of a Hindu invader.

Coming back to south India, Rajasimha, the man largely held as the inventor of the idea that the king was an embodiment of the divine, didn't just build temples to express this divinity. He also furnished these temples with artefacts pillaged during his military exploits. Besides adding insult to the loser's injury, this also served to establish the victor as the unambiguous sovereign with nothing short of a divine mandate. In other words, it legitimized the conquest.

One example of this can be seen in Rajasimha's exploits in the Chalukyan[7] capital of Vātāpi (today, Badami). The Chalukyas and the Pallavas had been rivals since forever. When the Cholas replaced the Pallavas, they also inherited, besides all else, this rivalry. Coming back to Vātāpi, the crowning jewel of the city was a stone Ganesha figure known to this day as Vātāpi Gaṇapati.

When Rajasimha's men invaded the city, they also plundered the temple that housed this figure. The raid was evidently aimed at the Gaṇapati. The figure was, claim oral traditions around the region, subsequently brought to Tanjavur by a Pallava general as a spoil of war.[8] A caveat here remains that oral accounts aren't always accurate, and the general's own list of war trophies does not mention this idol, something one would expect him to brag the most about. Having said that, Vātāpi's sack isn't up for debate: that did happen.

Back again in Madhya Pradesh, in the ruins of Khajurāho this time, sits a twenty-eight-line inscription that dates back to the year 1011. This inscription truly brings the whole subcontinent together. Referring to a solid gold Viṣṅu installed by Chandela king Yaśovarman in the nearby Lakṣmaṅa Temple, it recounts the deity's breath-taking journey all the way from the snowy heights of Kashmir to the tropical jungles of Madhya Pradesh. The temple itself was built around 950 CE, and for the sole purpose of housing this very precious object.

Viṣṅu Vaikuṅṭha, as the statue is referred to, began its journey in Kashmir, whence it then passed on to the Tibetans. Later, it landed in Kangra after its king, the Hindu Shahi dynast, received it as a gift. So far things seem peaceful and friendly. But then came the Gurjara-Pratihara dynast Herambapâla who became the first to snag it by unambiguous force. From him, the figure passed on to his son Devapâla who finally lost it to Yaśovarman. Again, by unambiguous force. The inscription is quite clear on the fact that military violence was involved in the last two transactions.[9] What makes the Chandela investment in this deity even more amusing is the fact that they were, in fact, Shaivites.

Also from Kashmir comes another episode involving the same deity. Same deity because the Hindu polity Kashmir has traditionally been Vaishnavite.

This account comes from the region's most important text, Rājataraṃgiṇī. In this account, a Bengali king is assassinated while on a trip through Kashmir. The hit is said to have been ordered by none other than the Kashmiri king Lalitāditya himself, despite an earlier promise not to do so. Livid at this treachery and eager for revenge, the people of Gaur, as Bengal was known at the time, prepared to sack Lalitāditya's capital.

So a contingent of armed men disguised as pilgrims entered Kashmir, while Lalitāditya himself was not in town. The object of their ire was not the town itself but its spirit. And that spirit was, of course, its patron deity.

The Parihāsakeśava Temple was the holiest of all in the capital, for it housed a solid silver Viṣṅu Vaikuṅṭha, the guardian deity of Lalitāditya's dynasty and, by extension, Kashmir. The complex also included a nearby shrine that housed another deity, Rāmasvāmi.

When the soldiers of Gaur surrounded the complex, Rājataraṃgiṇī says, the priest locked the gates from the inside. The soldiers, however, managed to soon overwhelm the defences and got hold of Rāmasvāmi. Mistaking it to be the patron deity, they proceeded to smash it into pieces right outside the gates.[10]

This is one of the strongest illustrations of temple desecration done by a Hindu mob. The statue, in this case, unlike in other examples so far, was not appropriated for later consecration. Nor was it Buddhist or Jain. No, this was a very Hindu deity suffering very incontestable desecration at the hands of a very Hindu force. This was at least two centuries before a Muslim invader from Afghanistan entered the scene and gave such desecrations a gargantuan proportion.

Speaking of which, Mahmud Ghaznavi, the most notorious of Muslim invaders, came to India only in the early decades of the eleventh century. About a hundred years before him, we find Indra III, the eighth Rashtrakuta king who inherited a troubled empire at a rather young age due to his father's abrupt passing. Among all the places he conquered and tamed in northern India was Kalpi, then known as Kalapriya. Here stood a prominent temple dedicated to the worship of its patron deity and namesake, Kalapriya. This temple was, at the time, among the biggest centres of sun worship on the subcontinent; Kalapriya was just another name for the Sun God here.

Contemporary epigraphic accounts describe the invasion in great detail. Part of this detail involves the temple. Here, the courtyard is said to have been destroyed by the invading army's elephants, hinting at a good amount of vandalism.[11]

Remember Pratāparudra, the Gajapati whose Bālakṛṣṇa was looted by his southern neighbour Kṛṣṇadevaraya at the beginning of the sixteenth century? While one still feels sorry for his loss, here's an account of something done by his grandfather, Kapilendra. His was the most ambitious of all Gajapati reigns. Under his watch, Orissa hit its territorial zenith that stretched from Ganga in the north to Kaveri in the south. Naturally, such ambitions come at a human cost. Kapilendra's campaigns in the south saw large-scale vandalism—vandalism, not mere loot or desecration—of temples all over what is today Tamil Nadu.

A most thorough account of the events during this period comes from Rāyavācakamu, a sixteenth-century Telugu prose piece by Vijayanagar's Vishvanatha Nayani. An account in this text refers to the time Kapilendra was travelling through Tamil territory. Kapilendra's men got out of hand and ended up sacking whole villages, groves and other infrastructure along the way. This included not only Brahmin settlements but also temples, both Shaivite and Vaishnavite. The sacrilege was far from religious and entirely borne out of political spite. Ironically, this happened when the troupe was on a pilgrimage.[12]

By this time, though, the Muslims had firmly taken over as the leaders of the vertical. Although it's unfair to entirely absolve religious zealotry as one of the drivers in their case, it is just as unfair to absolve politics. How the credit for temple desecration is divided between the two factors could be debated, but such debates are more often than not loaded with their own socio-political baggage on either side of the fence. Which is why we won't get into those debates here.

What we do need to understand, however, is that an abundance of indicators exists in favour of hegemonic motivations. Since places of worships were conflated with territorial sovereignty, it's only natural that they would suffer any blow dealt in the direction of such polities. Religious fanaticism becomes even harder to explain in cases like Ahobilam.

This story is from the sixteenth century; the Vijayanagar Empire was now in decline, and various Muslim rulers had taken large swathes of the subcontinent under their control. Hindu kingdoms were now ever-diminishing pockets of barely autonomous vassals in varying stages of decline.

Ahobilam is a holy township centred on a temple dedicated to the lion-headed avatar of Viṣṅu called Narasiṃha. This temple was built by the rulers of Vijayanagar at a time when the empire was ascendant. After almost a century of relative peace, the temple suffered its first desecration in the year 1579.

Vijayanagar in those days shared part of its borders with a burgeoning Muslim polity—the Golconda Sultanate. This Muslim polity was keen on expanding southward. The Sultan in question is Ibrahim Quli Qutb Shah Wali.

Fully aware of Vijayanagar's crumbling defence, thanks to very expensive prior conflicts with the Bahamani Sultanate, this man decided to make a move. A force was promptly dispatched to raid Ahobilam. Muslim raids were not new to Vijayanagar, but this was a first for Ahobilam. The Hindu dynasts' devotion to this deity and the primacy of this temple was public knowledge. Its destruction would have dealt a major strategic blow to the Raya.

The temple was completely demolished and its contents—it was an extremely well-endowed institution—plundered. As was routine, the deity became part of the loot. It was a dazzling figure made in gold and silver and studded with rubies all over. Needless to say, the crowning jewel of the plunder.

The prize was personally carried to Golconda and presented to the Sultan by his general, the man who led the whole campaign. His name? Murahari Rao, a Marathi Brahmin.[13]

The presence of a Hindu name—a Brahmin, no less—in the service of a Muslim invader among those leading an assault on a highly-revered Hindu temple sure complicates the discourse. And things only get more complicated over time because the subcontinent's history from that point on is filled with such episodes.

The incidents we discussed don't make up even a minuscule part of the whole list. So, did Hindus ever desecrate Hindu temples? The answer is a resounding and unfortunate yes. Were they motivated by religious fanaticism? Well, it's complicated.

Were Britain, France and Portugal Our Only Colonists?

First came the Portuguese, then the British, and finally the French. Of these, the British emerged the most successful. Our history has traditionally confined itself to these three entities when discussing the European colonization of India. What if there were others—the Danes, or the Dutch? Naysayers argue that their presence was too insignificant to consider. But was it?

ON 24 AUGUST 1608, A LARGE BOAT NAMED HECTOR dropped anchor off the mouth of the Tapti River, some fourteen miles from India's fast-silting mercantile metropolis, Surat.[1] This became the first ship flying the British standard to dock on an Indian coast. The man at the helm, Captain William Hawkins, was representing a very nascent business house with little in the way of prospects, the East India Company. The last bit would soon prove wrong against all odds, and as we all know, the enterprise went on to script a success story with no parallel in either British or world history.

India in those days was seen as this mythical land of elephants, spices and exotica that could feed the fortunes of entire nations. Much of Europe, on the other hand, lived in unfathomable squalor. Naturally, a trade link with this mythical land was every European royalty's Holy Grail. Charters were granted to whoever would dare make this oriental cornucopia more accessible. To that end, the East India Company opened up a whole new world of possibilities and, within decades, made Britain the wealthiest empire in human history.

In light of this success, it's hard to appreciate that the British were, in fact, among the last to the party. Almost every European empire of any reckoning was already in brisk business with India even before the East India Company was conceived. The latter just became so successful so quickly that others slowly faded away from public reckoning and memory. Except the French and the Portuguese, who continued to hold on to their colonies on the subcontinent for far longer than all others.

So we had the Portuguese in Goa, the French in Pondicherry and the British pretty much everywhere else. But who all, if at all, have we had besides these usual suspects? The scope of this question for our purposes is the early modern period which begins around 1530, so that rules out all ancient and medieval imperialists such as the Chinese, the Greeks, the Persians and the Mongols, among others. We are further narrowing it down to only European powers.

The East India Company saw its genesis in a Royal Charter titled 'Governor and Company of Merchants of London trading into the East Indies', on 31 December 1600, which issued to a group of 200-odd merchants the right to conduct business in the Indian Ocean under the British standard, and to raise funds for the same. India did not even figure on their list of business destinations at the time. Instead, for the first few years, all company ships sailed to and from what they called the 'Spice Archipelago', today's Indonesia.[2]

But in the bigger scheme of things, this charter did not exactly blaze any trails, for the Dutch had already been trading in those waters for over a quarter of a century. The only problem with the

Dutch, at least at the time, was their mercantile disarray. Commerce was dominated by tiny private businesses called *voorcompagnieën* (lit. 'pre-companies') with little imperial oversight and mighty cutthroat competition.

When the competition started affecting trade and peace, the national administrative body of the Dutch Republic, the States-General, decided to merge all these bickering businesses into a single megalith with complete monopoly to conduct business east of the Cape of Good Hope. They named this megalith *De Vereenigde Oost-Indische Compagnie* (lit. 'The United East India Company') or VOC.[3] This was two years after the British East India Company.

Although late to the game, the Dutch quickly proceeded to consolidate all opportunities in the East Indies and the VOC grew into the world's largest commercial entity of its time on every count that matters. Soon it went on to have its own standing army and a capital reserve that could bankroll not only other businesses but also nations. The enterprise also became history's first stock corporation to be publicly traded as securities in an exchange, when it floated the Amsterdam Bourse for the purpose in 1602.[4]

Three years down the line, a VOC commander named Paulus van Soldt arrived at Machilipatnam and, with the help of a Jewish local, set up a trading post for his company. This wasn't exactly a first for Dutch merchants, as earlier voorcompagnieën have been known to engage in business with partners in Coromandel since as early as 1603. But this certainly was the first permanent outpost, a precursor to later colonialism.[5]

What isn't commonly known about the Indian economy of the time is that the dominant commodity then wasn't really spices; it was textiles. Indian textiles, particularly muslin, was an object of desire among European royalties. And unlike spices that could be sourced from multiple regions, muslin couldn't. When the fabric reached Batavia through the Dutch, it found a whole new market of colonists there. To capitalize on the lucrative opportunity, van Soldt made another voyage to India, from Batavia. This time, instead of

Machilipatnam, his yacht reached a place further south, Pulicat. Although he didn't dwell on this find and eventually sailed further north reaching Petapuli, Pulicat would continue to figure in their story as a source of textile.

Both Machilipatnam and Petapuli were then parts of Golconda, and after a favourable negotiation with its ruler, the Dutch were soon running factories and warehouses at both ports. The local governors' extortionist behaviour, however, prompted the Dutch to also look elsewhere.

So they turned to southern Coromandel and rediscovered Pulicat as not only a source accessible via a middleman but also a trading base with direct control. Soon, the town became home to a third Dutch factory. Things looked upbeat at this point, but the Portuguese threat was not gone yet. In the summer of 1612, the Pulicat factory was raided by the Portuguese of San Thomé. To avoid a recurrence, the Dutch decided to build themselves a fort, paid for by a local Indian queen.

The structure was completed in a year and named Fort Geldria.[6] It became the capital and seat of what came to be known as Dutch Coromandel or Dutch India, a governing body administering all VOC possessions in India. The entity remained in existence until as late as 1825. Although far smaller than British India, the Dutch colony managed to stay not only afloat but highly profitable for its stakeholders for well over a century. Their downfall came when the British occupied the territory as a defence against the French towards the end of the eighteenth century. The fort itself was badly destroyed in 1804, and the Dutch rule in India completely ended twenty years later.[7]

So far, we have seen four different East India Companies, all independently invested in the colonization of the Indian subcontinent. Turns out, there were just as many more.

The profits generated by the Indian Ocean trade had convinced every European power that there was an unlimited amount of all things exotic to be had in those parts of the world for anyone adventurous enough. One such power was Denmark, more accurately the Dano-Norwegian Realm as it was officially called at the time.

In a rush not to miss the bus, King Christian IV ordered the incorporation of a *Dansk Ostindisk Kompagni* (lit. 'Danish East India Company') in 1616 to explore and exploit mercantile opportunities in South Asia and beyond. Interestingly, the two merchants who received the charter weren't even Danes—both Jan de Willum and Herman Rosenkranz were Dutch merchants settled in Denmark. After two years of enthusiastic preparations, the company finally launched its first expedition in 1618. It was not to India but Ceylon.[8]

By then, the Portuguese were already placed firmly in the region and prevented any Danish plans from taking off in Ceylon. Frustrated with the failures, yet unwilling to give up, the expedition then turned to the giant peninsula next door. But the Portuguese were here too and inflicted severe damage upon whatever remained of the Danish expedition.

Finally, after losing his ship and the bulk of his crew, commander Roland Crappe, also Dutch, wound up in Tanjore. Subsequently produced before the local king Raghunatha Nayak, Crappe then sold to the latter the idea of a lucrative trade deal with his company. The plan worked, and the Dutchman landed a land grant in Tranquebar, today's Tharangambadi, to build a trading outpost for an annual rent of a little over 3,000 rupees. Soon enough, Tranquebar was home to an imposing fort that served as the local administrative office as well as the warehouse of the Danish East India Company. Named Fort Dansborg,[9] it became the largest Danish fort in the world, second only to the Kronborg Castle in Helsingør, Denmark.

But business proved more challenging than originally thought. The competition was lethal and adversaries abundant. It took the Danes a good six years to finally turn a decent profit after losing a number of ships to both bad weather and the Portuguese. Even this ship, named Pearl, had barely made it with the cargo intact. Part of its exotic payload, accounts claim, was a piece of textile so fine they called it 'the flying wind'. We now know they were referring to Dhaka muslin.

From that point on, the company entered a spell of good business and concluded a number of profitable trades. For once, it looked like the Danes were finally back in the game. But this was temporary.

Crappe, by the way, knew of muslin and where it came from. And that's why he was quite keen on scoring trade deals in Bengal, a region then under the Mughals with some Portuguese presence, especially in Hooghly. Unfortunately, he lost his ships to bad weather and had to abandon his Bengal dreams as he had no money left to buy expensive gifts for the emperor in Delhi. But only for now. His past experiences with the VOC had given him precious insights into how India worked, and that's what the Danes banked on.

By 1624, the Danes had lost too many ships and too many trades. Things got so bad that they were no longer able to pay the rent for the Tranquebar property. This drove a big wedge between them and Nayak, who started attacking their fort and imprisoning their men in order to extort the rent. The Danes now needed a secondary property. Crappe came handy and helped the company establish factories at Machilipatnam, which, if you may recall, was already a Dutch stronghold.

This was followed by another venture into Bengal—this time a successful one. In quick succession came two new trading outposts at Balasore and Pipli. The following year, the local Mughal governor looted one of their ships in Balasore and caused a great deal of financial discomfort to the still fledgeling enterprise. This cargo was expected to be a rare windfall to the Danes. This was a big blow, given the difficulty with which they had managed to even enter Bengal.

In 1635, Berent Pessart, yet another Dutchman, was sent to India to replace Crappe. By now, the showdowns between the Danes and the Bengalis had become far too frequent. Frustrated and determined to recoup losses, Pessart declared war on the Mughals in 1642. By the end of the year, his men captured a large, fully-loaded Mughal vessel and brought it to Tranquebar. Here, the cargo was sold for a grand profit and the vessel itself incorporated into the Danish fleet as The Bengali Prize.[10] Even this big a loot, though, failed to help the sinking Danish economy beyond the immediate term, and the company once again slid back into decline and finally filed for bankruptcy three years later.

This did not mean the end of Danish presence in India, though. In 1670, the company was reincorporated, and trades with India resurrected. This time, they experienced a longer run that lasted well into the nineteenth century. For a while, even the Andaman and the Nicobar Islands were in their possession. The colonies were all eventually sold to the British East India Company, but the Danes had a good 250 years of presence in India.

Just as the first Danish venture filed for bankruptcy, another emerged to try its luck—this time in the most unexpected of places. Of all the imperial powers to have ever ventured into India, the least understood, if at all known, comes from Italy.

In 1649, the year following Christian IV's death, a group of prominent patricians came together to conduct business as *Compagnia Genovese delle indie orientali* (lit. 'Genoese East India Company'). The objective was the same as that of all other East India Companies so far—to explore and exploit trading opportunities in the resource-rich Orient and maximize returns by eliminating mutual rivalries.

The Republic was then in a period of steady decline thanks to repeated French assaults and the recently concluded Treaty of Münster that practically terminated its alliance with a financially ruined Castile.

Although the stated mission of this enterprise focused on the Japanese, the participants were initially far more interested in Macao, Indonesia and India. Just as was the case with their Danish counterparts, the Genoese, too, relied heavily on Dutch sailors for their maritime expertise. One such sailor was Jan Maas van Duijnkerken who had previously worked with the VOC. In fact, there was hardly any Genoese sailor in the entire fleet. Unfortunately, the Portuguese caught wind of the matter and spilt it to their Dutch friends.

Eager to keep any new player out of the region and maintain monopoly, the Dutch immediately swung into action. At first, a series of deals were signed, allowing the Genoese to conduct business in the Far East on a profit-sharing basis. Interestingly, one of the clauses also forbade the Genoese from hurting or punishing any Indian without express permission from the Dutch.[11]

Unfortunately, this arrangement didn't quite pan out as expected, and the expedition died at the hands of a far more powerful VOC in Batavia. Although at least one Genoese merchant was already stationed in Goa at the time, the venture could never really take off, given the dominance of far bigger players in the region.

The losses in Batavia doomed the company, and it folded operations in 1650. This was almost immediately followed by a second venture named *Compagnia Marittima di San Giorgio* (lit. 'Maritime Company of Saint George'). This entity started off with expeditions to Brazil under a Portuguese licence, only to raise enough capital to get back to the original plan—India. Promising as it seemed at the time, this venture too folded before it could see India.[12] Thus, we came pretty close to having an Italian presence on the subcontinent.

Coming back to Scandinavia, even Sweden tried its hand, unbeknownst to many today. The *Svenska Ostindiska Companiet* (lit. 'Swedish East India Company') was incorporated by royal charter in 1731 in the city of Gothenburg.[13]

This company quickly became the largest trading company in the region, but folded just as quickly. Late as they were in the business, the Swedes were naturally seen as unwelcome disruptors by other players and consequently discouraged from the arena. The first few expeditions suffered great adversities, and the environment that only grew more hostile by the day. Despite the name, however, the enterprise was mainly focused on China rather than India. In its entire 82-year existence, the Swedish East India Company only sent six expeditions to India, three each to Bengal and Surat.

Besides their focus on trading tea with China, a big reason they did not colonize India was that, of course, they could not. By the mid-eighteenth century, the subcontinent was already divvied up among imperial behemoths such as Britain, Portugal and France with little room to spare for a new aspirant.

And now we come to our last candidate, Austria. Here, the Österreichische Ostindien-Kompanie (lit. 'Austrian East India Company') was born when a certain William Bolts petitioned Empress Maria Theresa and secured a charter to float an Austrian mercantile base in India. The year was 1775.

The first Austrian factories to come up on the subcontinent were in Malabar, followed by more in Bengal. Earlier, Bolts had made a solo trip to India, landing in Surat. From there, he headed south to seek an audience with a local ruler whose rivalry with the British was public knowledge all over Europe. With the aim of capitalizing on this rivalry, Bolts headed straight to Seringapatnam, where he met with Hyder Ali and secured a trade deal that brought Austrian factories to Baliapatam, Mangalore and Karwar.[14]

Albeit reasonably threatened by this new development,[15] the British East India Company allowed the Austrians to take over Banki Bazaar,[16] a small township near Calcutta—now a suburb of Barrackpore. The only other territory the Austrians managed to capture in India was the Nicobar Islands.

All these possessions eventually went back to the British, and the Austrian East India Company went out of business in 1785, having suffered colossal losses in the tea trade thanks to stiff competition.

So these were some of the lesser-known imperial powers, who either colonized India or came temptingly close. On this side of the world, little is ever told of these Austrian, Genoese, Danish and Swedish expeditions, but it's worth noting that most of these businesses lasted well over a century. Or the fact that most of them failed to take root in India mainly because they were repelled by the Dutch—itself an entity with no significant foothold in the country.

Did We Really Invent the Musical Notation?

Sometime in the eleventh century, an Italian musician came up with the idea of writing down music using names for seven distinct notes. Today we call those notes do, re, mi, fa, so, la and ti. Indians have their own version that goes sa, re, ga, ma, pa, dha, ni. Both seven notes. Much of the world believes everyone learnt from the Italians, while India says it was from the Indians. Is there any merit to the Indian argument, or is it just historical appropriation?

THE STORY OF MUSIC IS PROBABLY AS OLD AS THE STORY of our species. But the story of written music certainly isn't. That's only reasonable since mankind went for millennia without writing anything down, much less music. Although future discoveries may or may not change this notion, some of the earliest uses of a script come from Ancient Egypt and Mesopotamia. And so does the earliest example of written music discovered so far. More specifically, Sumer.

In Philadelphia's Penn Museum sits N3354, an artefact from the ancient Sumerian city of Nippur. It's a clay tablet inscribed with an Akkadian-language text in the cuneiform script. Understood to be instructions for playing or singing a hymn to Lipit-Ištar, the inscription is understood to be the oldest written music discovered so far. The tablet is said to be from somewhere between 1900 and 1600 BCE.[1]

The problem with this tablet is that it lacks any kind of mensural information, i.e., specifics on the duration of each individual note relative to others. This defect makes it less than ideal as an expression of musical notations as understood today.

But Mesopotamia needn't lose heart, for there's another tablet that comes from Babylon and seems to hold up to scrutiny better. Those who question the integrity of the Nippur notations take this one as the oldest extant specimen of written music using notational symbols. The tablet's been dated to 1200 BCE. Studies have now established that Ancient lyre-playing Mesopotamians had an unbroken continuum of musical tradition and music theory, as early as the second millennium before the common era, maybe even earlier.[2] But this isn't the music that's survived to this day, as differences of opinion on how to interpret these inscriptions still exist. Although attempts have been made to recreate the music, much of it remains speculative rather than derivative.[3] That said, there's no dispute over them being musical notations, just that their reading isn't fully established as the tablets are highly fragmented with many pieces missing.

Music theory, as we know it, is traditionally traced to the Italians. They invented what music theorists call a *solfège*—a set of seven syllables, each representing a unique note on the musical scale. The solfège we're now most familiar with goes *do*, *re*, *mi*, *fa*, *so* (also sol), *la* and *ti*. Seven names for seven notes. In fact, that's where the name solfège comes from—a rough portmanteau of *sol* and *fa*.

But this wasn't always the case. When the idea of seven named notes first emerged, the syllables were *ut*, *re*, *mi*, *fa*, *sol*, *la*, and *si*.

The man credited with coming up with that one is a Benedictine monk from the late tenth, early eleventh century named Guido. He created the set from *Hymnus in Ioannem*, a Latin chant written by a historian from Lombardy 200 years earlier. Its first stanza is seven lines long. Guido took the first syllable from each of these lines to assemble his seven-note set.[4]

So we can safely place the origins of named musical notations in tenth-century Italy. However, that's just the names. The notes themselves go even further back in time, albeit still not far from Italy. Before the solfège, they used symbols. Of course, there was no means of referring to them in verbal communications as there were no names.

Before Guido, a primordial staff notation was employed where tones were represented pictorially using symbols placed directly above the words in the song lyrics. This was meant to serve as a guide for singers. This notation, however, only helped if the reader were already familiar with the actual music and its rhythm. The symbols were only there to remind him of what he was already expected to be aware of. To anyone who had never heard the song before, this system was of little help.[5]

The oldest extant piece of written music using such symbols for each of the seven notes comes from a Frankish music theorist named Aurelian of Réôme. He lived at the Moutiers-Saint-Jean Abbey in north-eastern France, albeit later expelled from there, and compiled *Musica disciplina*, a treatise on hymnal music as early as 850 CE.[6] This is the oldest piece that we have in entirety, although fragmented literature exists from even earlier times.

Tracing the origins of music theory, we finally come to a man named Isidore, the seventh-century Archbishop of Seville. Sometime in the early decades of the seventh century, Isidore of Seville compiled an etymological encyclopædia titled Etymologiae, covering a breathtakingly wide array of subjects. It was the most studied textbook in Europe during the Middle Ages. Among the subjects covered in this expansive twenty-volume work was music.

It's in this work that the suggestion to write down music was first made. Isidore defines music as the practical knowledge of sound modulation and traces the etymology of the word to the Ancient Greek goddess of arts, Múses. He goes on to warn that unless written down for posterity, music can easily fall out of memory.[7] This is the idea that drove the eventual development of musical notation, first as symbols, then as the solfège.

We could end the conversation here, but shouldn't. Because Italy seems to have a challenger in the Orient. Contrary to the popular notion, Italy or even Europe, are only recent players in the music theory game. Beating them to it by centuries are the Chinese.

In fact, just when Isidore was advancing the idea of writing down music, scholars and musicologists in the Tang dynasty were already doing exactly that as a common practice.[8] *Gongche*, their notation, consisted of seven notes just like the one in Italy—*shàng*, *chě*, *gōng*, *fán*, *liù*, *wǔ* and *yǐ*. The name of this arrangement comes from the second and third characters in the series in reverse order—gōng and chě. Back in the day, this notation was written in a vertical orientation, although these days, horizontal is preferred.

While this sounds pretty old, it's still not old enough. Not even for China. But before we delve deeper into this country's musical notation system, let's return to Europe for a quick minute.

Now Italy and its neighbourhood is believed to be the cradle of Western music and music theory as we know it today. Be it the familiar solfège, or the symbols representing it on the staff, it's this region that invented it all. But did it really? Remember, the Romans conquered Greece well before the common era and subsequently borrowed a lot from them. Including their very religion. The Ancient Greeks are known as the source of all things good in Europe anyway—government, history, arts, literature, probably even toilets. So why not music?

Turns out, that's exactly what happened. Music was being not only composed, but also written down in Ancient Greece long before there was an Italy, or even a Rome. They noted down aspects of their music in a system involving letters of the alphabet. With the Roman conquest, however, this system lost its place and slowly faded out of use. As music became more and more democratized, music theory and the system of notations shrank into the confines of monasteries and scholarly exercises.[9] The plebeian at large had little to do with how music was written or if it was. The system would only experience a revival towards the end of the eighth century with a fresh impetus from Isidore.

Greek musicologists seem to now come on top; they predate their Tang counterparts by nearly a millennium. But before we hand it to them, let's circle back to China, just to be sure.

While the Chinese started writing their compositions impressively early on, the gongche system that made it possible only evolved in the tenth century. But it did not come out of thin air. The system, revolutionary as it was, itself evolved out of something even older—the *wǔshèng* notation, also known as *wuyin*. Wu means five, which makes the system pentatonic. The first elaboration of this system comes from the works of a court theorist named Guanzi. The second appears in Erya, a dictionary that came two centuries later. Guanzi lived in the seventh century BCE.[10]

Suddenly, China seems to beat the Greeks by a large number of centuries, if not a whole millennium. But we're still not done. There exists a system that may or may not predate even the Chinese.

Just like the Europeans, Indians too write their music in seven notes. But this wasn't always the case. At first, there was just one note. Then four—*udatta*, *anudatta*, *madhyama*, and *svarita*. In Sanskrit, *svara* means note. Of the four, madhyama is the most neutral sound and all others identify themselves as relative to it. The note below is anudatta, the one above is udatta. Svarita is a circumflex, the musical equivalent of a diphthong, of both udatta and anudatta.

Singing was much simpler in the days of these four notes. Most singing used to be religious chants and required little in the way of melody or harmony. Much of it was just a few syllables, such as Ōṁ, chanted in repetition, so four pitches more than sufficed.

The system we are familiar with today involves seven notes and is called *sargam*. Just like the solfège came about as a combination of two Italian notes, sargam is a combination of (the first) four in India—*sa*, *re*, *ga*, *ma*, *pa*, *dha*, *ni*. Just as the notes of the solfège originated in the seven lines of a hymn, those of the sargam originate from a *śloka* in a Sanskrit treatise. But while Hymnus in Ioannem was a liturgical composition, the śloka that gives sargam isn't. Instead, the latter was composed specifically as an introduction to the musical notations. It lists out the full names of each note—*ṣaḍja*, *ṛṣabha*, *gāndhāra*, *madhyama*, *pañcama*, *dhaivata*, and *niṣāda*.

The text this śloka comes from—verse xxviii.21[11]—is called *Nāṭyaśāstra,* which is considered a seminal work on performing arts in India. It has been attributed to a sage named Bharata. Some really generous estimates place him in the fourth century BCE, but that hardly helps, given the uncertainty over the authorship itself. In other words, scholars aren't certain a figure named Bharata even existed.[12]

Despite its perceived vintage, the sargam still fails to beat the Chinese wǔshèng or even the Greek alphabetical notation. But that isn't the end of the India story here. The idea of notation, even if not seven, goes further back. As we've already noted, the name in Sanskrit is svara.

And svara isn't a Nāṭyaśāstra innovation. That credit goes to another work that most certainly came before Nāṭyaśāstra (if a more sober dating is considered for the latter). This work is titled *Jaiminīya Upaniṣad Brāhmaṇa.* Also known by other names, such as *Talavakāra Āraṇyaka* and *Jaiminīya Talvakāra Upaniṣad Brāhmaṇa*, this work is attributed not to Jaimini himself but one of his students by the name Talavakāra. Since Jaimini is said to have composed the Mīmāṁsā Sūtras around the third century BCE,[13] Talavakāra's work must have come within the same window, right after Mīmāṁsā's composition.

In the third adhyāya of Jaiminīya's Brāhmaṇa—there's four in all—there's a mention of svar in a musical context. It's in subchapter or *khaṇḍa* 33. The verse basically characterizes some celestial items, including the Sun. Air or *vāyu* is breath, fire or *agnī* is speech, the Moon or *candra* is mind, and then comes the Sun, which is characterized as svara. In this context, svara has been interpreted as tone. To further bolster this interpretation, the khaṇḍa adds that the Sun goes around as a tone, referring to its harmonic motion, leaving little to doubt.[14]

Beyond this one reference, however, the Upaniṣad fails to provide any practical details on its usage. It's quite likely music was being noted using symbols during the time, but this work doesn't say how.

Another reference to svara appears in a text not younger than the third century BCE called *Nāradīyaśikṣā*. Śikṣās are a highly specialized genre of ancillary works that serve to elaborate on the vocal aspect of the chants or mantras introduced in the Vedas. Nāradīyaśikṣā is the most well-known of these works and one of the very few still available in extant form. It deals with the phonetics and enunciation of the mantras in the Sāmaveda. The specific reference occurs in verse 1.2.1 where it stresses on the need for perfection in the chanting of Sāmavedic hymns.[15]

Just like the other work, Nāradīyaśikṣā also doesn't offer much in the way of technicalities. At least not beyond lexical terminology and semantics.

Going further back, we arrive at the big one itself—the Vedas. Remember udatta, anudatta and svarita—the three primordial notes India had long before sargam was developed? This is where they were born. More precisely, in the very first Veda, the Rig Veda. Here, the notes or svaras are not just defined but also explained with usage. Just to recap, udatta is defined as the rising note, anudatta as the falling, and svarita as a combination or circumflex of the two. Marks are prescribed to be placed on top of the syllables being modified to indicate the pitch. While udatta remains unmarked, anudatta and svarita are noted with horizontal and vertical lines, respectively. This may not sound very sophisticated, but that's all they needed back in the day. We're talking second millennium BCE here. The actual mantras, along with the prescribed notations, are listed in the many Samhitas and Brāhmaṇas.[16]

The musical and phonetic aspects are further explored and expounded in the Veda that was specially composed for this very purpose—the Sāmaveda. In fact, the very name comes from *sāman*, Sanskrit for song. Interestingly, the word is cognate with the Ancient Greek word *húmnos*, which gives us hymn. The shift from /s/ to /h/ is a known phenomenon with many words that moved from India to Persia and Greece.

So where does this leave us? As they say, music doesn't see barriers. Neither of language, nor of ethnicity. Every civilization developed its own theory independently before eventual mutual contacts fostered new improvisations. The Ancient Greeks are the established source of music theory, which was later co-opted by the Romans and subsequently standardized by later Italians. That said, however, they weren't exactly world pioneers because the Chinese have also had their own system independently, since as early as the pre-common era. And so have the Indians. While later Greek influences cannot be entirely ruled out in the development of the sargam, India's music theory is as independent and as ancient as the very first Veda.

Having said that, if one were to objectively locate the origin of musical notation in any form, with or without later influences, that credit has to go to India. That is, unless new breakthroughs hand it to the Mesopotamians someday. Because remember, they were the world's first musicologists, and the only reason they still don't get the title is that their tablets are far from intact.

Who Invented Sugar—China or India?

The Hindi name for sweet, Cīnī, directly takes after the name China, and there's a growing notion that it's because the Chinese introduced the practice of extracting juice from sugarcane and turning it into a sweetener. But then, saccharin comes from the Sanskrit śakkar, which would make India its birthplace. So who came first? Some say China; others say India. And both theories have some evidence. Yet, one is wrong.

SUGAR COMES FROM SUGARCANE. THERE'S ALSO THE kind that comes from other sources, such as beetroot, but for the purpose of this discussion, we'll restrict ourselves to the sweet, juicy reed that has, along with honeybees, fulfilled mankind's sweet cravings since early antiquity.

There was a time long ago, though, when there was no sugar, just sugarcane. The plant grew natively and in abundance both in the Orient and the New World for millennia. And the Europeans got a whiff more recently. Recently being a relative term, of course. Many historians place the origins of sugarcane, or at least the knowledge thereof, as a source of nutrition in India. There's an interesting legend in Hindu mythology that refers to the plant, perhaps the first such reference in any scriptural account.

The legend involves a king named Triśaṅku and a sage named Viśvāmitra. With nothing left to desire in the mortal world, the king wished to enter heaven with his body intact. So he contacted the sage for help. Instead of rebuking him for such an absurd and seemingly impossible demand, the sage agreed to help. But there was one problem—Indra. He offered stiff resistance. And Viśvāmitra couldn't go back on his promise to Triśaṅku. So he figured out an alternative. He conjured up an alternative heaven for the king.[1]

This faux heaven was then duly appointed with all the luxuries the privileged resident could possibly think of. Among those luxuries was a plant that would serve as the king's source of nutrition. This plant was specially created for Triśaṅku; it was not available to any mortal back on earth. Later, when the king died, Indra finally agreed to admit him into the real heaven. No longer needed, the faux heaven was then destroyed along with everything on it. Except for the plant.

This plant was sugarcane. Instead, it was brought down into the mortal world, and thus began the journey of its cultivation as a farm crop.[2]

The story of Triśaṅku comes from Vālmīki's Rāmāyaṇa, which itself has been dated to not beyond the fifth century BCE even by generous hypotheses.[3]

But the story does not begin there. The first historical reference to sugarcane goes further back to the eighth century BCE and comes from Chinese accounts. These accounts do, however, note that their knowledge of the plant came from India. By the third century, the commodity had become valuable enough to be used as the currency of tributes paid by feudatories to their overlords, a notable example being the Cambodian confederacy of Fúnán. Tributes of this kind were also made from Indian principalities to the Chinese during the reign of Emperor Taizong, co-founder of the Tang dynasty, which was in the first half of the seventh century.

Further bolstering the Indian claim to sugarcane cultivation are accounts of Alexander's campaigns in the Indus, from Greek and Roman sources such as Strabo, Dioskourídēs and Pliny. These accounts speak of a native Indian reed that produced 'honey' without the help of bees.[4]

The first Greek account comes from a Macedonian admiral sent down the Indus on a scouting mission by Alexander, ahead of his eventual campaign. His name was Nearchus. It's he who first noted sugarcane's cultivation around the river and called it 'honey reed'. This was in the fourth century before the common era. Later, towards the beginning of the common era, Dioskourídēs became the first to use the word *sákkharon* in writing. This is the word that later went on to become sugar. Dioskourídēs was a contemporary of the notorious Nero.

There's more. Even the Old Testament offers multiple mentions of a plant product imported from distant lands, probably in the East.[5]

In short, all roads lead to India, at least so far as sugarcane and its juice goes. Now the question that remains is, was India also the first to make sugar out of it? We know molasses have been an Indian mainstay for far longer than sugar. But who refined it into the crystals we're familiar with today?

Cheeni or cīnī, as mentioned earlier, is the Hindi for sweet as well as Chinese. This cannot be mere coincidence, so the Chinese seem to be the inventors of sugar, who subsequently exported either the technology or the product to India.

But there's far more to the Sino-Indian relationship under the Tang rule than what we just learnt. Taizhong's Indian contemporary was Emperor Harṣa, the last and the most notable of the Vardhanas. Turns out, the two monarchs shared a mighty cordial relationship and frequently exchanged tributes and embassies. Of interest to us is one such embassy from China to India in the year 643. The mission was headed by the Tang ambassador, Li Yibiao and involved multiple activities. The expressed brief was to escort a group of Brahmins visiting China on a diplomatic mission, representing Harṣa, back to

India. But the more crucial brief was to procure from India, a skill. In return, Taizhong sent thousands of pieces of silk. Chinese accounts place the destination of this mission in the kingdom of Mo Jia Ta, Chinese for Magadha. So whatever that skill was, it was desirable and scarce enough to command such a significant volume of the most precious commodity China had to offer at the time. What could that be?

Sugar making, of course.[6]

This changes things. The world's first sugar-manufacturing centre now suddenly shifts from China to Magadha, today's Bihar. Then why is it still called cīnī and not something Indian? Because it's more complicated than that. We'll get to it in a bit, but so far it seems clear that India is where sugarcane juice was first turned into something solid.

Another corroboration for this argument comes from the Byzantine or Eastern Roman Empire. In the seventh century, a physician named Paulus Aegineta produced his magnum opus, a medical treatise known for its comprehensiveness and meticulousness. It was titled *Epitomes iatrikes biblia hepta* (lit. 'Medical Compendium in Seven Books'). In this work, he prescribed a rather expensive substance imported from India as a cure for fever. But the idea wasn't his own. Nearly half a millennium earlier, the prescribed product had been recommended by the Roman Gaius Plinius Secundus, or Pliny the Elder. The substance that the compendium by Paulus referred to was Indian salt, which was, in fact, a type of sugar.[7] (More on this in a bit.)

There is, thus, little doubt that India was the world's sugar pioneer. For a final argument in its support, let's circle back to Dioskourídēs' sákkharon. The word's etymology brings us to a Sanskrit word for gravel, śarkarā. Incidentally, this word is also the source of Persian šakar, Arabic *'uššaq*, Andalusian *súkkar*, and Latin *zuccarum*, all cognates of the English *sugar* and Hindi *ṣakkar*.

While the Vedas are pretty much extensive and self-contained, many ancillary works also exist that attempt to further elaborate or comment on individual Vedic subjects in detail. These are the various

Brahmanas, Sutras and Aranyakas. The literature thus attached to the Atharva Veda is called the Pariśiṣṭas, plural because more than three dozen are known to exist. And one of these Pariśiṣṭas is the Āsurī-Kalpa.

The text is essentially a ritualistic elaboration of rites meant for exorcism and healing. One hymn speaks of a triangular firepit no larger than a man's palm used for ritualistic offerings to a certain goddess. Part of the ceremony involves an oblation into this firepit of a concoction called *ghṛtaçarkarāhōma*—a mixture of *ghṛta*, meaning ghee or clarified butter, and çarkarā, meaning sugar.[8] Assuming the text was composed around 600 to a thousand years before the common era, even by most conservative estimates,[9] sugar easily becomes an Indian invention with a head start of centuries.

This brings us back to the nagging question we left on the back-burner some time ago: why cheeni, and not ṣakkar? Lest there be any misunderstanding, ṣakkar still remains the most common word in Hindi and other tongues of its heritage, such as Marathi. But in a significant portion of the subcontinent, cheeni remains just as mainstream. This makes little sense if the item itself has no Chinese connection.

Here's something we ought to understand about sugar: it's dirty. Not in the form we buy it, but the one it's born in. The first stage of a long refinement process gives us a brown, rocky substance that's simultaneously ugly and sweet—jaggery. The Hindi word for this comes from Śaurasenī Prākṛta *guḍ*. From this to sugar is a long process of repetitive refinement and crystallization. The brown has to become white. An intermediary is something that's brown like jaggery but crystalline like sugar. We call it brown or Demerara sugar. Actually, even before jaggery comes something even more primitive that tastes sweet but looks exactly like very coarse and dull sand, brown with a slightly greenish tint. This is most likely what Indians made back in the day, as one of the things the Sanskrit word śarkarā stands for is gravel or pebbles. It was not white, because it was not clarified. The technology was rather primordial and involved nothing more than extracting the juice, sun-drying it to form a thick syrup, and boiling the result long enough to get a solid brownish residue. This residue is then shattered into pieces or ground to make what we know today as cane sugar—and almost never consume. When the Tang emperor imported sugar and its technology from Magadha, it's most likely this that they got. When the physicians in Ancient Rome prescribed a very expensive Indian 'salt' as medicine for fever, it was this. Note that no European account from the time makes any mention of the colour.

With time, the process was further fine-tuned with more steps to produce a better, clarified version. This involved placing some kind of aquatic plants on top of raw cane sugar and letting the whole thing stand for about three days. After three days, some sugar was removed and more was added, along with new plants. The process was repeated until all the sugar had been through it. How exactly this worked is beyond the scope of this discussion, but work, it seems, it did.

Later, in parts of Bihar, they started using milk and butter in lieu of plants. In others, they improvised with lime water and even ash. Bihar, as we've already noted before, used to be the fulcrum of sugar innovation back in the day. At some point in time, they even experimented with date palm as an alternative to sugarcane with reasonable success.[10]

Eventually, Bihar became a prominent producer and exporter of sugar. By the middle of the eighteenth century, Bihar, along with Bengal, was exporting more than four million pounds annually with a 50 per cent margin. In the space of twenty years, sugar merchants in the region brought in an eye-watering six million rupees in revenue.[11] And that's eighteenth-century rupees. But then came the fall.

As more and more sugar flooded the market, so did its demand back home. While internationally, newer sources started emerging and driving prices down, local demands kept rising. To add to the manufacturers' woes, transportation and logistics also started getting more expensive. Too many forces were now acting against the sugar business, especially in Bengal. By the end of the eighteenth century, exportation of sugar became untenable for most manufacturers given the steep rise in freight costs. So they cut down production. Many consumers, even within Bengal now started importing sugar from places such as Benaras. But no one Indian industry was big enough to satisfy the entire nation's sweet tooth.

As a result, wealthier consumers in places like Bombay started looking elsewhere. Bombay, for instance, looked to Batavia, Manila and China.[12] Of these, China rapidly emerged as the biggest source of a highly refined candied sugar, whiter than anything Bengal produced. This soon became the most sought-after variety in all of India, which further drove down prices, and before you knew it, sugar from China became the dominant sweetener in the Indian market.

The Chinese had been making innovations of their own since the Tang days to further refine the cane sugar they had learnt to manufacture from India. Eventually, they came up with a whiter, more crystalline form of it that looked more appealing without compromising on the sweetness. But the evolution from brown to white wasn't easy or quick. Until as late as the close of the thirteenth century, sugar was less than white in China. At best, it approximated white, a paler version of cane sugar, as reported by the celebrated Venetian traveller Marco Polo.[13] But the commodity had been thoroughly mainstreamed in the country by that time, even if in a dirtier form.

By the sixteenth century, though, things started changing rapidly. New industrial breakthroughs had now made truly white sugar a reality. Sugar, as we know it, started showing up at feasts, ceremonies and grocery stores. But it'd largely remain confined to China for another century or two. Demand at home was growing fast enough to prevent any large-scale export. By the seventeenth century, the Qing household alone was consuming upward of eighty tonnes of it annually. China was easily the world's largest producer of white refined sugar. And also its largest consumer.[14]

This Chinese innovation, white sugar, only came to India's notice after Bengal lost its business in the late eighteenth century. At first, they called it *cheeni ṣakkar*, i.e., Chinese sugar, which later came to be known as simply cheeni.

Long story short, no, China did not introduce us to sugar. We introduced them to it. Not just to them, but to the world. However, the sugar we know today is truly the product of team effort. We taught the world how to draw *honey* out of *reeds*, we taught the Chinese how to turn it into sweet pebbles, and the Chinese taught us how to refine it into the beautiful white crystals we so universally take for granted, while also loving and dreading it.

Is Sri Lanka Aryan, and If So, since When?

Sri Lanka's history has been a saga of bitter conflicts between two ethnic groups—the largely Hindu Tamils and the largely Buddhist Sinhala. The latter trace their history to the Aryans and claim to be the original inhabitants of the island nation. The former, on the other hand, are evidently Dravidian and claim to have been there before the Aryans came. This dispute isn't different from the Aryan–Dravidian dispute in our own country. Which is what makes it interesting and worth investigating.

IT'S BOTH IMPOSSIBLE AND UNREASONABLE TO DISCUSS Sri Lanka in an Indian book without bringing in a great Indian epic, the Rāmāyaṇa, into the equation. Not just as the site of the epic's climax, but also as the abode of its most central supervillain. The island-nation is as indispensable to Rāma's story as Rāma himself. Without getting into a history vs mythology debate right now, we can surely agree that the most popular version of the work is the one by Valmiki, which is Aryan. Across most versions, Rāma is thus an Aryan character.

What this means right off the bat is that the Aryans were surely aware of the island's existence. And that it had captured their imagination well enough for it to figure in one of their most pivotal stories. It is portrayed as an exotic land of gold and debauchery beyond the seas. The knowledge of its existence must, therefore, predate Rāmāyaṇa. The question is, by how much?

It's true that the island was once connected to the mainland Indian territory via a land-bridge—that bit is established in geology. What's also known, however, is that this land-bridge, called Adam's Bridge or Rāma Setū, went completely underwater thanks to a constellation of geological changes, mostly tectonic, more than 3,000 years ago.[1] So when did Rāma and, by extension, the Aryans, get acquainted with the place?

We need not rule out a pre-common era Aryan presence in Sri Lanka purely on the basis of this fact, though, for the distance is small enough for even the most primitive kinds of boats. A land-bridge sure makes it easier, but isn't indispensable for the supposed migration to have happened.

The island itself has been under continuous habitation even before the Toba super-eruption 75,000 years ago. Mesolithic hunter-gatherers were thus the earliest Sri Lankans. These early inhabitants were known as Veddas or *Wanniyala-Aetto.* Their descendants continue to live there, but they are not more than a few thousand today.[2]

This indigenous predominance stood undisturbed until as recently as 500 or 400 BCE, depending on how you interpret the Pali chronicle *Mahāvaṃsa*. (There are other texts too, more mythological than historical, but a near-unanimous agreement exists on Mahāvaṃsa and its 500–400 BCE mark.) That's when a bunch of intruders led by one Prince Vijaya show up on the island. These were from India, and they numbered about 700. This is the first literary record of someone from India visiting Sri Lanka, although earlier visits shouldn't be ruled out. Vijaya may or may not have been a historical figure, depending on whom one asks: the Mahāvaṃsa was composed almost a thousand years after this event, so there's that.[3]

Vijaya's entourage reached Sri Lanka after being expelled from his kingdom, largely displaced the aborigines and established a brand new kingdom of his own. Modern Sinhalese people trace their ancestry to Vijaya and his men. It's worth noting here that Sri Lanka isn't the name anyone used back in the day. Vijaya called the place *Tambapaṇṇī,*[4] a Pali corruption of *Tāmraparṇī*, itself a Sanskrit compound meaning 'tree with red leaves'. This is the name that first spread to Europe after the famed Greek Indologist Megasthenes reported it as *Taprobana*. This was more than a century after Vijaya's fabled arrival.

The name *Siṃhala* goes back to the legend of Vijaya's father Siṃhabāhu, who is said to have been born of a human mother and a lion father.[5] Of course, modern historians interpret this 'lion' as a mere metaphor for some kind of a savage outlaw, rather than a literal jungle cat. Be that as it may, it's safe to assume that these new immigrants from India were Aryans. Over time, as is often the case with such ethnic confluences, these Indo-Aryans started mixing with the local Vedda people and created a whole new kind of gene pool unique to the island. So the modern Sinhalese peoples can be seen as a wide array of this admixture. The Indo-Aryans that came with Vijaya were either already Buddhists or became Buddhist shortly after arrival. The Mahāvaṃsa chronicles three visits by Gautama Buddha.

The chronicle refers to the indigenous peoples not as Vedda, but as *yakṣa*.[6] This is interesting as the name originally comes from a number of post-Vedic texts, including works such as Nāṭyaśāstra, the Mahābhārata, the Skanda Purāṇa, and many others. The name carries many connotations, ranging from very benign and friendly to very hostile and evil.

Closely associated with the *rākṣasas*, yakṣas are generally described as feral, uncivilized, dark and carnivorous—at times even cannibalistic. It's easy to read this as an Indo-Aryan prejudice against an aboriginal people, aided by the striking difference in the two groups' physical and aesthetic attributes. However, there also exist historians who posit a whole other theory on their origins.

Sure, everyone ultimately came out of Africa, and so did the Veddas, but that's not what we're talking about here. We're talking about something more recent. This line of hypothesis places the first yakṣas not in Sri Lanka but all the way in the Himalayas.[7] If that's the case, what the Mahāvaṃsa calls the yakṣas could actually be a separate group from the Veddas and less indigenous; likely, also Indo-Aryan. Just as the Zoroastrians entered India in two batches, the first being Parsis and the second being Iranis, it's possible the Indo-Aryans entered Sri Lanka in two batches, if not more, Vijaya's entourage being the second. All this is still an educated guess, though.

Now, whether Vijaya and his group adopted Buddhism upon arrival or arrived as Buddhists, Sri Lanka was most certainly Buddhist by the third century BCE. Devānaṃpiya Tissa reigned over Anuradhapura, one of the earliest kingdoms on the island, between 307 and 267 BCE. He is recorded in the Mahāvaṃsa as a friend of Aśoka, himself a known Buddhist evangelist. It's during Devānaṃpiya's reign that Aśoka's son Mahinda and daughter Saṅghamittā are said to have introduced Theravāda Buddhism to Sri Lanka. The island also finds a mention as an exporter of pearls in Chanakya's Arthashastra.[8]

But Vijaya of the Mahāvaṃsa and Rāma of the Rāmāyana are both more likely mythological than historical, which makes it difficult to conclude that they are the progenitors of Sri Lankan Aryans. Don't forget that the Mahāvaṃsa was composed almost a thousand years after the purported Vijaya episode,[9] which somewhat diminishes its utility as a historical chronicle. And that brings us back to the question we started with: Is Sri Lanka Aryan, and if so, since when? The epics, even if fictional, sure establish that the Aryans were aware of Sri Lanka's existence. Did they pay a visit and settle down? That warrants a more scientific examination. But before we get there, let's get acquainted with the third, and final, contender in this debate.

Around the middle of the third century, the first Dravidians make an appearance in the Sri Lankan story in the form of two horse merchants, named Sena and Guttika. The man on Anuradhapura's throne at the time was Sūratissa. Sena and Guttika were on the Sinhalese king's payroll, likely managing his stables for him. But the duo was ambitious, or grew ambitious, and constantly conspired to somehow usurp Anuradhapura for themselves. Finally, in the year 236 BCE, they found a window of opportunity and took out the king.[10] Sena and Guttika now became co-rulers of what was so far a Sinhalese polity. This inaugurated the first Tamil reign on the island of Sri Lanka, although it didn't last long, and the novelty was quickly deposed by Sūratissa's nephew Asela.

The landscape, however, had changed now. The Tamils were firmly in Sri Lanka and they were eager to establish their own authority. Asela's reign only lasted about a decade before his kingdom was invaded, and he was killed by a powerful Chola monarch named Ellāḷaṉ. This time, the rule lasted more than four decades. From here on, the story of Sri Lanka is all about the Sinhalese–Tamil power struggle.

In simple terms, an Aryan–Dravidian power struggle. It's not that there was no Dravidian presence in the region before the two horse traders. The fact that they were employed by the king means they had already arrived in the city and had already settled there. If they were there, others could be there too. In fact, Sinhalese rulers have been known to take Tamil brides.[11] So the island wasn't exactly a stranger to the Dravidians before; what the usurpation and the subsequent Chola invasion did was establish a Dravidian prominence in the region's lore.

By the end of the first millennium CE, almost the entirety of Sri Lanka had been absorbed into the Chola empire. Over the following five centuries, the island consistently shuffled between Dravidian and Sinhalese powers, its history littered with brutal conflicts, both ethnic and political.

Now that we have all three players of the story in place (the Veddas, the Sinhalese, and the Dravidians), we can finally pick up on the promised scientific examination.

Let's start with language. This is arguably the easiest way to map a region's ethnicity and the relationship between different peoples. The

Sinhala script looks very similar to the script used to write several south Indian languages, and that's because it experienced heavy influence from the *Granta eḻuttu* or the Grantha script, the progenitor of both Tamil and Malayalam writing systems. Grantha itself developed from Pallava, a Brāhmī derivative.[12] Interestingly, Brāhmī is not a Dravidian writing system at all and originated in the northern reaches of the Indian subcontinent. The Devanāgarī script of modern Hindi is also a Brāhmī derivative. In other words, all languages in question use scripts that originated up north in the edicts of Aśoka. Which means we can't rely on how the language looks in order to ascertain its ethnicity. But we certainly can rely on how it sounds. After all, languages are spoken for centuries before they're written down.

Sri Lanka has two major tongues—Tamil and Sinhala. Tamil is Dravidian, so everything hinges on Sinhala. If that's also Dravidian, so are its speakers. But if it's an Indo-Aryan tongue, things change.

Right off the bat, we can note some Tamil (technically southern Dravidian since the words entered Sri Lanka long before the Tamil–Malayalam split) influence on much of Sinhala vocabulary. Most vocabulary relating to common household items, especially culinary ones, seem to come from Tamil. As do many words of kinship.

One interesting study on the subject comes from a pioneering Catholic priest from Jaffna, Nallur Swami Gnana Prakasar.[13] A widely-recognized scholar of both Dravidian and Sinhalese traditions, Prakasar published a paper on the Dravidian elements in Sinhalese in 1936. Therein he posited, with remarkable certainty, that Sinhala is a Dravidian tongue. To bolster his hypothesis, Prakasar noted the conspicuous absence of central Pali features from Sinhala, Pali being representative of the Indo-Aryan family in Sri Lanka. Careful to not leave anything to coincidence, he only considered features missing in both Tamil and Sinhala—aspirated consonants, optative or subjunctive mood, and several other features both syntactical and morphological.

Furthermore, Pali uses as many as eight tenses, whereas Tamil and Sinhala make do with just three. The languages also differ in how they treat their adjectives. While Pali adjectives must agree with the subject on gender and number, Tamil and Sinhala adjectives have no such need. Sinhala, thus, seems more Dravidian than Aryan. This has obvious implications. But before we conclude anything, let's investigate the matter further.

Prakasar's idea did not go unchallenged. The very year after his thesis, a counterargument emerged in the same journal. This was by Wilhelm Ludwig Geiger, a German linguist noted for his specialization in both Sinhalese and Pali.[14] Dismissing Prakasar's hypothesis right off the bat, Geiger observed that of the twelve Pali features listed as missing from Sinhalese, nine are actually not. The *de-aspiration* of Pali consonants, he noted, was a local development with Dravidian influence rather than a direct Dravidian import. As an example, he offers the Kashmiri language, which also lost its aspiration despite being an Indo-Aryan tongue. In this paper, Geiger provides a comprehensive list of similarities between Sinhala and what he calls Modern Indo-Aryan Vernaculars or MIAV, placing the language in question firmly in the Aryan territory.

This is the view currently maintained by most scholars and linguists of note, as well as the overwhelming majority of Sri Lankans, so this is what we'll go with—Sinhala is an Indo-Aryan tongue, just like Bengali, Gujarati, Hindi and so on.

And nearly two-thirds of the country being Sinhala speakers, we should safely be able to conclude that the nation is, at least as it stands today, Aryan.

But who was there first? What we have so far indicates that the Aryans—that is, Vijaya and his men—got there centuries before the Dravidians. To recall, Vijaya is understood to have arrived in the fifth century BCE, whereas the two Tamil usurpers only came in the third. That's a gap of at least two centuries, if not more. But, again, Vijaya may or may not have been real.

This is where epigraphical records come in handy. While a vast body of Buddhist works referenced in extant Pali texts corroborate the earlier Sinhalese development, almost all such referenced works have been lost to time. The oldest Sinhala inscription, on the other hand, has been dated to the third century BCE.[15] While the script used is Brāhmī, the language is Eḷu, an ancestral Prakrit tongue that later got corrupted to form Sinhala.

Thus, at least based on irrefutable linguistic indicators, Sinhala is an Indo-Aryan tongue. And based on irrefutable epigraphical evidence, it's at best 2,300 years old.

So then the question now is, does that make Sinhala older than Tamil in Sri Lanka? Because if yes, it establishes the primacy of the Aryan claim over the island.

This is where things get interesting. One of the oldest Tamil-language inscriptions also dates to the third century BCE. It's a neolithic black and red potsherd, unearthed in a town called Tissamaharama in the Southern Province. Archaeologists have catalogued this artefact as the Tissamaharama Inscription No. 53. While considerable differences of opinion exist on its interpretation, there are few (in academic circles) in relation to its language. The scholarship also seems unanimous on the script being Tamil–Brāhmī. Some see this as evidence of a thriving Tamil guild in the region, while others see it as that of the presence of Tamil commoners—peasants, villagers and so on—instead. Both opinions agree on Tamil.[16]

So this makes Tamil and Sinhala of similar vintage, leaving the question of who came first unanswered. So let's go further back in time.

In 1997, archaeologists digging for protohistoric artefacts near Colombo found a large cache of black and red ware again. This time engraved with symbols that weren't Brāhmī of any kind. Generally interpreted as potter's marks, these symbols offer an important clue as to the ethnicity of their makers. The potsherds have been dated to the neolithic times or even earlier, placing them clearly ahead of Vijaya's trip, likely by centuries. What's special about these engravings is that the exact same symbols have also been found on the exact same kind of black and red ware potsherds unearthed in the Erode district of Tamil Nadu.[17]

This is taken, oftentimes with a measure of political enthusiasm, as a smoking-gun indicator of prehistoric Dravidian presence in Sri Lanka. If true, it makes this ethnic group the island's original inhabitants; at least more so than the Indo-Aryan Sinhalese.

The mere presence of similar artefacts could, however, also be due to a thriving commercial contact between the two territories, rather than a Tamil cultural hegemony over the island. That said, even a mercantile exchange would surely involve some kind of cross-migration, ergo a Dravidian presence in the region. Either way, the idea that the Dravidians were in Sri Lanka before the Aryans seems more plausible than otherwise, owing not only to the archaeological and epigraphical corroborations, but also to the geographical proximity between Tamil Nadu and Sri Lanka.

What we have unfairly ignored so far in this Aryan–Dravidian debate is the third claimant to the title—the Veddas. Whichever way we slice it, these remain the original inhabitants. Endangered in their own land today, they were here before everyone else.

This was a ridiculously simplified account of one of South Asia's bloodiest ethnic flashpoints. Now here's a presumably related question: Whom does Sri Lanka belong to—Buddhist (Aryan) Sinhalese, Hindu (Dravidian) Tamils, or the indigenous Veddas? We will leave you to try to answer that.

Did Hindus Ever Invade Other Nations?

India is generally considered a peaceful, non-imperialist nation. Sure, we were once a confusing collection of kingdoms and principalities with constant infighting, but we never invaded anyone outside the subcontinent. But then if that's true, how did places like Bali end up so characteristically Hindu? Hinduism sure did reach those distant lands. Was it peaceful or violent? Did the Hindus, a large majority in India, invade them or simply settle there?

WHEN WE SWEEP THROUGH THE HISTORY OF Southeast Asia, we run into a long list of place names that sound less foreign than they ought to. There's an Ayutthaya in Thailand, a Châmpa in Vietnam, a Śrīvijaya in Indonesia, a Tāmbraliṅga in Malaysia, and a whole array of Hindu temples and statuary scattered all over the region. This abundance of Hindu names and structures in a place that is politically separate from India is bound to trigger a question: how did Hinduism get that far? And that question, in turn, triggers another: did we invade them?

In a distant past, Indians engaged in routine maritime commerce with their Indonesian counterparts. They traded spices, gold and much else. This has often been understood to be the primary reason behind the 'Indianization' of the archipelago, starting with Java.

When two mutually unintelligible cultures meet, a degree of intermingling is inevitable. This is what happened over the decades following the first Indian arrival in Java. These foreign merchants found it difficult to do business with the locals, thanks to the enormous cultural and linguistic barriers. So they spent time learning and assimilating. Eventually, some married into influential local families, which helped introduce and normalize Hindu traditions and practices in the region. The process was organic. That's the view held by some scholars, such as Gabriel Ferrand and Richard Winstedt.

The view, however, finds resistance among those who doubt the merchants' ability to exert such a lasting influence. The ubiquity Hinduism seems to have enjoyed in the region could only be the product of something stronger, something more hegemonic. And that's where the Brahmins and the Kshatriyas come in.

These immigrants brought to the region the Shaivite creed and quickly grew to dominate the cultural landscape using esoteric ideas and socioeconomic prosperity.[1] The presence of Kshatriyas in the equation does facilitate speculation of some kind of violence, ergo invasion. But we need more than just that to establish the hypothesis.

~

The thousand-Rupiah bills from the 1980s carry a portrait of the 'National Hero of Indonesia' on the obverse. His name is Patuan Besar Ompu Pulo Batu, better known as Singamangaraja XII. The man died fighting Dutch imperialism in the early years of the twentieth century and is thus celebrated as a venerable martyr. But who was he?

Singamangaraja XII was the last in a long line of sacral kings in Sumatra that started with Singamangaraja I. The latter may or may not have been a real, flesh-and-blood individual, but the legend surrounding his birth prevails among the Batak natives of the island. According to this legend, the king's birth was foretold by a shaman after his mother, Boru Pasaribu, was impregnated by Debata Batara Guru, the supreme deity in the local pantheon. The king was subsequently born after four years, bringing with him calamitous disasters and disarray. That's when the boy's mortal father received a book of commandments from Batara Guru himself, and the first instruction was to name the child Singamangaraja.[2]

What makes the story interesting is not only the supernatural elements therein, but also the multiple Hindu connections it makes. Singamangaraja is a portmanteau of the Sanskrit words *singha*, meaning lion, and *maharaja*, meaning king, and Debata Batara Guru is a direct derivation of the name Śhiva. Debata is a slightly corrupted version of *devta*, a rough Sanskrit equivalent of demigod. The supremacy accorded to this deity in the Batak pantheon is a clear indication of its Shaivite influences.

The legend of Singamangaraja firmly establishes the Batak tribes as Hindus, and yet finds no parallel in any Hindu scripture or epic from mainland India. The story seems entirely indigenous with little foreign equivalence. Other than Śhiva, that is. Scholars argue that this is only possible if the development of the local creed was organic and free from military influence. A religion cannot diversify and new legends cannot emerge when the propagation is done under duress.

Now let's travel a little further north, to Cambodia, known at one time as Kâmpŭchéa locally and Kāmbōja in India.

The capital city Phnom Penh has an etymology of import to this discussion, for here began, some two millennia ago, what scholars believe to be the first distinctly Indian polity outside of India. It was the kingdom of Fūnān.

According to some experts, Fūnān is the Mandarin pronunciation of the original Old Khmer name, *B'iu-nâm*. It's this original name that modern Khmer registers as Phnom, meaning 'mountain'. Back in the day, the territory was ruled by a dynasty of Hindu kings called Śailēndra, Sanskrit for 'king of the mountains'. Its capital city was named Vyādhapūra (lit. 'city of hunters'). This leaves little doubt that Hinduism not only thrived in the region but enjoyed a rather dominant status, complete with royal patronage. As for the beginnings of the religion in the region, multiple theories exist. While they differ greatly on the question of the Śailēndras and whether or not they were indigenous, they do mostly agree on one name—Kauṇḍinya, also known as Añña Koṇḍañña.

Kauṇḍinya was a Brahmin contemporary of Gautama Buddha who renounced Hinduism to become one of the first apostles of what would later grow into Mahayana Buddhism. So what's a Buddhist evangelist from Bihar doing in Khmer country?

Mỹ Sơn is a cluster of Hindu temples in central Vietnam, dating all the way to the fourth century when the region was ruled by a Hindu Cham dynasty. Here lies a Sanskrit inscription from the seventh century that briefly describes a legend.

A Brahmin named Kauṇḍinya, the story goes, once came to Bhavapura carrying a javelin he was gifted by Aśvatthāma, son of the Mahābhārata's Droṇācārya. Here, he took as wife the local queen Somā and the two ruled happily.[3]

Bhavapura, here, is the capital of Zhēnlà, a Hindu–Buddhist polity that succeeded Fūnān in the Indochina region. How Kauṇḍinya got there, we don't know for sure. But the inscription makes it abundantly clear that he did. Several other epigraphical and textual references corroborate the idea in both Chinese and Khmer contexts.

What's also interesting here is that many peoples of distinctly oriental features, especially in north-east India, are still referred to as nāgas in both Hindu and Buddhist chronicles. And that's the descent Somā has been accorded in the inscription we just noted.

But nowhere do these references indicate any military conflict. Kauṇḍinya was never a ruler back home. His intercourse with Fūnān royalty was no conquest, but a peaceful marital alliance. Accounts differ on the circumstances of this alliance, but they all agree on there being no military conflict.

So, although Indochina gradually came under the Indian sphere of influence, it did so without resistance and without violence. Hindus never invaded or colonized them. In fact, they enjoyed quite the esteem under the Chinese too. In the areas ruled by the Jìn dynasty, Brahmins were held in high regard for their perceived healing and mystical powers. Consequently, they got appointed to designations of higher social order and enjoyed privileges and prestige unavailable to most others. Naturally, many locals adopted the Hindu way of life, seeking upward mobility, which further accelerated the 'Indianization' of the region.[4]

Over time, the Śailēndras helped carve out a strong Hindu identity in Indochina that, despite tracing origins in India, had a character of its own. Enormous temple complexes such as those at Angkor and Borobudur came up as expressions of this cultural autonomy. Built as odes to the dynasty's divine kingship, these complexes grew as centres of Hindu theology independent of any overarching Indian influence. In fact, the construction of Angkor Wat ironically coincided with the destruction of temples back in India, thanks to violent incursions from the emergent Islamic world.

So, once again, we see that the spread and adoption of the Hindu creeds throughout the Southeast Asia was organic, peaceful and involved no conflict. The only 'invasion' here was cultural. What resulted was not the dominance of Hindu traditions as often assumed, but the emergence of a unique blend of Hindu, Buddhist and local animist traditions not found anywhere else in the world. The same happened in the case of Singamangaraja, where Shaivism entered Sumatra and blended with local lore, resulting in a flavour of Hinduism that seems familiar and yet carries a strong independent identity of its own.

This merger of traditions and ceremonies almost rules out any armed conflict or religious zealotry. Almost because the story doesn't end here.

Between the third and the ninth centuries, much of southern India was ruled by a line of kings called the Pallavas. This was a Hindu dynasty where religion and royalty expressly shared territorial and moral sovereignty, and where temple complexes were expressions of this collaboration.

The fourth member of this dynasty was SimhaViṣṅu: the king largely held responsible for much of the empire's territorial gains. Before him, they were confined to a small pocket around Kāñcipuram.

In an attempt to consolidate power, the Pallavas made generous land grants to influential Brahmin families and commissioned a large number of temple complexes all over the empire. These grants were often conveyed in the form of imperial charters inscribed on copper plates. Mostly in Sanskrit but sometimes also in Tamil, such plates have been found all over south India and beyond. Besides grant announcements, these inscriptions also carried accounts, often highly exaggerated ones, of the rulers' military accomplishments.

One such example comes from Kasakudi, a small town 25 miles south of Pudukkottai in Tamil Nadu. These bilingual inscriptions, collectively called the Kasakudi plates, talk about a series of ambitious naval campaigns by SimhaViṣṅu. These plates, more hagiographic than historical, speak of how the Pallava king took on and valiantly defeated all his adversaries and challengers—both in the neighbourhood and at large. In the latter category are the kings of Ceylon (noted as Simhala) and Malaysia (noted as Malaya).[5]

This is one of the earliest accounts of an Indian king launching a military expedition against a non-Indian polity. Scholars stand divided on the accuracy of these claims, and many believe it all to be mere braggadocio motivated by politics. Nevertheless, the inscriptions still establish Indian kings' interest in annexing distant lands. Whether the Pallavas had the kind of naval prowess that could successfully be deployed on campaigns as far as the Malay Peninsula is contentious at best. Mercantile seafaring is vastly different from military seafaring, and there simply exists no strong evidence the Pallavas had any expertise in the latter. That said, the possibility of attempts to launch a military attack cannot be entirely ruled out either, for there is one such attempt that does find historical backing from a later dynasty.

In 1025, Mahmud Ghaznavi raided Somnath, plundered its famous Ŝhiva temple and ended the Chalukyas' reign in the region. The same year, a Hindu king also launched a similarly ambitious raid on a piece of land hitherto untouched by an Indian naval force.

But while Mahmud's campaign was a blend of political aspirations and religious zeal, the maritime expedition was purely commercial. The man we're talking about is Rajendra Chola I, arguably the single most influential member of the single most influential dynasty in all of Medieval south India.

The Cholas were no strangers to maritime expeditions, just as their Pallava predecessors engaged in routine commercial exchanges with distant lands, most notably Śrīvijaya.

Śrīvijaya was an ethnic Malay thalassocracy based on the island of Sumatra that, owing to its Buddhist and Hindu character, fell in the Indian sphere of cultural influence.[6] Politically, though, it was part of the Śailēndra realm.

China is to the north of India and Indonesia to the south. And yet, paradoxically, it's Śrīvijaya (Indonesia) that enjoyed better proximity to China than India did, thanks to the mostly unbroken link through Indochina, bypassing India. This created problems.

Southern China, then under the Sòng dynasty, was the economic powerhouse every nation on earth aspired to have close ties with. It was a great consumer market, and both India and Sumatra had a whole lot of spices, textile and other stuff to sell.[7]

A natural outcome of situations like this are business rivalries. And those days, it wasn't uncommon for business rivalries to burgeon into political and, even worse, military rivalries. That's when Rajendra Chola decided to destroy the competition with brute force.

Another theory suggests a more geopolitical driver and holds that the Chola king was merely helping an ally. Sūryavarman I, the Buddhist king of the Khmer Empire at the time, was in conflict with the Tāmbraliṅga kingdom on the Malay Peninsula. Suryavarman was friends with Rajendra Chola, and the Tāmbraliṅga king was friends with Sangrama Vijayatunggavarman, the king of Śrīvijaya. So the conflict between Khmer and Tāmbraliṅga translated into one between the Cholas and Śrīvijaya.[8]

Yet another theory calls the whole exercise merely hegemonic and driven by the Chola king's territorial ambitions, the geopolitical circumstances being mere alibis.[9] Whichever be the case, the invasion happened.

It was a swift exercise with a singular objective to plunder and weaken the adversary. What the Cholas lacked in naval experience, they made up for in stealth and speed. Bypassing traditional waypoints and skipping replenishments, the fleet took the Sumatrans by surprise and proceeded to plunder the whole state, one city after another. By the time it was over, the Śailēndra rule had ended, its king taken hostage,[10] and the kingdom plundered dry. Rajendra Chola also took the defeated king's daughter as his wife.[11]

The invasion did not result in a Chola rule over Sumatra, but it did foster a change in the island's demographic makeup. More Tamils started streaming in and acquiring positions of influence now.

About forty years down the line, another Chola launched a second invasion in the region, this time as an ally of Śrīvijaya; the campaign was against the neighbouring Kedah and ended in victory for the Chola–Śrīvijaya alliance.[12]

So, as we see, the notion that India has never invaded others is less than accurate and, to an extent, even absurd. The further back we go in time, the more frequent such invasions become. And kingdoms on the Indian subcontinent have been at war with each other since the time of the Vedas. So there's no reason they'd see non-subcontinent polities any differently.

While such invasions have become progressively rarer with time, there do exist instances in post-Medieval times as well. Take the Sino-Sikh War, for example. Also known as the Dogra–Tibetan War, this was as recent as the mid-nineteenth century. The conflict was between a relatively autonomous Gulab Singh of Jammu and Dàoguāng Dì of the Qing Dynasty. Tibet, in those days, was a vassal of the Chinese, just as Jammu was of the Sikh Empire. The campaign lasted over a year and ended inconclusively.

Sure, the Indian side did not do as well against the Chinese as it did against the Indonesians, but it tried nonetheless. Remember, all invasions are not and need not be conquests.

References

Is Damascus Steel Really from India?

1 Waring, JB. 'Museum of Ornamental Art.' In *Catalogue of the Art Treasures of the United Kingdom Collected at Manchester in 1857* (Manchester: Bradbury and Evans, Manchester, 1857), p. 171.

2 Manning, Charlotte Speir. 'Commerce and Manufactures.' In *Ancient and Mediaeval India, II, Wm. H.* (London: Allen & Co., London, 1869), p. 365.

3 Craig, Will and Ashley Leonard. 'Chapter 5: Ferrous Metals and Alloys.' In *Manufacturing Engineering & Technology* (Essex: Ed-Tech Press, 2020), p. 202.

4 Davidson, Hilda Ellis. 'The Making of the Sword.' In *The Sword in Anglo-Saxon England: Its Archaeology and Literature* (Suffolk: Boydell Press, 1998), p. 18.

5 Burton, Richard Francis. 'The Proto-Sideric or Early Iron Age of Weapons.' In *The Book of the Sword* (London: Chatto and Windus, 1884), pp. 108–111.

6 Davidson, Hilda Ellis. 'The Making of the Sword.' In *The Sword in Anglo-Saxon England: Its Archaeology and Literature* (Suffolk: Boydell Press, 1998), p. 20.

7 Durand-Charre, Madeleine. 'Of Swords and Swordmaking.' In *Microstructure of Steels and Cast Irons*, trans. James H. Davidson (New York: Springer-Verlag Berlin Heidelberg, 2013), pp. 20–21.

8 Panseri, Carlo. 'Damascus Steel in Legend and in Reality.' In *Gladius* IV (1965), pp. 9–12, https://doi.org/10.3989/GLIUS.1965.188.
9 Feuerbach, Ann. 'Damascus Steel and Crucible Steel in Central Asia.' *American Society of Arms Collectors Bulletin* 82 (2000), p. 38, https://americansocietyofarmscollectors.org/wp-content/uploads/2019/06/2000-B82-Damascus-Steel-and-Crucible-Steel-in-Cen.pdf.

China Gave Us Silk, but Who Gave Them Cotton?

1 Cameron, Judith Anne. 'Textile Technology in the Prehistoric Southeast Asia, vol. I.' (Canberra: Australia National University, 2002), pp. 39–49.
2 Good, I. L, et al. 'New Evidence for Early Silk in the Indus Civilization.' *Archaeometry* 51, no. 3 (2009), pp. 459–461, https://doi.org/10.1111/j.1475-4754.2008.00454.x.
3 Fagan, Brian M. 'The First Farmers and Civilizations.' In *Ancient Lives: An Introduction to Archaeology and Prehistory, 5th ed.* (New York: Taylor & Francis, 2016), p. 296.
4 Kvavadze, Eliso, et al. '30,000 Years Old Wild Flax Fibers—Testimony for Fabricating Prehistoric Linen.' *Science* 325, no. 1359 (2009), pp. 1–3, https://doi.org/10.1126/science.1175404.
5 Robson, E. Iliff, trans. 'Indica Book VIII.' In *Arrian: Anabis Alexandri (Books V–VII), Indica (Book VIII), II* (London: William Heinemann Ltd, 1949), p. 353.
6 Jones, Horace Leonard, trans. 'Book XV.' In *The Geography of Strabo, VII* (London: William Heinemann Ltd, 1930), p. 33.
7 De Sélincourt, Aubrey, trans. 'Book Seven.' In *Herodotus: The Histories* (Middlesex: Penguin Books, 1955), p. 439.
8 Singh, Upinder. 'The Harappan Civilization, c. 2600–1900 BCE.' In *A History of Ancient and Early Medieval India: From the Stone Age to the 12th Century* (New Delhi: Pearson Education, 2008), p. 163.
9 Roche, Julian. 'History and Background of Cotton.' In *The International Cotton Trade* (Cambridge: Woodhead Publishing Limited, 1994), p. 5.
10 Schoff, Wilfred H., trans. 'The Periplus of the Erythraean Sea.' In *The Periplus of the Erythraean Sea: Travel and Trade in the Indian Ocean* (New York: Longmans, Green, and Co., 1912), p. 24.
11 Goodrich, Carrington L. 'Cotton in China.' *Isis*, 34, no. 5 (1943), p. 408, https://doi.org/10.1086/347858.

Is India Truly the Birthplace of Toilets?

1 Harrington, Sir John. 'Advertisement.' In *The Metamorphosis of Ajax; a Cloacinean Satire: With the Anatomy and Apology* (Chiswick: C. Whittingham, 1814), p. vi.

2 Brooks-Tyreman, Alan, et al. 'Harrington's Toilet.' In *Britain 1500-1750, vol. 2, Digging Deeper* (Oxford: Heinemann Educational Publishers, 2005), p. 26.

3 Rogers, Dylan Kelby. 'Categories of Water Usage: Archeological Evidence.' In *Water Culture in Roman Society* (Leiden: EJ Brill, 2018), p. 45.

4 Fracchia, Helena. 'Etruscan and Roman Cortona: New Evidence from the Southeastern Val Di Chiana.' In *Etruscan Italy: Etruscan Influences on the Civilizations of Italy from Antiquity to the Modern Era*, ed. John F. Hall (Provo, UT: Museum of Art, Brigham Young University, 1996), p. 206.

5 Burn, Robert. 'The Velabrum, Vicus Tuscus, Forum Boarium, and Circus Maximus.' In *Rome and the Campagna: An Historical and Topographical Description of the Site, Buildings, and Neighbourhood of Ancient Rome* (Cambridge: Deighton, Bell, and Co., 1876), pp. 279–286.

6 Koloski-Ostrow, Ann Olga. 'Understanding Roman Sanitation from Archeology.' In *The Archaeology of Sanitation in Roman Italy: Toilets, Sewers, and Water Systems* (Chapel Hill, NC: University of North Carolina Press, 2015), p. 55.

7 Meyer, Susan. 'Hideous Hygiene.' In *The Totally Gross History of Ancient Greece* (New York: The Rosen Publishing Group, Inc., 2016), pp. 9–10.

8 Sorek, Shaul. 'Fundamentals of Hydrodynamic Modeling in Porous Media.' In *Handbook of Engineering Hydrology, vol. 1*, ed. Saeid Eslamian (Boca Raton, FL: CRC Press, 2014), vol. 1, p. 172.

9 Farsy, Muhammad Saleh. 'I. Keeping of Places and Bodies Clean and Tidy.' In *Islam and Hygiene* (Leiden: E. J. Brill, 1964), pp. 84–85.

10 Cullen, Carla Luna, et al. '19. Perfume Flasks.' In *Serçe Limani, the Glass of an Eleventh-Century Shipwreck, vol. 2* (Texas: Texas A&M University Press, 2010), p. 241.

11 Ataie-Ashtiani, Behzad, and Craig T. Simmons. '"The Millennium Old Hydrogeology Textbook" "The Extraction of Hidden Waters" by the Persian Mathematician and Engineer Abubakr Mohammad Karaji (c. 953 – c. 1029).' Hydrology and Earth System Sciences Discussions, 15 August 2019, pp. 1–19, https://doi.org/10.5194/hess-2019-407.

12 Clarke, David V and Patrick Maguire. 'The Cells.' *Skara Brae: Northern Europe's Best Preserved Neolithic Village*, ed. Chris Tabraham (Edinburgh: Historic Scotland, 2000), p. 14.

13 De Feo, Giovanni, et al. 'Historical Development of Wastewater Management.' In *Handbook of Engineering and Hydrology*, ed. Saeid Eslamian (Raton, FL: CRC Press, 2014), p. 168.

14 McIntosh, Jane R. 'Resources, Trade, and Communications.' In *The Ancient Indus Valley: New Perspectives* (Santa Barbara, CA: ABC-CLIO, Inc., 2008, p. 184). Understanding Ancient Civilizations series.

Was the World's First University Indian?

1 Bose, Sudhindra. 'Some Aspects of British Rule in India (Bulletin of the State University of Iowa).' *Studies in the Social Sciences* V, no. 1 (1916), p. 138.

2 Shephard, Roy J. 'The Emergence of Health Science Education.' In *A History of Health & Fitness: Implications for Policy Today* (Cham: Springer International Publishing AG, 2018), p. 258.

3 Kia, Mehrdad. 'Kings and Queens of the Sasanian Dynasty.' In *The Persian Empire: A Historical Encyclopedia, I* (Santa Barbara: ABC-CLIO, LLC, 2016), p. 261. Empires of the World series.

4 Datta, Surja. 'Introduction.' In *A History of the Indian University System: Emerging from the Shadows of the Past* (London: Palgrave Macmillan, 2017), pp. 3–4.

5 Godley, AD, trans. 'Book VII.' In *Herodotus, III* (Cambridge, MA: Harvard University Press, 1938), p. 379.

6 Perrin, Bernadotte, trans. 'Alexander.' *Plutarch's Lives, VII* (Cambridge, MA: Harvard University Press, 1967), pp. 405–407.

7 Sastri, KA Nilakanta. 'Chapter III: India in Early Greek and Latin Literature.' In *Age of the Nandas and Mauryas*, ed. KA Nilakanta Sastri (Delhi: Motilal Banarsidass, 1988), pp. 105–106.

8 Balfour, Edward. The Cyclopaedia of India and of Eastern and Southern Asia, 3rd ed., I. *A—Gyrocarpus* (London: Bernard Quaritch, 1885), p. 434.

9 Trainor, Kevin. 'Buddhist Relic Veneration in India.' In *Relics, Ritual, and Representation in Buddhism: Rematerializing the Sri Lankan Theravada Tradition* (Cambridge: Cambridge University Press, 1997), p. 34. Cambridge Studies in Religious Traditions series.

10 Lahiri, Nayanjot. 'An Expansive Imperial Articulation.' In *Ashoka in Ancient India* (Cambridge, MA: Harvard University Press, 2015), p. 181.

11 Monroe, Paul. 'Buddhist Universities—I.' In *Encyclopaedia of History of Education, I* (New Delhi: Cosmo Publication, 2000), p. 166.

12 Pinkney, Andrea Marion. 'Looking West to India: Asian Education, Intra-Asian Renaissance, and the Nalanda Revival.' *Modern Asian Studies* 49, no. 1 (2014), p. 119, https://doi.org/10.1017/s0026749x13000310.
13 Marshall, John. 'Historical.' In *A Guide to Taxila, 4th ed.* (Cambridge: Cambridge University Press, 2013), p. 11.
14 Petrie, Cameron A. 'Taxila.' In *History of Ancient India III: The Texts, and Political History and Administration till C.200 BC*, ed. DK Chakrabarti and M Lal (Delhi: Vivekananda International Foundation and Aryan Books International, 2013), p. 656.
15 Altekar, AS. 'Educational Centres and Institutions.' In *Education in Ancient India* (Benaras: Nand Kishore & Bros., 1944), pp. 105–109.
16 Nepo, Mark. 'Learning Together.' In *More Together than Alone: Discovering the Power and Spirit of Community in Our Lives and in the World* (New York: Atria Books, 2019), p. 78.

Who Truly Owns Biryani?

1 Sathya, A. 'The Art of Naming Traditional Rice Varieties and Landraces by Ancient Tamils.' *Asian Agri-History* 18, no. 1 (2014), p. 8, https://www.researchgate.net/publication/287564599_The_art_of_naming_traditional_rice_varieties_and_landraces_by_ancient_Tamils.
2 Nabhan, Gary Paul. 'Merging the Spice Routes with the Silk Roads.' In *Cumin, Camels, and Caravans: A Spice Odyssey* (Oakland: CA: University of California Press, 2014), p. 135.
3 Ibid.
4 Westfahl, Gary. 'The Islamic World, 600–1500.' In *A Day in a Working Life: 300 Trades and Professions Through History, I* (Santa Barbara, CA: ABC-CLIO, 2015), p. 398.
5 Al-Warrāq, Al-Muẓaffar ibn Naṣr Ibn Sayyār and Saḥbān Murūwah. 'Medieval Baghdad and Food Culture.' In *Annals of the Caliphs' Kitchens: Ibn Sayyār Al-Warrāq's Tenth-Century Baghdadi Cookbook*, trans. Nawal Nasrallah (Leiden: Brill, 2007), p. 30.
6 Hodgson, Marshall GS. 'II: The Indian Timuri Empire: Coexistence of Muslims and Hindus, 1526-1707.' In *The Venture of Islam: Conscience and History in a World Civilization, 3: The Gunpowder Empires and Modern Times* (Chicago, IL: The University of Chicago Press, 1977), pp. 62–63.
7 Muhammad, Zahīr ud-Dīn. 'The Genghisid and Timurid: Background of Iran and Central Asia.' In *The Baburnama: Memoirs of Babur, Prince and*

Emperor, ed. & trans. by Wheeler M Thackston (New York: The Modern Library, 2002) p. xlvi.
8 Collingham, Elizabeth M. 'Biryani: The Great Mughals.' In *Curry: A Tale of Cooks and Conquerors* (Oxford: Oxford University Press, 2006), pp. 17–18.
9 Jamison, Stephanie W, and Joel P. Brereton, trans. 'X.85 (911) Wedding.' *Rigveda: The Earliest Religious Poetry of India* (Oxford: Oxford University Press, 2014), p. 1522.
10 Sharma, Chaturvedi Dwarkaprasad, trans. 'Verse 82.' Sachitra Srimadvalmiki-Ramayan: Ayodhyakand–2; Purvardh (Allahabad: Ramnarayan Lal, 1927), p. 549; Sharma, Chaturvedi Dwarkaprasad, translator. 'Verse 56.' Sachitra Srimadvalmiki-Ramayan: Ayodhyakand–3; Uttarardh (Allahabad: Ramnarayan Lal, 1927), pp. 588–591; Sharma, Chaturvedi Dwarkaprasad, trans. 'Verse 47.' In Sachitra Srimadvalmiki-Ramayan: Aranya Kand (Allahabad: Ramnarayan Lal, 1927), pp. 393–394.
11 Sharma, PV, trans. 'On Vajikarana (Aphrodisiac Treatment).' In *Charaka Samhita Text with English Translation, 4th ed*, (Varanasi: Chaukhambha Orientalia, 1998), pp. 41, 43, 48–49.
12 'Allami, Abu'l-Fazl. 'The Imperial Kitchen.' In *Ain-i-Akbari*, ed. Lt. Col. D. C. Phillott, trans. H Blochmann (New Delhi: Oriental Books Reprint Corporation, 1927), pp. 59–60.
13 'Allami, Abu'l-Fazl. 'Recipes for Dishes.' In *Ain-i-Akbari*, ed. Lt. Col. D. C. Phillott, trans. H Blochmann (New Delhi: Oriental Books Reprint Corporation, 1927), p. 61.
14 Mayrhofer, Manfred. 'Eltere Teil: Ältere Sprache, Schluß (N–H).' In *Etymologisches Wörterbuch Des Altindoarischen* (Heidelberg: Universitätsverlag C. Winter, 1996), p. 597.

Aryans: How Indian or Foreign Are They Anyway?

1 Arvidsson, Stefan. 'From Noah's Sons to the Aryan Race: The Foundation Is Laid.' In *Aryan Idols: Indo-European Mythology as Ideology and Science*, trans. Sonia Wichmann (Chicago, IL: University of Chicago Press, 2006), p. 20.
2 Thapar, Romila. 'The Theory of Aryan Race and India: History and Politics.' *Social Scientist* 24, no. 1/3 (1996), p. 5, https://doi.org/10.2307/3520116.
3 Tilak, Bal Gangadhar. 'The Arctic Home in the Vedas: Being Also a New Key to the Interpretation of Many Vedic Texts and Legends.' *Kesari*, 1903.
4 Jennings, Cecilia. 'Chapter One: Early Empires.' In *India in Ancient Times* (New York: Greenhaven Publishing, LLC, 2018), p. 16.

5 Possehl, Gregory L. 'Chapter 13. The Transformation of the Indus Civilization.' In *The Indus Civilization: A Contemporary Perspective* (Walnut Creek, CA: Rowman & Littlefield Publishers, Inc., 2002), p. 238.
6 Schug, Gwen Robbins, et al. 'Infection, Disease, and Biosocial Processes at the End of the Indus Civilization.' *PLOS ONE 8*, no. 12 (2013), p. 2, https://doi.org/10.1371/journal.pone.0084814.
7 Jacobson, Roni. 'New Evidence Fuels Debate over the Origin of Modern Languages.' *Scientific American*, 1 March 2018, https://www.scientificamerican.com/article/new-evidence-fuels-debate-over-the-origin-of-modern-languages/.
8 Lamberg-Karlovsky, CC. 'Archaeology and Language: The Indo-Iranians.' *Current Anthropology* 43, no. 1 (2002), p. 82, https://doi.org/10.1086/324130.
9 Ibid, p. 66.
10 Greenberg, Joseph. 'Genetic Linguistics and Human History.' In *Genetic Linguistics: Essays on Theory and Method*, ed. William Croft (Oxford: Oxford University Press, 2005), p. 362.
11 Mallory, JP and Douglas Q Adams, eds. 'Indo-European Homeland.' In *Encyclopedia of Indo-European Culture* (Chicago, IL: Fitzroy Dearborn Publishers, 1997), p. 292.
12 Ibid, p. 292.
13 Witzel, Michael. 'Early Loan Words in Western Central Asia: Indicators of Substrate Populations, Migrations, and Trade Relations.' In *Contact and Exchange in the Ancient World*, ed. Victor H. Mair (Honolulu: University of Hawai'i Press, 2006), p. 160.
14 Luckenbill, DD. 'Hittite Treaties and Letters.' *The American Journal of Semitic Languages and Literatures* 37, no. 3 (1921), p. 175.
15 Witzel, Michael. 'Autochthonous Aryans? The Evidence from Old Indian and Iranian Texts.' *Electronic Journal of Vedic Studies* 7, no. 3 (2001) p. 7, https://doi.org/10.11588/ejvs.2001.3.830.
16 'What Are Single Nucleotide Polymorphisms (SNPs)?' MedlinePlus, U.S. National Library of Medicine, 18 September 2020, https://medlineplus.gov/genetics/understanding/genomicresearch/snp/.
17 Reich, David, et al. 'Reconstructing Indian Population History.' *Nature* 461, no. 7263 (2009), pp. 489–494, https://doi.org/10.1038/nature08365.
18 ABC News. 'Three Chariots Dating Back to Bronze Age Unearthed by Archaeologists.' *ABC News*, 8 June 2018, https://www.abc.net.au/news/2018-06-08/bronze-age-chariots-point-to-ancient-warrior-class-india-claims/9848232.

19 Librado, Pablo, et al. 'The Origins and Spread of Domestic Horses from the Western Eurasian Steppes.' *Nature* 598 (2021), pp. 634–640, https://doi.org/10.1038/s41586-021-04018-9.
20 Lindner, Stephan. 'Chariots in the Eurasian Steppe: A Bayesian Approach to the Emergence of Horse-Drawn Transport in the Early Second Millennium BC.' *Antiquity* 94, no. 374 (2020), pp. 361–380, https://doi.org/10.15184/aqy.2020.37.
21 Parpola, Asko. 'The Rigvedic Indo-Aryans and the Dāsas.' In *The Roots of Hinduism: The Early Aryans and the Indus Civilization* (Oxford: Oxford University Press, 2015), p. 185.
22 Ibid, pp. 185–186.
23 Ibid, p. 191.

Is the Swastika Exclusively Hindu?

1 Lankester, Edwin Ray. 'The Origin of the Swastika.' In *Secrets of the Earth and Sea* (London: Methuen and Co. Ltd, 1920), p. 207.
2 Wilson, Thomas. 'Different Forms of the Cross.' In *The Swastika: The Earliest Known Symbol, and Its Migrations with Observations on the Migration of Certain Industries in Prehistoric Times* (Washington, DC: Government Printing Office, 1896), p. 765.
3 Wilson, Thomas. 'Names and Definitions of the Swastika.' In *The Swastika: The Earliest Known Symbol, and Its Migrations with Observations on the Migration of Certain Industries in Prehistoric Times* (Washington, DC: Government Printing Office, 1896), p. 770.
4 'Textile Fragment: Unknown: V&A Explore the Collections.' Victoria and Albert Museum: Explore the Collections, Victoria and Albert Museum, 22 January 2009, https://collections.vam.ac.uk/item/O184378/textile-fragment-unknown/.
5 Pāṇini. 'Tritiya Pāda.' *The Ashtādhyāyī of Pānini*, trans. Srisa Chandra Vasu, VI (Benaras: Sindhu Charan Bose, 1897), p. 1243.
6 Yvanez, Elsa. 'Spinning in Meroitic Sudan: Textile Production Implements from Abu Geili.' *Dotawo: A Journal of Nubian Studies* 3 (2016), p. 170, https://doi.org/10.5070/d63110031.
7 Baldwin, Agnes. 'Symbolism on Greek Coins.' *The American Journal of Numismatics* 49 (1915), p. 136.
8 Kenoyer, Jonathan Mark. 'The Indus Valley Tradition of Pakistan and Western India.' *Journal of World Prehistory* 5, no. 4 (1991), pp. 337–338, https://doi.org/10.1007/BF00978474.

9 Kenoyer, Jonathan Mark. 'Indus Seals: An Overview of Iconography and Style.' *Ancient Sindh Annual Journal of Research* 9, no. 1 (2006), p. 23, http://ancientsindh.salu.edu.pk/index.php/ancientSindh/article/view/65/62.

How Integral Are Temples to Hinduism?

1 Carroll, Maureen. 'Sacred Gardens.' In *Earthly Paradises: Ancient Gardens in History and Archaeology* (Los Angeles, CA: J. Paul Getty Museum, 2003), p. 60.

2 Maniscalco, Katya. 'Access to Heritage: The Role of the Maltese National Cultural Heritage Agency.' *WIT Transactions on the Built Environment*, vol. 191 (Southampton: WIT Press, 2020), p. 247.

3 'Gobekli Tepe: The World's First Temple?' Smithsonian Institution, Smithsonian Institution, 1 November 2008, https://www.smithsonianmag.com/history/gobekli-tepe-the-worlds-first-temple-83613665/.

4 Burkert, Walter. 'The Meaning and Function of the Temple in Classical Greece.' In *Temple in Society*, ed. Michael V. Fox (Winona Lake, IN: Eisenbrauns, 1988), p. 28.

5 'Maa Mundeshwari Temple (Bhagwanpur).' Maa Mundeshwari Temple (Bhagwanpur) | District Kaimur, Government of Bihar | India, Government of Bihar, https://kaimur.nic.in/tourist-place/maa-mundeshwari-temple-bhagwanpur/.

6 Punjabi, Mona. 'Tirupati Balaji - History of Tirupati Balaji Temple.' *The Times of India*, 21 April 2019, https://timesofindia.indiatimes.com/religion/religious-places/history-of-tirupati-balaji-temple/articleshow/68206101.cms.

7 Maity, Biswajit. 'Severe Situations Frequently Faced by the Toiling Tribes in India.' *Tribal Perspectives in India: Critical Responses*, ed. Dipak Giri (Bilaspur: Booksclinic Publishing, 2020), p. 106.

8 Lipner, Julius J. 'In Retrospect: The Trajectory of Image-Worship in the Light of Yāmuna's Āgamaprāmāṇya.' In *Hindu Images and Their Worship with Special Reference to Vaisnavism: A Philosophical-Theological Inquiry.* (New York: Routledge, 2017), pp. 38–40. Routledge Hindu Studies series.

9 Sikora, Jack. 'Appendix. Sacrifice and Service: An Observation on the Religion of Nanak and the Hindu Tradition.' In *Religions of India: A User Friendly and Brief Introduction to Hinduism, Buddhism, Sikhism, and the Jains* (Lincoln, NE: Writers Club Press, 2002), p. 86.

10 Keith, Arthur Berriedale. 'The Ritual in the Rigveda.' In *The Religion and Philosophy of the Veda and Upanishads*, ed. Charles Rockwell Lanman, vol.

31 (Delhi: Motilal Banarsidass Publishers Private Limited, 1989), p. 254. The Harvard Oriental series.

11 Elgood, Heather. 'Village and Tribal Patrons and Their Religious Arts.' In *Hinduism and the Religious Arts* (London: Cassell, 2000), p. 194.

12 Varadpande, Manohar Laxman. 'Dionysus in India.' In *History of Indian Theatre* (New Delhi: Abhinav Publications, 1987), p. 249.

13 Sparreboom, M. 'The Use of the Chariot in Ritual.' In *Chariots in the Veda* (Leiden: E. J. Brill, 1985), pp. 63–64.

14 Acharya, Prasanna Kumar. 'Text of the Encyclopaedia.' *An Encyclopaedia of Hindu Architecture, VII* (Oxford: Oxford University Press, 1946), pp. 178–179. Manasara series.

15 Ibid, p. 178.

16 Raman, Sita Anantha. 'Vedic Goddesses and Women.' In *Women in India: A Social and Cultural History, vol. 1* (Santa Barbara, CA: ABC-Clio, LLC, 2009), p. 35.

17 Halbfass, Wilhelm. 'Tradition and Indian Xenology.' In *India and Europe: An Essay in Philosophical Understanding* (Delhi: Motilal Banarsidass Publishers Private Limited, 1990), p. 176.

18 Shah, Priyabala, trans. 'Adhyāya 93.' In *Shri Vishnudharmottara (A Text on Ancient Indian Arts)* (Ahmedabad: The New Order Book Co, 1990), p. 275.

19 Pragiter, Frederick Eden. 'The Puranas and Their Genealogical Texts.' In *Ancient Indian Historical Tradition* (Oxford: Oxford University Press, 1922), pp. 79–80.

20 Hazra, Rajendra Chandra. 'The Upapurānas.' In *The Cultural Heritage of India*, ed. Sarvepalli Radhakrishnan (Calcutta: The Ramkrishna Mission Institute Of Culture Calcutta, 1975), p. 272.

21 Vaidya, Chintaman Vinayak. 'The Kainakila Yavanas of Āndhra.' In *History of Medieval Hindu India (Being a History of India from 600 to 1200 A.D.), I* (Poona: The Oriental Book-Supplying Agency, 1921), p. 352.

22 Olivelle, Patrick. 'Introduction.' *Manu's Code of Law: A Critical Edition and Translation of the Mānava-Dharmaśāstra*, ed. Suman Olivelle (Oxford: Oxford University Press, 2005), pp. 24–25.

23 Narayanan, Vasudha and Katherine K. Young. 'Brimming with Bhakti, Embodiments of Shakti: Devotees, Deities, Performers, Reformers, and Other Women of Power in the Hindu Tradition.' In *Feminism and World Religions*, ed. Arvind Sharma (Albany, NY: State University of New York Press, 1999), p. 48.

24 Menon, Srikumar M. 'From Megaliths to Temples in South India: Astronomy in the Lithic Record of South India.' The Growth and Development of Astronomy and Astrophysics in India and the Asia-Pacific

Region. Astrophysics and Space Science Proceedings of the 9th International Conference on Oriental Astronomy, ed. W Orchiston et al. 54 (June 2019), p. 246, https://doi.org/10.1007/978-981-13-3645-4_27.

25 Sreedharan, E. 'Chapter 16.' In *A Textbook of Historiography, 500 BCE to CE 2000* (Hyderabad: Orient Longman Private Limited, 2004), p. 476.

26 Acharya, Prasanna Kumar, trans. 'Preface.' In *Architecture of Mānasāra (Translated from Original Sanskrit)* (Oxford: Oxford University Press, 1933), p. lvii.

27 Devadevan, Manu V. 'Religious Identities in Times of Indumali's Grief.' In *The 'Early Medieval' Origins of India* (Cambridge: Cambridge University Press, 2020), p. 335.

28 Sutton, Nicholas. 'Session One: Devotion, Worship, and Ritual.' Course: Understanding Hinduism: Ritual, Yoga, Caste, and Gender. Course no HS108, Oct. 2015, Oxford, Oxford Center for Hindu Studies.

29 Ernst, Carl W. 'Admiring the Works of the Ancients: The Ellora Temples As Viewed by Indo-Muslim Authors.' In *Refractions of Islam in India: Situating Sufism and Yoga* (New Delhi: SAGE Publications India Private Limited, 2016), p. 172.

Āryabhata Gave Us Zero, but Did He Invent It?

1 Hayes, John L. 'Appendix One: History of Sumerian.' In *A Manual of Sumerian Grammar and Texts, 2nd ed.* (Malibu, CA: Undena Publications, 2000), p. 385.

2 Stephen, Chrisomalis. 'Mesopotamian Systems.' In *Numerical Notation: A Comparative History* (Cambridge: Cambridge University Press, 2010), p. 247.

3 Ifrah, Georges. 'Mesopotamian Numbering after the Eclipse of Sumer.' In *The Universal History of Numbers: From Prehistory to the Invention of the Computer*, trans. David Bellos et al. (New York: John Wiley and Sons, Inc., 2000), p. 152.

4 Agarwal, Ravi P, and Syamal K Sen. 'History of Zero Including Its Representation and Role.' *Zero: A Landmark Discovery, the Dreadful Void, and the Ultimate Mind.* (Cambridge, MA: Elsevier Science, 2015), p. 38.

5 Imhausen, Annette. 'The Egyptian Number System.' In *Mathematics in Ancient Egypt: A Contextual History* (Princeton, NJ: Princeton University Press, 2020), p. 20.

6 Joseph, George Gheverghese. 'The Beginnings of Written Mathematics: Egypt.' In *The Crest of the Peacock: Non-European Roots of Mathematics*, 3rd ed. (Princeton, NJ: Princeton University Press, 2011), p. 67.

7 Plofker, Kim. 'Mathematical Traces in the Early Classical Period.' In *Mathematics in India* (Princeton, NJ: Princeton University Press, 2009), p. 55–56.
8 O'Connor, John and Edmund F Robertson. 'The Bakhshali Manuscript.' Maths History, School of Mathematics and Statistics, University of St Andrews, Scotland, November 2000, https://mathshistory.st-andrews.ac.uk/HistTopics/Bakhshali_manuscript/.
9 Kaplan, Robert. 'Eastward.' In *The Nothing That Is: A Natural History of Zero* (London: Allen Lane The Penguin Press, 1999), p. 43.
10 Smith, David Eugene. 'The Period from 500 to 1000.' In *History Of Mathematics: General Survey of the History of Elementary Mathematics, I* (New York: Dover Publications, Inc., 1958), p. 167.

Was Vasco the First European to Reach India by Sea?

1 Velho, Alvaro and João De Sá. 'Calecut.' In *A Journal of the First Voyage of Vasco Da Gama (1497–1499)*, trans. EG Ravenstein, vol. XCIX (London: The Hakluyt Society, 1958), p. 48.
2 Ibid, p. 46.
3 Ibid, pp. 49–51.
4 Di Santo Stefano, Hieronimo. 'Account of the Journey of Hieronimo Di Santo Stefano, 'A Genovese.' In *India in the Fifteenth Century. Being a Collection of Narratives of Voyages to India, in the Century Preceding the Portuguese Discovery of the Cape of Good Hope; from Latin, Persian, Russian, and Italian Sources, Now First Translated into English*, ed. Richard Henry Major (London: The Hakluyt Society, 1857), pp. 3–10.
5 'Afanasy Nikitin's Voyage Beyond Three Seas.' History of Russian Literature, RusLiterature.org, http://www.rusliterature.org/afanasy-nikitins-voyage-beyond-three-seas/#.YYosT2BBxPb.
6 Laparyonok, Leonid. 'Prominent Russians: Afanasy Nikitin.' Afanasy Nikitin – Russiapedia Geography and Exploration Prominent Russians, RT, https://russiapedia.rt.com/prominent-russians/exploring-russia/afanasy-nikitin/.
7 Bracciolini, Poggio. 'De Varietate Fortvnae: Edizione Critica Con Introduzione e Commento a Cura Di Outi Merisalo.' *Annales Academiæ Scientiarum Fennicæ* 265 (1993): pp. 153–156.
8 Arbuthnot, John. 'Of the Interest of Money.' In *Tables of Ancient Coins, Weights and Measures, Explain'd and Exemplify'd in Several Dissertations* (London: J Tonson, London, 1727), p. 269.

9 Mandeville, John. 'Of the Customs of Isles about Ind.' In *The Travels of Sir John Mandeville: The Version of the Cotton Manuscript in Modern Spelling*, trans. Alfred W Pollard (London: Macmillan and Co. Limited, 1900), p. 109.

10 Hunter, William Wilson. 'Chapter XIV. Early European Settlement (1498 to 18th Century A.D.).' In *The Indian Empire, Its Peoples, History, and Products, Third ed.* (London: W.H. Allen & Co. Ltd, 1893), p. 417.

11 Arora, Namit. 'Marco's Malabar.' *Open The Magazine*, 29 January 2021, https://openthemagazine.com/lounge/books/marcos-malabar/.

12 Harvey, Schoff Wilfred, trans. 'Introduction.' In *The Periplus of the Erythraean Sea: Travel and Trade in the Indian Ocean* (New York: Longmans, Green, and Co., 1912), pp. 8–10.

Was Ujjain the World Capital of Timekeeping?

1 Rossi, Cesare, and Flavio Russo. 'Measuring Time.' In *Ancient Engineers' Inventions: Precursors of the Present, 2nd ed.* (Cham: Springer International Publishing, 2017), p. 41.

2 'How Do Sundials Work?' *Yale Scientific*, 22 November 2008, https://www.yalescientific.org/2008/11/how-do-sundials-work/.

3 'Equatorial Sundials.' *Sundials Australia*, https://www.sundialsaustralia.com.au/equatorial-sundials.

4 Ibid.

5 Bernard, Paul. 'Aï Khanoum En Afghanistan Hier (1964–1978) Et Aujourd'hui (2001): Un Site En Péril. Perspectives D'avenir (Information).' *Comptes Rendus Des Séances De L'Acad*émie Des Inscriptions Et Belles-Lettres 145, no. 2 (2001), p. 971.

6 Bosworth, A.B. 'B. Alexander and His Empire.' In *Conquest and Empire: The Reign of Alexander the Great* (Cambridge: Cambridge University Press, 1988), p. 248.

7 Thapar, Romila. 'Appendix III. The Geographical Locations of the Edicts.' In *Aśoka and the Decline of the Mauryas* (Oxford: Oxford University Press, 1961), p. 237.

8 Kumar, Alok. 'Astronomy.' Ancient Hindu Science: Its Transmission and Impact on World Cultures (Willistin, VT: Morgan & Claypool Publishers, 2019), p. 68.

9 Wilhelm, Ernst. 'Vara.' In *Classical Muhurta: Vedic Electional Astrology* (San Diego, CA: Käla Occult Publishers, 2003), p. 44.

10 Eratosthenes. 'Eratosthenes and the History of Geography.' In *Eratosthenes' Geography*, trans. Duane W. Roller (Princeton, NJ: Princeton University Press, 2010), pp. 4–5.
11 Bell, James. 'Geography of the Ancients.' In *A System of Geography, Popular and Scientific, or a Physical, Political, and Statistical Account of the World and Its Various Divisions, V* (Glasgow: Archibald Fullarton and Co., 1832), p. 418.
12 Burgess, Ebenzer, trans. 'Introduction.' In *The Sûrya-Siddhânta A Text-Book of Hindu Astronomy*, ed. Phanindralal Gangooly (New Delhi: Motilal Banarsidass Publishers Private Limited), 1997, p. ix.
13 Wright, John Kirtland. 'Notes on the Knowledge of Latitudes and Longitudes in the Middle Ages.' *Isis* 5, no. 1 (1923), p. 89, https://doi.org/10.1086/358121.
14 Gregory, John, and John Gurgany. 'The Description and Use of the Terrestrial Globe.' In *Gregorii Posthuma: Or, Certain Learned Tracts* (London: Thomas Williams, 1671), p. 276.
15 Alcock, Susan E. 'Breaking Up the Hellenistic World: Survey and Society.' In *Classical Greece: Ancient Histories and Modern Archaeologies*, ed. Ian Morris (Cambridge: Cambridge University Press, 1994), p. 186.
16 Burgess, Ebenzer, trans. 'Of the Mean Motion of the Planets.' In *The Sûrya-Siddhânta A Text-Book of Hindu Astronomy*, ed. Phanindralal Gangooly (New Delhi: Motilal Banarsidass Publishers Private Limited, 1997), p. 46.
17 Mayall, R Newton, and Margaret Mayall. 'The Development of the Sundial.' In *Sundials: Their Construction and Use* (Mineola, NY: Dover Publications, 2000), p. 13.
18 Rohr, René R. 'A Unique Greek Sundial Recently Discovered in Central Asia.' *Journal of the Royal Astronomical Society of Canada* 74 (1980), pp. 271–278.
19 Ibid, pp. 275–276.
20 Ibid, p. 275.
21 Wright, Colin. 'Sind Club, Karachi.' The British Library, The British Library, 12 September 2008, https://www.bl.uk/onlinegallery/onlineex/apac/photocoll/s/019pho0000940s1u00041000.html.
22 Hannah, Robert. 'Conceptions of Time.' In *Time in Antiquity* (Oxford: Routledge, 2009), p. 121.

How Homogeneous Is the Rajput Bloodline?

1 Mitchiner, John E., trans. 'The Historicity of the Account.' *The Yuga Purāṇa*, ed. John E. Mitchiner (Calcutta: The Asiatic Society, 1986), p. 44. Bibliotheca Indica—A Collection of Oriental Works series.

2 Beckwith, Christopher I. 'Prologue. Scythian Philosophy: Pyrrho, the Persian Empire, and India.' In *Greek Buddha: Pyrrho's Encounter with Early Buddhism in Central Asia* (Princeton, NJ: Princeton University Press, 2015), pp. 5–6.

3 Eastwick, Edward Backhouse. 'Introduction: Scythian Invasion.' *Handbook of the Panjáb, Western Rajpútáná, Kashmír and Upper Sindh* (London: John Murray, 1883), p. 6.

4 Marshall, John, et al. 'Inscriptions of the Kushān, Gupta and Later Periods.' In *The Monuments of* Sāñchī, I (New Delhi: Archeological Survey of India, 1902), p. 392.

5 Majumdar, RC. 'The Gupta Empire.' In *A Comprehensive History of India*, ed. RC Majumdar and KK Dasgupta (New Delhi: Three, People's Publishing House, 1960), pp. 53–54.

6 Tod, James. 'History of the Rajpoot Tribes.' In *Annals and Antiquities of Rajast'Han, or, The Central and Western Rajpoot States of India, 2nd ed.* (Madras: Higginbotham and Co., 1873), p. 22.

7 Bhandarkar, RG. 'Foreign Elements in the Hindu Population.' *The Indian Antiquary, a Journal of Oriental Research* XL (1911), p. 21.

8 Vaidya, Chintaman Vinayak. 'Are Agnikulas Gujars?' In *History of Medieval Hindu India (Being a History of India from 600 to 1200 A.D.), II* (Poona: The Oriental Book-Supplying Agency, 1924), p. 29.

9 *The Mahābhārata: Text As Constituted in Its Critical Edition, I* (Poona: Bhandarkar Oriental Research Institute, 1971), pp. 188, 231, 331, 437, 458 and 479.

10 Raychaudhuri, HC. 'India in the Age of the Nandas.' In *Age of the Nandas and the Mauryas*, ed. KA Nilakanta Sastri (Delhi: Motilal Banarasidass, 1988), p. 13.

11 Sharma, Dasharatha. 'The Origin and Original Habitat of the Chauhans.' In *Early Chauhān Dynasties (a Study of Chauhān Political History, Chauhān Political Institutions and Life in the Chauhān Dominions from c. 800 to 1316 A.D.)* (Delhi: S. Chand & Co., 1959), p. 9.

12 Sircar, Dinesh Chandra. *The Guhilas of Kiṣkindh*ā (Calcutta: Sanskrit College, 1965), pp. 4–5.

13 Asher, Catherine B and Cynthia Talbot. 'North India between Empires: History, Society, and Culture, 1350–1550.' In *India Before Europe* (Cambridge: Cambridge University Press, 2006), p. 99.

14 Hiltebeitel, Alf. 'The Myth of the Agnivaṃśa.' In *Rethinking India's Oral and Classical Epics: Draupadi among Rajputs, Muslims, and Dalits* (Chicago, IL: University of Chicago Press, 2009), p. 448.

15 Talbot, Cynthia. 'The Heroic Vision of an Elite Regional Epic.' In *The Last Hindu Emperor: Prithviraj Chauhan and the Indian Past, 1200–2000* (Cambridge: Cambridge University Press, 2016), p. 120.

16 Bannerman, AD. 'Chapter IX. Castes, Tribes and Races.' Census of India, 1901, 25, no. 1, 1902, p. 138.

Did We Invent Our Script, or Import It?

1 Hiralal, Rai Bahadur. 'Tiwarkhed Plates of the Rashtrakuta Nannaraja, Saka 553.' In *Epigraphia Indica and Record of the Archeological Survey of India*, ed. E Hultzsch, XI (Calcutta: Bombay Education Society's Press, 1911), pp. 276–277.

2 Fischer, Steven Roger. 'Three: Speaking Systems.' In *A History of Writing* (London: Reaktion Books Ltd, 2003), pp. 10–12.

3 Salomon, Richard. 'Writing and Scripts in India.' In *Indian Epigraphy: A Guide to the Study of Inscriptions in Sanskrit, Prakrit, and Other Indo-Aryan Languages* (Oxford: Oxford University Press, 1998), p. 39.

4 Deambi, BK Kaul. '3The Sharada Script: Origin and Development.' In *Jammu, Kashmir & Ladakh: Linguistic Predicament*, ed. PN Pushp and K Warikoo (New Delhi: Har-Anand Publications, 1996), p. 82.

5 Verma, Thakur Prasad. 'The Period of Accelerated Development (from A.D. 78 to A.D. 200).' In *The Palaeography of Brāhmī Script in North India (from c. 236 B.C. to c. 200 A.D.), 1st ed.* (Varanasi: Siddharth Prakashan, 1971), p. 109.

6 Sircar, Dines Chandra. 'Chapter III. Miscellaneous Inscriptions.' In *Select Inscriptions Bearing on Indian History and Civilization, from the Sixth Century B.C. to the Sixth Century A.D., vol. 1*, ed. Dines Chandra Sircar (Kolkata: University of Calcutta, 1942), p. 85.

7 Salomon, Richard. 'Writing and Scripts in India.' In *Indian Epigraphy: A Guide to the Study of Inscriptions in Sanskrit, Prakrit, and Other Indo-Aryan Languages* (Oxford: Oxford University Press, 1998), pp. 52–53.

8 Kak, Subhash. 'The Evolution of Early Writing in India.' *Indian Journal of History of Science* 28 (1994), pp. 380–382.

9 Coningham, RAE, et al. 'Passage to India? Anuradhapura and the Early Use of the Brahmi Script.' *Cambridge Archaeological Journal* 6, no. 1 (1996), p. 77, https://doi.org/10.1017/S0959774300001608.

10 Salomon, Richard. 'Writing and Scripts in India.' In *Indian Epigraphy: A Guide to the Study of Inscriptions in Sanskrit, Prakrit, and Other Indo-Aryan Languages* (Oxford: Oxford University Press, 1998), pp. 20–21.

11 Chakravarti, Niranjan Prasad. 'The Minor Rock Edicts of Aśoka and Some Connected Problems.' *Ancient India: Bulletin of the Archeological Survey of India*, no. 4 (1948), p. 19.

12 Falk, Harry. 'The Creation and Spread of Scripts in Ancient India.' In *Literacy in Ancient Everyday Life*, ed. Anne Kolb Berlin (Boston: De Gruyter, 2018), pp. 55–59, https://doi.org/10.1515/9783110594065-004.
13 Hultzsch, E. 'Description of the Inscriptions.' In *Corpus Inscriptionum Indicarum*, I (Oxford: Clarendon Press, 1925), p. xiii.
14 Bühler, Georg. 'The Derivation of the Brāhma Letters from the Most Ancient North-Semitic Signs.' In *On the Origin of the Indian Brāhma Alphabet, 2nd ed.* (Strassburg: Karl J. Trübner, 1898), p. 84.
15 Ibid, pp. 54–59.

Is Roma the Only Medieval Diaspora from India?

1 Hancock, Ian. 'Romanies and the Holocaust: A Re-Evaluation and Overview.' In *The Historiography of the Holocaust*, ed. Dan Stone (New York: Palgrave Macmillan, 2004), p. 392.
2 Szombati, Kristóf. 'The Limits of Racist Mobilization: The Case of Devecser.' In *The Revolt of the Provinces: Anti-Gypsyism and Right-Wing Politics in Hungary* (New York: Berghahn Books, 2018), p. 206.
3 Pisharoty, Sangeeta Barooah. 'The Modi Government, and RSS, Are Keen to Claim the Roma as Indians, and Hindus.' *The Wire*, https://thewire.in/diplomacy/the-modi-government-and-rss-are-keen-to-claim-the-roma-as-indians-and-hindus.
4 Mendizabal, Isabel, et al. 'Reconstructing the Population History of European Romani from Genome-Wide Data.' *Current Biology* 22, no. 24 (2012), p. 2347, https://doi.org/10.1016/j.cub.2012.10.039.
5 Hugo, Victor. 'History of the Mystery Concluded.' In *The Hunchback Or Bell-Ringer of Notre Dame* (London: T. Allman & Charles Daly, 1840), p. 63.
6 Kenrick, Donald. 'Under Arab Rule: 642–C.900.' In *Gypsies: From the Ganges to the Thames* (Hertfordshire: University of Hertfordshire Press, 2004), pp. 20–21.
7 De Goeje, Michael Jan and J Snijders. 'A Contribution to the History of the Gypsies.' In *Accounts of the Gypsies of India*, ed. David MacRitchie, K Paul (Hertfordshire: Trench, 1886), pp. 11–13.
8 Meyer, Frank. 'Biography and Identity in Damascus: A Syrian Nawar Chief.' In *Customary Strangers: New Perspectives on Peripatetic Peoples in the Middle East, Africa, and Asia*, ed. Joseph C Berland and Aparna Rao (Westport, CT : Praeger Publishers, 2004), pp. 72–74.
9 Cockburn, Andrew and Patrick Cockburn. 'The Origins of Saddam Hussein.' In *Saddam Hussein: An American Obsession* (London: Verso, 2002), p. 76.

10 Cockburn, Patrick. 'The Siege of Najaf.' In *Muqtada Al-Sadr and the Battle for the Future of Iraq* (New York: Scribner, 2008), p. 143.
11 Sati, Vishwambhar Prasad. 'Chapter 7: Change in Culture and Custom.' *Himalaya on the Threshold of Change* (Cham: Springer International Publishing, Cham, 2020), p. 110.
12 Das, K. C., ed. 'Dom.' North Indian Dalits Ethnography, vol. I (New Delhi: Global Vision Publishing House, 2007), p. 264.
13 Phillips, David J. 'A World Survey of Pastoral and Peripatetic Peoples.' In *Peoples on the Move: Introducing the Nomads of the World* (Carlisle: Piquant, 2001), p. 431.
14 Marushiakova, Elena and Vesselin Popov. 'Gypsies of the Caucasus.' In *Gypsies in Central Asia and the Caucasus* (London: Palgrave Macmillan, 2016), pp. 67–75.
15 Hancock, Ian. 'On Romani Origins and Identity.' In *Danger! Educated Gypsy: Selected Essays,* ed. Dileep Karanth (Hertfordshire: University of Hertfordshire Press, 2010), pp. 54–94.

Are Sanskrit and Persian Related?

1 Rocher, Rosane. 'The Knowledge of Sanskrit in Europe until 1800.' In *History of the Language Sciences, vol. 2.* (Berlin: Walter De Gruyter GmbH, 2001), p. 1159.
2 Müller, Max. 'Chips from a German Workshop. Essays on the Science of Religion, &c. &c.' In *The Christian Remembrancer: A Quarterly Review, LVI* (London: John and Charles Mozley, 1868), p. 147.
3 Tavakoli-Targhi, Mohamad. 'Orientalism's Genesis Amnesia.' In *Refashioning Iran: Orientalism, Occidentalism and Historiography* (New York: Palgrave Macmillan, 2001), p. 26.
4 Martínez, Gerardo. 'Origin Theories of the Korean Language.' Origin Theories, Brigham Young University, 24 February 1998, https://linguistics.byu.edu/classes/Ling450ch/reports/korean.html.
5 Bandhu, Vishva, ed. 'Saptamam Mandalam.' Ṛgvedā, 1st ed., vol. 23 (Hoshiarpur: Vishveshvaranand Vedic Research Institute, 1964), p. 2412. Vishveshvaranand Indological series.
6 Everson, Michael and Roozbeh Pournader. 'Proposal for Encoding the Inscriptional Parthian, Inscriptional Pahlavi, and Psalter Pahlavi Scripts in the SMP of the UCS.' Script Encoding Initiative, 18 September 2007, p. 10, https://escholarship.org/uc/item/2hm6b38h.

7 Cheung, Johnny. 'On the (Middle) Iranian Borrowings in Qur'ānic (and Pre-Islamic) Arabic,' 2016, p. 14, https://halshs.archives-ouvertes.fr/halshs-01445860. Preprint.
8 Burrows, T. 'Spontaneous Cerebrals in Sanskrit.' *Bulletin of the School of Oriental and African Studies, University of London* 34, no. 3 (1971), pp. 538–559, http://www.jstor.org/stable/613901.
9 Jahanshiri, Ali. 'Grammatical Cases—Persian Grammar.' Personal Website of Ali Jahanshiri, Ali Jahanshiri, 3 April 2021, https://www.jahanshiri.ir/fa/en/grammatical-case.
10 Jackson, Abraham Valentine Williams. 'Introduction: The Avesta and Zoroaster.' An Avesta Grammar in Comparison with Sanskrit, I, W. Kohlhammer, Stuttgart, 1892, p. xxxii.

Algebra Came from India ... or Did It?

1 Oaks, Jeffrey A. 'Polynomials and Equations in Arabic Algebra.' Archive for History of Exact Sciences, vol. 63, 14 Nov. 2008, p. 171, https://doi.org/10.1007/s00407-008-0037-7.
2 Boyer, Carl B. 'Chhapter 13, The Arabic Hegemony.' In *A History of Mathematics, 2nd ed.* (New York: John Wiley & Sons, Inc., 1991), pp. 228–229.
3 Gupta, RC. 'History of Mathematics in India.' In *Students' Britannica India, Six* (New Delhi: Encyclopaedia Britannica [India] Pvt. Ltd., 2000), p. 329.
4 Colebrooke, Henry Thomas. 'Algebra (Cuṭṭaca).' In *Algebra, with Arithmetic and Mensuration, from the Sanscrit of Brahmegupta and Bháscara* (London: John Murray, 1817), pp. 325–373.
5 O' Connor, JJ and EF Robertson. 'Wang Xiaotong.' Wang Xiaotong (580 - 640) - Biography - MacTutor History of Mathematics, School of Mathematics and Statistics, University of St. Andrews, Scotland, December 2003, https://mathshistory.st-andrews.ac.uk/Biographies/Wang_Xiaotong/.
6 Oaks, Jeffrey A. 'Diophantus, Al-Karajī, and Quadratic Equations.' In *Revolutions and Continuity in Greek Mathematics*, ed. Michalis Sialaros (Berlin: Walter De Gruyter GmbH, 2018), pp. 271–272.
7 Eves, Howard. 'The Syncopation of Algebra.' In *Great Moments in Mathematics (before 1650), vol. 5* (Washington, DC: The Mathematical Association of America, Inc., 1983), p. 126. The Dolciani Mathematical Expositions series.
8 Fine, Henry Burchard. 'Origin of the Negative and the Imaginary.' In *The Number-System of Algebra: Treated Theoretically and Historically* (Boston, MA: Leach, Shewell, & Sanborn, 1890), pp. 100–101.

9 Hart, Roger. 'Fangcheng, Chapter 8 of the Nine Chapters.' In *The Chinese Roots of Linear Algebra* (Baltimore, MD: The John Hopkins University Press, 2011), pp. 67–70.
10 Joseph, George Gheverghese. 'Ancient Indian Mathematics.' In *The Crest of the Peacock: Non-European Roots of Mathematics, 3rd ed*, (Princeton, NJ: Princeton University Press, 2011), p. 349.
11 Boyer, Carl B. 'Euclid of Alexandria.' In *A History of Mathematics, 2nd ed.* (New York: John Wiley & Sons, Inc., 1991), p. 109.
12 Rooney, Anne. 'The Magic Formula.' In *The History of Mathematics* (New York: Rosen Publishing Group, Inc., 2013), p. 123.
13 Clagett, Marshall. 'Document IV.4 The Berlin Papyrus 6619.' In *Ancient Egyptian Science: Ancient Egyptian Mathematics, III* (Philadelphia: American Philosophical Society, 1999), pp. 249–253.
14 Friberg, Jöran. 'Three Old Babylonian Mathematical Problem Texts from Uruk.' In *A Remarkable Collection of Babylonian Mathematical Texts: Manuscripts in the Schøyen Collection: Cuneiform Texts I* (New York: Springer Science+Business Media, LLC, 2007), p. 245.

Is Hindu Atheist Really an Oxymoron?

1 Flood, Gavin. 'Ancient Origins.' In *An Introduction to Hinduism* (Cambridge: Cambridge University Press, 1996), p. 37.
2 Dasgupta, Surendranath. 'The Vedas, Brahmanas and Their Philosophy.' In *A History of Indian Philosophy*, I (Cambridge: Cambridge Univ. Press, 1957), p. 18.
3 Kaegi, Adolf and Robert Arrowsmith. 'The Vedic Belief.' In *The Rigveda: The Oldest Literature of the Indian, Authorised Translation, with Additions to the Notes*, trans. R. Arrowsmith (Boston: Ginn & Co., 1886), pp. 33–34.
4 Ibid, p. 89.
5 Hume, Robert Ernest. 'Maitri Upanishad.' In *The Thirteen Principal Upanishads: Translated from the Sanskrit with an Outline of the Philosophy of the Upanishads and an Annotated Bibliography* (London: Humphrey Milford, Oxford University Press, 1921), pp. 422–423.
6 Nicholson, Andrew J. 'Āstika and Nāstika in the Late Medieval Period.' In *Unifying Hinduism Philosophy and Identity in Indian Intellectual History* (New York: Columbia University Press, 2010), pp. 179–180.
7 Larson, Gerald James. 'A Critical Review of the History of Interpretations of the Sāṁkhya.' In *Classical Sāṁkhya: An Interpretation of Its History and Meaning* (Delhi: Motilal Banarsidass Publishers, 1998), p. 34.
8 Sinha, Nandalal. 'Preface.' In *The S*āṁkhya Philosophy (Allahabad: Panini Office, 1915), p. xiii.

9 Perrett, Roy W. 'Sāṃkhya-Yoga Ethics.' In *Indian Ethics: Classical Traditions and Contemporary Challenges*, ed. Purusottama Bilimoria et al., (Hampshire: Ashgate, 2007), p. 151.
10 Larson, Gerald James and Ram Shankar Bhattacharya, eds. 'Proto-Sāṃkhya and Pre–Kārikā-Sāṃkhya.' In *Encyclopedia of Indian Philosophies, vol.* 4 (Delhi: Motilal Banarsidass, 1987), p. 6.
11 Müller F Max. In *The Six Systems of Indian Philosophy* (London: Longmans, Green and Co., 1899), pp. 258–259.
12 Dasgupta, Surendranath. 'Mīmāṃsā Philosophy.' In *A History of Indian Philosophy, I* (Cambridge: Cambridge University Press, 1957), p. 370.
13 Ibid, pp. 402–403.
14 Basu, Baman Das. 'Of Existence of God.' In *The Vaisesika Sūtra of Kaṇāda*, trans. Nandalal Sinha (Allahabad: The Pānini Office, 1923), pp. 65–66.
15 Perrett, Roy W. 'Volume Introduction.' In *Philosophy of Religion: Indian Philosophy* (New York: Taylor & Francis, 2013), pp. xiii-xiv.
16 Basham, Arthur Llewellyn and Lionel David Barnett. 'Other Doctrines of the Ājīvikas.' In *History and Doctrines of The Ājīvikas: A Vanished Indian Religion*, ed. Satya Ranjan Banerjee (Delhi: Motilal Banarsidass Publishers Pvt. Ltd, 2002), pp. 272–273.
17 Āchārya Mādhava and Archibald Edward Gough. 'The Chārvāka System.' In *The Sarva-Darśana-Saṃgraha, or Review of the Different Systems of Hindu Philosophy*, trans. Edward B Cowell (London: Trübner & Co., 1882), pp. 2–11.
18 Larson, Gerald James and Lloyd W Pflueger. 'Person, Purity, and Power in the Yogasūtra.' In *Theory and Practice of Yoga: Essays in Honour of Gerald James Larson*, ed. Knut A Jacobsen (Delhi: Motilal Banarsidass, 2008), pp. 38–39.
19 Patañjali. 'Book I.' In *The Yoga Sutr*ās of Patanjali; *'the Book of the Spiritual Man; an Interpretation*, trans. Charles Johnston (New York: Charles Johnston, 1912), p. 14.
20 Clooney, Francis Xavier. 'Arguing the Existence of God: From the World to Its Maker.' In *Hindu God, Christian God: How Reason Helps Break Down the Boundaries between Religions* (Oxford: Oxford University Press, 2010), p. 37.

Was There Ever a River Named Sarasvatī?

1 Caland, W, trans. 'Twenty-Fifth Chapter. The Sattras, Concluded.' In *Pañcaviṃśa Brāhmaṅa—the Brāhmaṅa of Twenty-Five Chapters* (Calcutta: Asiatic Society of Bengal, 1931), p. 636.
2 Macdonell, AA. 'Parjanya.' *Vedic Mythology* (Delhi: Motilal Banarsidass Publishers Private Limited, 2002), pp. 83–86.

3 Valdiya, KS. 'Tracing the Course of River Saraswati.' In *Saraswati, the River That Disappeared* (Hyderabad: Universities Press, 2002), p. 23.
4 Possehl, Gregory L. 'Ancient Indian Civilization.' In *The Indus Civilization: A Contemporary Perspective* (Walnut Creek, CA: Rowman & Littlefield Publishers, Inc., 2002), pp. 8–9.
5 Hanifi, M. Jamil and EIr. 'Helmand River I. Geography.' Encyclopaedia Iranica Foundation, 15 December 2003, www.iranicaonline.org/articles/helmand-river-i.
6 Monier-Williams, Monier. *A Sanskrit–English Dictionary, Etymologically and Philologically Arranged with Special Reference to Cognate Indo-European Languages* (Delhi: Motilal Banarsidass, 1986), p. 355.
7 Darmesteter, James, trans. 'Fargard I: An Enumeration of Sixteen Lands Created by Ahura Mazda, and of as Many Plagues Created in Opposition by Angra Mainyu.' In *The Zend–Avesta; Part I: The Vendidad* (Oxford: The Clarendon Press, 1880), p. 8. The Sacred Books of the East series.
8 Ibid, p. 7.
9 Oldham, Richard Dixon. 'On Probable Changes in the Geography of the Punjab and Its Rivers: An Historico-Geographical Study.' *Memoirs–Geological Society of India* no. 4 (December 1886), pp. 341–342.
10 Ghose, Bimal, et al. 'The Lost Courses of the Saraswati River in the Great Indian Desert: New Evidence from Landsat Imagery.' *The Geographical Journal* 145, no. 3 (1979), pp. 448–450, https://doi.org/10.2307/633213.
11 Ibid, p. 450, https://doi.org/10.2307/633213.
12 Ibid, p. 450, https://doi.org/10.2307/633213.
13 Mukherjee, Ashoke. 'Rigvedic Saraswati: Myth and Reality.' *Breakthrough* 9, no. 1 (2001), p. 5.

Trojan Horse, but Trojan Elephant?

1 'A Relief Carving Showing a Trojan Horse on Wheels. Gandhara School, Pakistan C.2nd-3rd Century.' British Museum Images, The Trustees of the British Museum, https://www.bmimages.com/preview.asp?image=00100175001.
2 Stewart, Peter. 'The Provenance of the Gandhāran "Trojan Horse" Relief in the British Museum.' *Arts Asiatiques* 71, no. 1 (2016), pp. 6–7, https://doi.org/10.3406/arasi.2016.1923.
3 Rogers, Henry Thomas, trans. 'The Story of Queen Samavati, Queen Magandiya, and the Slave Khugguttara.' In *Buddhaghoṣa's Parables* (London: Trübner and Co., 1870), pp. 33–39.

4 Johnson, Helen M. 'The Udayana-Vāsavadattā Romance in Hemacandra.' *Journal of the American Oriental Society* 66, no. 4 (1946), p. 296, https://doi.org/10.2307/596408.
5 Cowell, Edward B and Frederick William Thomas, trans. 'Chapter VI.' *The Harṣa-Carita of Bāṇa* (London: Royal Asiatic Society, 1897), p. 192.
6 Varadpande, Manohar Laxman. 'Dionysus in India.' In *History of Indian Theatre* (New Delhi: Abhinav Publications, 1987), p. 249.

How Akhand Was Bharat Anyway?

1 Sayeed, Khalid bin. 'Conflicting Views about the Origin of Pakistan.' In *Pakistan The Formative Phase, 1857–1948* (Oxford: Oxford University Press, 1968), p. 4.
2 Ambedkar, Bhimrao. 'Hindu Alternative to Pakistan.' In *Pakistan or Partition of India, 2nd ed.* (Bombay: Thacker and Company Limited, 1945), p. 131.
3 Savarkar, Vinayak Damodar. 'Ahmedabad (Karnavati).' In *Hindu Rashtra Darshan: A Collection of the Presidential Speeches Delivered from the Hindu Mahasabha Platform* (Bombay: LG Khare, 1949), p. 4.
4 Richardson, John. 'Anglo-Indian Empire: British Empire in India—Hindustan.' In *A Smaller Manual of Modern Geography: Physical and Political, John Murray* (London: Albemarle Street, 1880), pp. 145–146.
5 Oka, Krishnaji Govind. 'Dwitiyam Kandam.' In *The N*âmalingânusâ*sana (Amarakosha) of Amarasimha with the Commentary (Amarakoshodgh*âtana*) of Ksh*îrasvâ*min* (Poona: Law Printing Press, 1913), p. 47.
6 Parpola, Asko. 'The Rigvedic Indo-Aryans and the Dāsas.' In *The Roots of Hinduism: The Early Aryans and the Indus Civilization* (Oxford: Oxford University Press, 2015), p. 94.
7 Singh, Upinder. 'War.' In *Political Violence in Ancient India* (Cambridge, MA: Harvard University Press, 2017), p. 253.
8 Jha, Dwijendra Narayan. 'Deconstructing Hindu Identity.' In *Rethinking Hindu Identity* (New York: Routledge, 2014), p. 12.
9 Rocher, Ludo. 'Individual Purāṇas (in Alphabetical Order).' In *The Purāṇas*, ed. Jan Gonda, II (Wiesbaden: O. Harrassowitz, 1986), p. 249. A History of Indian Literature series.
10 Wilson, Horace Hayman. 'Preface.' In *The Vishnu Purán: A System of Hindu Mythology and Tradition*, ed. Fitzedward Hall, I (London: Trubner and Co., 1864), p. CXII.
11 Hall, Daniel George Edward. 'The Pre-Pagan Period.' In *Burma* (Redditch: Read Books Ltd., 2013), p. 3.

12 Savada, Andrea Matles, ed. 'Bhutan.' In *Nepal and Bhutan: Country Studies, 3rd ed.* (Washington, DC: Federal Research Division, Library of Congress, 1993), p. 254. Area Handbook series.

13 Shaha, Rishikesh. 'The Licchavi Era (5th Century AD to Mid-9th Century).' In *Ancient and Medieval Nepal* (New Delhi: Manohar Publications, 1992), p. 13.

14 Senaveratna, John M. 'King Vijaya.' In *The Story of the Sinhalese from the Most Ancient Times Up to the End of 'The Mahavansa or Great Dynasty* (Madras: Asian Educational Services, 1997), p. 11.

Did bin Qasim Introduce India to Islam?

1 Asani, Ali. 'Muhammad Ibn Al-Qasim.' In *Medieval Islamic Civilization: An Encyclopedia, vol. 2*, ed. Jsef W. Meri (New York: Routledge, 2006), p. 524.

2 This work was named after Chach of Alor, a Brahmin chamberlain who rose to become the ruler of Sind. The book opens with his story.

3 Manan, Ahmed. 'Chachnama: A New Frontier History.' In *The Many Histories of Muhammad B. Qasim: Narrating the Muslim Conquest of Sindh* (Chicago, IL: Department of South Asian Languages and Civilizations, University of Chicago, 2008), pp. 118–114.

4 H-Iram, and Laura Veccia Vaglieri. 'Ibn Al-Ashʿath.' In *The Encyclopaedia of Islam*, ed. B Lewis et al., III (London: Luzac & Co., 1986), pp. 715–719.

5 MacLean, Derryl N. 'Ismāʿīlism in Arab Sind.' In *Religion and Society in Arab Sind* (Leiden: EJ Brill, 1989), p. 126.

6 Ahmed, Mukhtar. 'Related Ethnic Communities.' In *The Arains: A Historical Perspective* (Realsville, NC : CreateSpace Independent Publishing Platform, 2016), p. 45.

7 Wink, André. 'The Frontier of Al-Hind.' In *Al-Hind: Early Medieval India and the Expansion of Islam, 7th–11th Centuries* (Boston, MA: Brill Academic Publishers, Inc., 2002), p. 120.

8 Titus, Murray T. *Islam in India and Pakistan* (Calcutta: YMCA Publishing House, 1959), p. 3. The Heritage of India series.

9 Miller, Roland E. 'The Heritage of the Past.' In *Mappila Muslims of Kerala: A Study in Islamic Trends* (Bangalore: Orient Longman, 1976), pp. 40–41.

10 Koyippally, Joseph. 'Mappila': Identity and Semantic Narrowing.' *IOSR Journal Of Humanities And Social Science*, vol. 22, no. 1, Jan. 2017, p. 8., https://doi.org/10.9790/0837-2201060813.

11 Ibid.

12 Geaves, Ron. 'Introduction.' In *Islam and Britain Muslim Mission in an Age of Empire* (New York: Bloomsbury Publishing, 2019), p. 6.

Was Urdu Always a 'Muslim' Tongue?

1 Woolner, Alfred C. 'Subject Defined.' *Introduction to Prakrit* (Delhi: Motilal Banarsidass, 1986), pp. 3–4.
2 Ogilvie, Sarah, et al. 'Hindustani.' In *Concise Encyclopedia of Languages of the World* (Oxford: Elsevier Science, 2010), p. 498.
3 Alam, Muzaffar. 'The Pursuit of Persian: Language in Mughal Politics.' *Modern Asian Studies* 22, no. 2, 1998, p. 319, http://www.jstor.org/stable/313001.
4 Ahmad, Aziz. 'Safawid Poets and India.' *Journal of the British Institute of Persian Studies* 14, no. 1 (1976), p. 117, https://www.tandfonline.com/doi/abs/10.1080/05786967.1976.11834212.
5 Ahmad, Aziz. 'Safawid Poets and India.' *Journal of the British Institute of Persian Studies* 14, no. 1 (1976), pp. 327–328, https://www.tandfonline.com/doi/abs/10.1080/05786967.1976.11834212.
6 Ogilvie, Sarah, et al. 'Hindustani.' In *Concise Encyclopedia of Languages of the World* (Oxford: Elsevier Science, 2010), p. 497.
7 Ayres, Alyssa. 'Articulating a New Nation.' In *Speaking Like a State: Language and Nationalism in Pakistan* (Cambridge: Cambridge University Press, 2009), p. 19.
8 Diamond, Jeffrey M. 'A "Vernacular" for a «New Generation»? Historical Perspectives about Urdu and Punjabi, and the Formation of Language Policy in Colonial Northwest India.' In *Language Policy and Language Conflict in Afghanistan and Its Neighbors, vol. 2,* ed. Harold Schiffman (Leiden: Brill, 2012), pp. 282–283. Brill's Studies in South and Southwest Asian Languages series/collection, https://doi.org/10.1163/9789004217652_010.
9 Desai, Rakesh. 'Scripting a Region: Narmad's Idea of Gujarat.' *Indian Literature* 58, no. 3 (2014), p. 184.
10 Ibid, p. 181.
11 Nyrop, Richard F. 'Communications and the Arts.' In *Area Handbook for Bangladesh* (Washington, DC: US Government Printing Office, 1975), p. 152.
12 Mehta, Alka and BL Grover. 'Cultural Awakening, Religious and Social Reforms.' In *A New Look at Modern Indian History (from 1707 to the Modern Times), 32nd ed.* (New Delhi: S Chand and Company Limited, 2018), p. 281.

13 Rai, Alok. 'The MacDonnell Moment.' In *Hindi Nationalism* (New Delhi: Orient Longman, 2001), p. 41.

14 Ramusack, Barbara N. 'Princely States, Society and Politics.' In *The New Cambridge History of India (The Indian Princes and Their States)* (Cambridge: Cambridge University Press, 2004), p. 210.

15 Everaert, Christine. 'Two Sister Languages.' In *Essential Hindi Grammar: With Examples from Modern Hindi Literature* (Honolulu, HI: University of Hawaii Press, 2017), p. 7.

How Many Temples Did Tipu Destroy?

1 Mitra, RC. 'Some Light on the Third Anglo-Mysore War from French Sources.' *Proceedings of the Indian History Congress* 14 (1951), p. 232, http://www.jstor.org/stable/44303974.

2 Sinha, Narendra Krishna. 'Relations with the Marathas, 1776–1778.' In *Haidar Ali, vol. 1* (Calcutta: Calcutta Oriental Press, 1941), pp. 217–218.

3 Kirkpatrick, William, trans. 'Letter III. To Mahommed Ghâyas.' In *Select Letters of Tippoo Sultan to Various Public Functionaries: Including His Principal Military Commanders; Governors of Forts and Provinces; Diplomatic and Commercial Agents; &c. &c. &c. Together with Some Addressed to the Tributary Chieftains of Shânoor, Kurnool, and Cannanore, and Sundry Other Persons* (London: Black, Parry, and Kingsbury, 1811), pp. 7–8.

4 Duff, James Grant. 'From A. D. 1784 to A. D. 1787.' In *A History of the Mahrattas, 3rd ed.* (Bombay: The Times of India Office, 1873), p. 466.

5 Kincaid, Charles Augustus and Dattatray Balwant Parasnis. 'Wars against Tipu.' In *A History of the Maratha People, III* (London: Humphrey Milford, 1925), p. 148.

6 Sultan, Tipu and William Kirkpatrick. 'Letter CXVII: To Meer Zynûl Aabideen, Sipahdár of a Kushoon; Dated 8th Wásaaley (17th September).' In *Select Letters of Tippoo Sultan to Various Public Functionaries*, trans. William Kirkpatrick (London: Black, Parry, and Kingsbury, 1811), pp. 150–151.

7 Ibid, p. 236.

8 Wilks, Mark. 'Chapter XXX.' In *Historical Sketches of the South of India: In an Attempt to Trace the History of Mysoor*, ed. Murray Hammick, II (Mysore: Government Branch Press, 1932), pp. 282–283; Mehendale, Gajanan Bhaskar. 'Kodagu's War of Independence.' In *Tipu As He Really Was* (Mehendale: Gajanan Bhaskar, 2018), pp. 28–29.

9 Kirmani, Hussain Ali Khan. 'Chapter VI.' In *The History of the Reign of Tipú Sultán, Being a Continuation of the Neshani Hyduri*, trans. W Miles

(London: The Oriental Translation Fund of Great Britain and Ireland, 1864), pp. 81–82.

10 Sen, Surendranath. 'Portuguese Records of Hyder and Tipu.' In *Studies in Indian History* (Calcutta: University of Calcutta, 1930), p. 174.

11 Ibid, p. 174.

12 Ibid, p. 161.

13 Ibid, p. 164.

14 Kirkpatrick, William, trans. 'Letter CLXIX. To Bûrhânûddeen.' In *Select Letters of Tippoo Sultan to Various Public Functionaries: Including His Principal Military Commanders; Governors of Forts and Provinces; Diplomatic and Commercial Agents; &c. &c. &c. Together with Some Addressed to the Tributary Chieftains of Shânoor, Kurnool, and Cannanore, and Sundry Other Persons* (London: Black, Parry, and Kingsbury, 1811), p. 207.

15 Hasan, Mohibbul. 'Appendix E.' In *A History of Tipu Sultan* (Calcutta: The Bibliophile Ltd, 1951), pp. 397–399.

16 Rao, Ram Chandra. *Memoirs of Hyder Ali Bahadur and His Son Tippoo Sultan*, trans. Charles Philip Brown, III (Madras: Simkins and Co., 1840), p. 37.

17 Khare, Vasudev Vaman. 'Tipoochi Nargundavar Swari.' In *Etihasik Lekh Sangrah*, VIII (Pune: Aryabhushan, 1915), pp. 3906–3907.

18 Girish, MB. 'Tipu Sultan's Hanuman Temple to Make Way for Highway.' *Deccan Chronicle*, 13 December 2019, https://www.deccanchronicle.com/nation/current-affairs/131219/tipu-sultans-hanuman-temple-to-make-way-for-highway.html.

19 Complete Guide to Mookambika Temple Kollur—Mookambika Info, https://www.mookambika.co/#rec49999066.

20 Donahaye, Guy and Eddie Stern. 'Saraswathi Rangaswamy.' In *Guruji: A Portrait of Sri K. Pattabhi Jois through the Eyes of His Students* (New York: North Point Press, 2010), p. 117.

Did Rajputs Always Stand Up to Aurangzeb?

1 Webb, William Wilfrid. 'Jaipur or Dhundar: Old Capital Ambér, Modern Capital Jaipur.' In *The Currencies of the Hindu States of* Rájput*ána* (London: Archibald Constable and Co., 1893), p. 69.

2 Sarkar, Jadunath. 'How Akbar Won the Kachhwas Over.' In *A History of Jaipur, c. 1503–1938*, ed. Raghubir Sinh (Hyderabad: Orient Longman, 1994), p. 31.

3 Sarda, Har Bilas. 'Ajmer–Merwara.' In *Ajmer: Historical and Descriptive* (Ajmer: Scottish Mission Industries Company Limited, 1911), p. 1.

4 Sarkar, Jadunath. 'How Akbar Won the Kachhwas Over.' In *A History of Jaipur, c. 1503–1938*, ed. Raghubir Sinh (Hyderabad: Orient Longman, 1994), p. 31.
5 Bhatnagar, VS. 'The Family.' In *Life and Times of Sawai Jai Singh 1688–1743* (Delhi: Impex India, 1974), p. 6.
6 Hooja, Rima. 'Rajasthan between c. CE 1500 – CE 1600.' In *A History of Rajasthan* (New Delhi: Rupa & Co., 2006), p. 482.
7 Ibid, p. 481.
8 Majumdar, AK. 'Mewār.' In *History and Culture of the Indian People; the Mughul Empire*, ed. RC Majumdar et al. (Bombay: Bharatiya Vidya Bhavan, 1974), pp. 331–332.
9 Kloff, Dirk HA. 'The Rajput of Pre-Mughal North India.' In *Naukar, Rajput and Sepoy; the Ethnohistory of the Military Labour Market in Hindustan, 1450–1850* (Cambridge: Cambridge University Press, 1990), p. 104.
10 Hooja, Rima. 'Rajasthan between c. CE 1500 – CE 1600.' In *A History of Rajasthan* (New Delhi: Rupa & Co., 2006), p. 482.
11 Sehgal, KK, ed. 'History.' In *Rajasthan District Gazetteers Bikaner* (Jaipur: Directorate, District Gazetteers, 1962), p. 28.
12 Hooja, Rima. 'Rajasthan between c. CE 1500 – CE 1600.' In *A History of Rajasthan* (New Delhi: Rupa & Co., 2006), p. 482.
13 Khan, Refaqat Ali. 'Chapter IV.' In *The Kachhwahas under Akbar and Jahangir* (New Delhi: Kitab Publishing House, 1976), p. 133.
14 Sarkar, Jadunath. 'How Akbar Won the Kachhwas Over.' In *A History of Jaipur, c. 1503–1938*, ed. Raghubir Sinh (Hyderabad: Orient Longman, 1994), p. 33.
15 Mukherjee, Soma. 'The Ladies of the Mughal Harem.' In *Royal Mughal Ladies and Their Contribution* (New Delhi: Gyan Publishing House, 2001), p. 23.
16 Hooja, Rima. 'Rajasthan between c. CE 1500 – CE 1600.' In *A History of Rajasthan* (New Delhi: Rupa & Co., 2006), p. 482.
17 Khan, Refaqat Ali. 'Chapter I.' In *The Kachhwahas under Akbar and Jahangir* (New Delhi: Kitab Publishing House, 1976), p. 3.
18 Sarkar, Jadunath. 'How Akbar Won the Kachhwas Over.' In *A History of Jaipur c. 1503–1938*, ed. Raghubir Sinh (New Delhi: Orient Longman, 1994), p. 35.
19 Hooja, Rima. 'Rajasthan between c. CE 1500 – CE 1600.' In *A History of Rajasthan* (New Delhi: Rupa & Co., 2006), p. 483.
20 Ibid, p. 483.
21 Ibid, p. 483.

22 Sarkar, Jadunath. 'How Akbar Won the Kachhwas Over.' In *A History of Jaipur c. 1503–1938*, ed. Raghubir Sinh (New Delhi: Orient Longman, 1994), pp. 35–36.
23 Latif, Syad Muhammad. 'Akbar and His Court.' In *Agra, Historical & Descriptive, with an Account of Akbar and His Court and of the Modern City of Agra* (Calcutta: Calcutta Central Press Company, 1896), p. 283.
24 Prasad, Beni. 'Youth.' In *History of Jahangir, 2nd ed.* (Allahabad: The Indian Press, Ltd, 1930), p. 29.
25 Sarkar, Jadunath. 'Battle of Haldighat, 1576.' In *Military History of India* (Calcutta: MC Sarkar & Sons, Private Ltd., 1960), p. 75.
26 Sarkar, Jadunath. 'Interlude and Mirza Raja Jai Singh (First Phase): 1614–1657.' In *A History of Jaipur c. 1503–1938*, ed. Raghubir Sinh (New Delhi: Orient Longman, 1994), p. 97.
27 Ibid, p. 98.
28 Ibid, p. 98.
29 Gupta, Savitri. 'History.' In *Rajasthan District Gazetteers* (Jaipur: Government of Rajasthan, 1960), p. 42.
30 Baruah, Amlan, and SB Roy Choudhury, eds. 'History.' In *Assam State Gazetteer, I* (Guwahati: Government of Assam, 1999), p. 136.
31 Bond, JW and Arnold Wright. 'The State of Jaipur.' In *Indian States, a Biographical, Historical, and Administrative Survey* (New Delhi: Asian Educational Services, 2006), p. 175.
32 Temple, Richard Carnac. 'Râjâ Prithî Singh of Jôdhpûr, As Told by a Bard at Ambâlâ.' In *The Legends of the Panjâb, III* (London: Kegan Paul, Trench, Trübner, and Co., Ltd, 1884), p. 252.
33 Richards, John F. 'Chapter 8: Imperial Expansion under Aurangzeb 1658–1689.' In *The Mughal Empire, vol. 5*, ed. Gordon Johnson (Cambridge: Cambridge University Press, 2001), p. 181. The New Cambridge History of India series, Part I.

Did Hindus Ever Desecrate Hindu Temples?

1 Vasudevan, Geeta. 'The Temple in Pre–Rajaraja Period—A Background Study.' In *The Royal Temple of Rajaraja; An Instrument of Imperial Cola Power* (New Delhi: Abhinav Publications, 2003), p. 31.
2 Luders, H. 'Amravati Inscription of Krishnaraya of Vijayanagara; Saka–Samvat 1437.' In *Epigraphia Indica and Records of the Archæological Survey of India, VII*, ed E Hultzsch (Calcutta: Office of the Superintendent of Government Printing, 1903), p. 19.

3 Hultzsch, E, trans. 'Miscellaneous Inscriptions from the Tamil Country.' In *South Indian Inscriptions III*, ed. E Hultzsch (Madras: Archaeological Survey of India, 1899), p. 53. New Imperial series.
4 Ibid, pp. 52–53.
5 Mirashi, Vasudev Vishnu, ed. 'No. 45; Plate XXXV: Bilhari Stone Inscription of Yuvarajadeva II.' In *Inscriptions of the Kalachuri–Chedi Era, Part I, IV* (Otacamund: Government Epigraphist for India, 1955), p. 204. Corpus Inscriptionum Indicarum series.
6 Ibid, p. 207.
7 Not the same as the Western Chalukyas, who came much later and were based in Kalyani in today's Bidar.
8 Catlin, Amy. '"Vātāpi Gaṇapatim»: Sculptural, Poetic, and Musical Texts in a Hymn to Gaṇeśa.' In *Ganesha: Studies of an Asian God*, ed. Robert L Brown (New York: State University of New York Press, 1991), p. 142.
9 Kielhorn, E. 'Inscriptions from Khajuraho.' In *Epigraphia Indica: A Collection of Inscriptions Supplementary to the Corpus Inscriptionum Indicarum of the Archæological Survey, I*, ed. Jass Burgess et al. (Calcutta: The Superintendent of Government Printing, 1802), p. 134.
10 Dutt, Jogesh Chunder, trans. 'Book IV.' In *Kings of Káshmíra Being a Translation of Sanskrit Work* Rájatarangginí of Kalhana Pandita, vol. 1 (Calcutta: IC Bose & Co., 1879), p. 78.
11 Mahajan, Vidya Dhar. 'The Tripartite Struggle for Supremacy.' In *Ancient India, 14th ed.* (New Delhi: S Chand and Company Limited, 1962), p. 581.
12 Wagoner, Phillip B, trans. 'The Gajapati Campaign.' In *Tidings of the King, a Translation and Ethnohistorical Analysis of the* Rāyavācakamu (Honolulu, HI: University of Hawaii Press, 1993), p. 146.
13 Vasantha, R. 'Tradition and History.' In *Ahobilam Sri Narasimha Swamy Temple* (Tirupati: Tirumala Tirupati Devasthanams, 2001), p. 72.

Were Britain, France and Portugal Our Only Colonists?

1 Foster, William, ed. '1608–13 William Hawkins.' In *Early Travels in India 1583–1619* (Oxford: Oxford University Press, 1921), p. 62–63.
2 Hunter, William Wilson, and PE Roberts. 'The Early European Settlements.' In *The Imperial Gazetteer of India, New* ed., *II* (Oxford: The Clarendon Press, 1908), pp. 454–455.
3 Prakash, Om. 'The Company in Asian Trade.' In *The Dutch East India Company and the Economy of Bengal, 1630–1720* (Princeton, NJ: Princeton University Press, 1985), pp. 9–10.

4 Petram, Lodewijk. 'A New Company.' In *The World's First Stock Exchange*, trans. Lynne Richards (New York: Columbia University Press, 2014), pp. 12–13.
5 Roychaudhuri, Tapan. 'The First Phase, 1605–1629.' In *Jan Company in Coromandel; 1605–1690* (The Hague: Martinus Nijhoff, 1962), p. 15.
6 Ibid, p. 122.
7 Kemp, PH van der. 'De Nederlandsche Factorijen in Vóór-Indië in Den Aanvang Der 19e Eeuw.' *Bijdragen Tot De Taal-, Land- En Volkenkunde / Journal of the Humanities and Social Sciences of Southeast Asia* 53, no. 1 (1901), pp. 364–368, https://doi.org/10.1163/22134379-90002075.
8 Bredsdorff, Asta. 'Leyel Arrives.' In *The Trials and Travels of Willem Leyel: An Account of the Danish East India Company in Tranquebar, 1639–48* (Copenhagen: Museum Tusculanum Press, 2009), pp. 10–11.
9 Ibid, p. 11.
10 Bredsdorff, Asta. 'Leyel Arrives.' In *The Trials and Travels of Willem Leyel: An Account of the Danish East India Company in Tranquebar, 1639–48* (Copenhagen: Museum Tusculanum Press, 2009), p. 86.
11 Subrahmanyam, Sanjay. 'Europeans and Asians in an Age of Contained Conflict.' In *The Political Economy of Commerce: Southern India 1500–1650* (Cambridge: Cambridge University Press, 2002), p. 289.
12 Ibid, pp. 294–295.
13 Milburn, William. 'Isle of France, St. Helena, &c.' In *Oriental Commerce, vol. 2* (London: Black, Parry, & Co., 1813), pp. 575–577.
14 Markov, Walter. 'La Compagnia Asiatica Di Trieste (1775–1785).' *Studi Storici* 2, no. 1 (1961), p. 14.
15 Say, Edward. *The Importance of the Ostend-Company Consider'd* (Oxford-Arms: Edward Say, 1726), pp. 3–55.
16 Firminger, Walter Kelly. 'River Trip No. 2.—Bandel, Hughli, Chinsurah, Chandernagore, Etc.' In *Thacker's Guide to Calcutta* (Calcutta: Thacker, Spink & Co., 1906), pp. 241–242.

Did We Really Invent the Musical Notation?

1 'Tablet Fragment.' N3354 | Collections—Penn Museum, Penn Museum, 6 April 2021, https://penn.museum/collections/object/527649.
2 West, ML. 'The Babylonian Musical Notation and the Hurrian Melodic Texts.' Music and Letters 75, no. 2 (1994), pp. 161, 179, https://doi.org/10.1093/ml/75.2.161.
3 Kilmer, Anne and Steve Tinney. 'Old Babylonian Music Instruction Texts.' *Journal of Cuneiform Studies* 48 (1996), pp. 54, 56, https://doi.org/10.2307/1359769.

4 Fétis, François-Joseph. 'Object of Music. Its Origin. Its Means.' In *Music Explained to the World; or, How to Understand Music and Enjoy Its Performance* (Boston, MA: Benjamin Perkins, 1842), p. 6.
5 McNaught, WG. 'The History and Uses of The Sol-Fa Syllables.' *Proceedings of the Musical Association for the Investigation and Discussion of the Subjects Connected with the Arts and Science of Music* 19 (January 1893), p. 35.
6 Rose, Hugh James, et al., eds. 'A Biographical Dictionary.' In *A New General Biographical Dictionary, II* (London: T Fellows, 1857), p. 363.
7 Barney, Stephen A, et al., eds. 'Mathematics, Music, Astronomy.' In *The Etymologies of Isidore of Seville* (Cambridge: Cambridge University Press, 2006), p. 95.
8 Ho, Wai-Chung. 'China: Socio-Political Constructions of School Music.' In *The Origins and Foundations of Music Education; Cross-Cultural Historical Studies of Music in Compulsory Schooling*, ed. Gordon Cox and Robin Stevens (London: Continuum International Publishing Group, 2010), p. 190.
9 Seebass, Tilman. 'Notation and Transmission in European Music History.' In *The Garland Encyclopedia of World Music*, ed. Timothy Rice et al. (New York: Garland Publishing, Inc., 2000), p. 49.
10 Thrasher, Alan R. 'Yuelü: Music Theory and Practice.' In *Sizhu Instrumental Music of South China: Ethos, Theory and Practice* (Leiden: Koninklijke Brill NV, 2008), pp. 83–85.
11 Ghosh, Manomohan, trans. 'On the Instrumental Music.' In *The Nāṭyaśāstra: A Treatise on Hindu Dramaturgy and Histrionics Ascribed to Bharata–Muni, II* (Calcutta: The Asiatic Society, 1961), p. 5.
12 Ley, Graham. 'Aristotle's Poetics, Bharatamuni's Natyasastra, and Zeami's Treatises: Theory As Discourse.' *Asian Theatre Journal* 17, no. 2 (2000), p. 194.
13 Dasgupta, Surendranath. 'Mīmāṃsā Philosophy.' In *A History of Indian Philosophy, I* (Cambridge: Cambridge University Press, 1957), p. 370.
14 Oertel, Hanns. 'Article IV. The Jāiminīya or Talavakāra Upaniṣad Brāhmaṇa: Text, Translation, and Notes.' *Journal of the American Oriental Society* 16 (1896), p. 192.
15 Sudhākaraśukla, Pandit, ed. 'Prathamaḥ Prapathakaḥ.' In *Nāradīyaśikṣā, Sripitambarapeeth* (Datia: Sanskrit Parishad, 1990), p. 7.
16 Beck, Guy L. 'Ancient India: Yajna and Sama–Gana.' In *Sonic Liturgy: Ritual and Music in Hindu Tradition* (Columbia, SC: University of South Carolina Press, 2012), p. 91.

Who Invented Sugar—China or India?

1 Singh, Shivam Shankar and Anand Venkatanarayanan. 'The Conjuring of Another Star.' In T*he Art of Conjuring Alternate Realities: How Information Warfare Shapes Your World* (Noida: HarperCollins Publishers, 2021), pp. 3–4.
2 Sabel, IAE. 'The History of Sugar.' *The Australian Woman's Mirror* 15, no. 13 (1939), p. 7.
3 Berriedale, Keith A. 'The Date of the Ramayana.' *The Journal of the Royal Asiatic Society of Great Britain and Ireland* 1 (1915), pp. 318–328.
4 Rolph, George M. 'Early History.' In *Something about Sugar: Its History, Growth, Manufacture and Distribution* (San Francisco, CA: John J. Newbegin Publishers, 1917), p. 119.
5 Reed, William. 'Sugar, Its Origin, and Earliest Introduction into Various Countries.' In *The History of Sugar and Sugar Yielding Plants, Together with an Epitome of Every Notable Process of Sugar Extraction, and Manufacture, from the Earliest Times to the Present* (London: Longmans, Green, and Co., 1866), pp. 1–2.
6 Yuan, Zhang. 'Harṣa and China: The Six Diplomatic Missions in the Early 7th Century.' *The Delhi University Journal of Humanities and Social Sciences* 2 (2015), pp. 7–8.
7 Reed, William. 'Sugar, Its Origin, and Earliest Introduction into Various Countries.' In *The History of Sugar and Sugar Yielding Plants, Together with an Epitome of Every Notable Process of Sugar Extraction, and Manufacture, from the Earliest Times to the Present* (London: Longmans, Green, and Co., 1866), pp. 1–2.
8 Magoun, HW. 'Translation and Commentary.' In *The Āsurī-Kalpa: A Witchcraft Practice of the Atharva-Veda, with an Introduction, Translation, and Commentary* (Baltimore, MD: Press of Isaac Friedenwald, 1889), p. 17.
9 Flood, Gavin. 'Ancient Origins.' In *An Introduction to Hinduism* (Cambridge: Cambridge University Press, 1996), pp. 37–38.
10 Singh, NP. 'Growth of Sugar Culture in Bihar (1793–1913).' *Proceedings of the Indian History Congress* 45 (1984), p. 588.
11 Milburn, William. 'Isle of France, St. Helena & co.' In *Oriental Commerce, vol. 2* (London: Black, Parry, & Co., 1813), p. 270.
12 Ibid, p. 271.
13 Sabel, IAE. 'The History of Sugar.' *The Australian Woman's Mirror* 15, no. 13 (1939), p. 7.
14 Perdue, Peter C. 'China and the World Economy: Exports, Regions, and Theories.' *Harvard Journal of Asiatic Studies* 60, no. 1 (2000), p. 260, https://doi.org/10.2307/2652706.

Is Sri Lanka Aryan, and If So, since When?

1 Ramasamy, SM. 'Facts and Myths about Adam's Bridge.' *GIS@Development* 7, no. 12 (2003), p. 44.

2 Indigenous Peoples Planning Framework Sri Lanka—Asian Development Bank. Road Development Authority, Ministry of Higher Education and Highways. https://www.adb.org/sites/default/files/linked-documents/50301-001-ippfab.pdf. Accessed 7 January 2022.

3 Sen, Sailendra Nath. 'New Religious Movements.' In *Ancient Indian History and Civilization, 2nd ed.* (New Delhi: New Age International [P] Limited Publishers, 1999), p. 91.

4 Obeyesekere, Gananath. 'The Conscience of the Parricide: A Study in Buddhist History.' *Man* 24, no. 2 (1989), p. 239, https://doi.org/https://doi.org/10.2307/2803304.

5 Wright, Arnold, ed. 'Agriculture.' In *Twentieth Century Impressions of Ceylon: Its History, People, Commerce, Industries, and Resources* (New Delhi: Asian Educational Services, 1999), p. 332.

6 Manogaran, Chelvadurai. 'Sinhalese-Tamil Ethnic Differences and the Beginnings of Conflict.' In *Ethnic Conflict and Reconciliation in Sri Lanka* (Honolulu, HI: University of Hawaii Press, 1987), p. 21.

7 Vashisth, Sudarshan. 'Kimpurish Varsh: Kinnaur.' In *Himalaya Gatha* (Delhi: Suhānī Books, 2008), p. 14.

8 Tyagi, Manisha. 'Commercial Relations between North India and Sri Lanka in Ancient Period: A Study.' *Proceedings of the Indian History Congress* 67 (2006), p. 107.

9 Sen, Sailendra Nath. 'New Religious Movements.' In *Ancient Indian History and Civilization, 2nd ed.* (New Delhi: New Age International [P] Limited, Publishers, 1999), p. 91.

10 Abeykon, John. 'The Progress of the Sinhalese in Literature, Arts, and Sciences.' In *The Orientalist, a Monthly Journal of Oriental Literature, Arts and Sciences, Folklore, &c., &c., &c.,* ed. William Goonetilleke (Bombay: Education Society's Press, 1884), p. 83.

11 Trawick, Margaret. 'The Past.' In *Enemy Lines: Warfare, Childhood, and Play in Batticaloa* (Berkeley, CA: University of California Press, 2007), p. 40.

12 Ghosh, Lipi and Kanokwan Jayadat. 'Thai Language and Literature: Glimpses of Indian Influence.' In *India-Thailand Cultural Interactions: Glimpses from the Past to Present,* ed. Lipi Ghosh (Singapore: Springer Nature Singapore Pte. Ltd, 2017), p. 142.

13 Prakasar, S Gnana. 'The Dravidian Element in Sinhalese.' *The Journal of the Ceylon Branch of the Royal Asiatic Society of Great Britain & Ireland* 22, no. 89 (1936), pp. 233–253.
14 Geiger, Wilhelm. 'The Linguistic Character of Sinhalese.' *The Journal of the Ceylon Branch of the Royal Asiatic Society of Great Britain & Ireland* 34, no. 90 (1937), pp. 16–43.
15 Gair, James W. 'Sinhala.' In *The Indo-Aryan Languages*, ed. George Cardona and Dhanesh Jain (New York: Routledge, 2007), p. 847. Routledge Language Family series.
16 Ragupathy, P. 'Tissamaharama Potsherd Evidences Ordinary Early Tamils among Population.' *TamilNet*, 28 July 2010, https://www.tamilnet.com/art.html?catid=79&artid=32303.
17 Bopearachchi, Osmund. 'Ancient Sri Lanka and Tamil Nadu: Maritime Trade.' In *South-Indian Horizons: Felicitation Volume for François Gros on the Occasion of His 70th Birthday*, ed. Jean-Luc Chevillard and Eva Wilden (Pondicherry: Institut Français De Pondichery and École Française D'Extreme-Orient, 2004), p. 541.

Did Hindus Ever Invade Other Nations?

1 Coedès, G and Susan Brown Cowling. 'Indianization.' In *The Indianized States of Southeast Asia*, ed. Walter F Vella (Canberra: Australian National University Press, 1975), pp. 22–24.
2 Andaya, Leonard Y. 'The Batak Malayu.' In *Leaves of the Same Tree: Trade and Ethnicity in the Straits of Melaka* (Honolulu, HI: University of Hawaii Press, 2008), p. 163.
3 Finot, ML. 'Notes D'Épigraphie: XI. Les Inscriptions De Mi-Sơn.' *Bulletin De l'École* Française d'*Extrême-Orient* no. 4 (1904), pp. 919–920.
4 Coedès, G and Susan Brown Cowling. 'Indianization.' In *The Indianized States of Southeast Asia*, ed. Walter F Vella (Canberra: Australian National University Press, 1975), p. 23.
5 Rasanayagam, Mudaliyar C. 'Sources and Synchronisms.' In *Ancient Jaffna: Being a Research into the History of Jaffna from Very Early Times to the Portuguese Period* (New Delhi: Asian Educational Services, 2003), pp. 231–232.
6 Kulke, Hermann. 'Śrīvijaya Revisited: Reflections on State Formation of a Southeast Asian Thalassocracy.' *Bulletin De l'École Fran*çaise d'*Extrême-Orient* 102, no. 1 (2016), pp. 47–48, https://doi.org/10.3406/befeo.2016.6231.

7 Ibid, p. 65.
8 Hall, Kenneth R. 'Khmer Commercial Development and Foreign Contacts under Sūryavarman I.' *Journal of the Economic and Social History of the Orient* 18, no. 1 (1975), pp. 331–333, https://doi.org/10.1163/156852075x00164.
9 Kulke, Hermann. 'Śrīvijaya Revisited: Reflections on State Formation of a Southeast Asian Thalassocracy.' *Bulletin De l'École Française d'Extrême-Orient* 102, no. 1 (2016), p. 68.
10 Susanti, Ninie. 'Rajendra Chola's Invasion and the Rise of Airlangga.' In *Nagapattinam to Suvarnadwipa: Reflections on the Chola Naval Expeditions to Southeast Asia*, ed. Hermann Kulke et al. (Singapore: Institute of Southeast Asian Studies, 2009), pp. 230–232.
11 Spencer, George Woolley. '7. Rajendra and Maritime Southeast Asia.' In *The Politics of Expansion: The Chola Conquest of Sri Lanka and Sri Vijaya* (Madras: New Era Publication, 1983) pp. 147–148.
12 Sen, Tansen and Noboru Karashima. 'Appendix II: Chinese Texts Describing or Referring to the Chola Kingdom As Zhu-Nian.' In *Nagapattinam to Suvarnadwipa: Reflections on the Chola Naval Expeditions to Southeast Asia*, ed. Hermann Kulke et al. (Singapore: Institute of Southeast Asian Studies, 2009), p. 305.

Acknowledgements

MUCH GRATITUDE IS OWED TO THE ACADEMIC behemoths whose work has helped make this book eminently more enjoyable. The reference section here lists more than 400 entries from scores of authors, a vast majority of whom worked and died long before our times, leaving behind a rich corpus of meticulous research.

Thanks go out to my family, especially mom, without whose motivation and unconditional support, I would've long given up. Their encouragement meant I could live and breathe nothing but this book for a while. Also a big shoutout to Nisha, who kept me from the myriad distractions of life.

I'd like to thank the team at HarperCollins India, too, especially my editor, Prema. She did a spectacular job of bringing this book to you in the best form possible.

And finally, the biggest thanks to the individual who seeded the idea in the first place, who quite literally made it all happen—Devdutt Pattanaik!

Acknowledgements

About the Author

Amit Schandillia is a language enthusiast and history communicator, with a background in computers and finance. Besides language, Amit has a long relationship with history, and has produced hundreds of popular Twitter threads on the subject, both Indian and otherwise. Of particular interest to him is the making of history accessible to laypersons by breaking down stories into thrilling, enjoyable reads. Amit also authors *India Uncharted*, an audio series on Indian history, with Storytel.